'This is an important book. For people ~ '   atter of lived experience that cr ''   this book will inspire hope and   an spirit to recover. And for thos   of childhood adversity this book   e depth of knowledge shared an   ...any stories illuminating the impact of traum   , ...in everyday life. I hope that it will be read by many, and ...am sure that those who do read it will treasure it.'

     — Kate Cairns, Director of KCA

'This clear, concise, cutting-edge collection of chapters by a wide range of skilled contributors demonstrates how insights from contemporary evidence-based research may be used to enable healing for traumatized children who are not able to live with their birth parents. Its relevance is far-reaching and makes it a "must-have" book for all who work with patients who struggle to overcome the effects of early relational trauma.'

     — Margaret Wilkinson, Training Analyst in the Society of Analytical Psychology and author of Coming Into Mind: The Mind-Brain Relationship: A Jungian Clinical Perspective *and* Changing Minds in Therapy: Emotion, Attachment, Trauma, and Neurobiology

'This is a brilliant book bringing together innovative creative therapies for adopted and fostered children and their families by specialists who have many years of experience of working with distressed or troubled children. If you are an adopter or foster carer you must use therapists who have both read this book and apply the principles.'

     — Helen Oakwater: Author of Bubble Wrapped Children: How Social Networking is Transforming the Face of 21st Century Adoption

'*Creative Therapies for Complex Trauma* is a very useful addition to the literature on this subject. It draws on the practice experience of an impressive range of therapists, and makes very effective use of case studies to exemplify and explore theoretical issues. Of use to both readers who are new to this area of work and to more experienced practitioners, it is certainly going to be on the reading list for my courses.'

     — Dr Kathy Evans, Senior Lecturer at the University of South Wales

CREATIVE THERAPIES
FOR COMPLEX TRAUMA

CREATIVE THERAPIES FOR COMPLEX TRAUMA

HELPING CHILDREN AND FAMILIES IN FOSTER CARE, KINSHIP CARE OR ADOPTION

EDITED BY ANTHEA HENDRY AND JOY HASLER

FOREWORD BY COLWYN TREVARTHEN

Jessica Kingsley *Publishers*
London and Philadelphia

The quote on p.22 has been reproduced with kind permission on behalf of
Bessel van der Kolk.
The quote on p.55 from *What Every Parent Needs to Know* by Margot Sunderland,
copyright © 2006, 2007, has been reproduced by permission of Dorling Kindersley Ltd.

First published in 2017
by Jessica Kingsley Publishers
73 Collier Street
London N1 9BE, UK
and
400 Market Street, Suite 400
Philadelphia, PA 19106, USA

www.jkp.com

Copyright © Jessica Kingsley Publishers 2017
Foreword copyright © Colwyn Trevarthen 2017
Front cover image titled 'Hope' copyright © Anthea Hendry

Library of Congress Cataloging in Publication Data
A CIP catalog record for this book is available from the Library of Congress

British Library Cataloguing in Publication Data
A CIP catalogue record for this book is available from the British Library

ISBN 978 1 78592 005 9
eISBN 978 1 78450242 3

Printed and bound in Great Britain

CONTENTS

FOREWORD

COLWYN TREVARTHEN

This book celebrates a shift in medical and psychological understanding of human nature. The therapeutic practice of the authors accepts that we build trust actively and responsively, and they adapt this principle to offer sensitive care when hopes for kindness and joyful sharing of experience have been betrayed. This supports the conviction that behavioural science, occupied with its various special techniques for measuring perception and intelligence, and for testing and imaging brain activity, must accept that we are from the start conscious selves making efforts to discover the meaning of life with rhythms of imagination for artful movement full of feeling. We bring to life not just an organism dependent on maternal nurturing, with growing cerebral cortices that will require instruction to become records of how to be conscious partners in mastery of artificial practices and symbolic conventions. As the paediatrician T. Berry Brazelton made clear, we are born as persons who, if we are not distressed, can share curiosity with mother and father in minutes after birth.

The alert newborn knows no facts, but he or she may imitate and synchronize with actions presented as signals for an imaginative dialogue, demonstrating aesthetic grace in movement and moral impulses of love that look for sympathetic confirmation from affectionate company. These are innate strengths for convivial vitality at the core of our being, formed before birth. The important message supported by the case studies presented here is that, given kind and thoughtful companionship after neglect or abuse, a child's hope for shared life can overcome hurt and recover well-being, and join with friends to contribute to a strong society. The professional support of foster care, kinship care, adoptive parenting and responsive teaching offers to overcome the sadness of increasing numbers of young children who experience life as confused, challenging and fearful, in their families, in the wider community and at school.

The revelation by René Spitz and John Bowlby of the distress and trauma newborn babies suffer if they are deprived of intimate affectionate care with their mothers from birth inspired attachment theory, leading to a more 'relational' or 'dialogical' approach in psychiatry. In the 1970s a descriptive developmental psychology re-examined age-related changes in initiatives, emotions and social understanding through the early years. The findings, inspired, for example, by research of Jerome Bruner and T. Berry Brazelton collaborating at Harvard, reformed education and pediatrics, and the training of teachers and clinicians. Daniel Stern, complementing his training as a child psychiatrist, analysed games that mothers played with young infants and was led to a new theory of the constructive powers of innate 'vitality dynamics' shared as in the performing arts. In the introduction to the second edition of *The Interpersonal World of the Infant*, Stern said:

> One consequence of the book's application of a narrative perspective to the nonverbal has been the discovery of a language useful to many psychotherapies that rely on the nonverbal. I am thinking particularly of dance, music, body, and movement therapies, as well as existential psychotherapies. This observation came as a pleasant surprise to me since I did not originally have such therapies in mind; my thinking has been enriched by coming to know them better. (Stern 2000, p.xiv)

In recent decades brain science has taken various routes to understand the process that coordinates and regulates acting human in healthy ways. Mine Conkbayir, a teacher in a state-maintained nursery school, a head trainer of teachers for the London Early Years Foundation and the author, with Chris Pascal, of a book about early childhood theories and contemporary issues, published in 2014, relates her practical knowledge of the child's playful zest for a life of learning to current neuroscience in this new book. She warns against acceptance of ideas about the fragility of brain circuits and their dependence on input of information based on restricted methods of analysis and observation. Neurodata needs to be interpreted in an open-minded way to relate to the well-being of a whole child alive in relations with parents and teachers.

The organization Attachment in Action, that some of these authors co-founded, supported development of services to improve the life of early years, and helped lead to the recognition of varieties of 'complex trauma' resulting from chaotic, neglectful or abusive parenting that affects a child's hope for a rewarding life in community. Anthea Hendry describes the 'complex therapies' required to aid recovery from this trauma, referring to the developmental brain theories of Allan Schore, Bruce Perry and Bessel van der Kolk, and the need for relational therapy, exemplified by Dan Hughes' Dyadic Developmental Psychotherapy. The Conversational Model of psychotherapy to strengthen self-confidence, created by the English psychiatrist Robert Hobson with attention to 'forms of feeling', was developed by the Australian psychiatrist Russell Meares, who eloquently describes how the poetry or 'making' of a therapeutic relationship may be applied to assist recovery from disorganized attachment. Fostering and adoption of traumatized young people supported by the vitality dynamics of relational therapy has become an important element for social policy in the world of modern industrial culture.

The veterinarian and phenomenological philosopher Barbara Goodrich welcomes the work of Rodolfo Llinás and György Buszáki as a new brain science that goes beyond attention restricted to cognitive functions of the individual thinker to appreciate the fundamental dimensions of movement and time. This gives value to the playful movements that regulate feelings and intelligence in creation of body-related time and space of an individual Self, and clarifies how these are communicated in intimate relations of artful performances of dance, music and drama that adapt their rhythms to encourage self-confident sharing and learning in affection and joy.

Joy Hasler, an expert in music therapy, and Sarah Ayache, an expert in art therapy, appreciate the work of Jaak Panksepp and Stephen Porges on the role of the subcortical brain, which is described as an integrated Self with emotions for learning in intimate relationships by natural impulses to signal pleasure in inner states of the body. These feelings are inhibited by negative, vitality-protecting, emotions of loneliness, anger and fear. Panksepp, defining an affective neuroscience, goes so far as to identify this core affective brain with the spiritual 'soul'. Hasler and Ayache relate their practice also with the findings of Daniel Stern who revolutionized psychoanalytic theory by recording that young infants assume leadership in play with their mothers. They note that Allan Schore identifies the affectionate relating that develops in the first three years of childhood with rapid growth of the right cerebral hemisphere, which establishes the foundations of prosody and syntax in language before the semantics of a vocabulary is learned. This accompanies accelerating growth of the left hemisphere in years three to five.

The musician Stephen Malloch applied rigorous methods of musical acoustics to analyse the vitality of a proto-conversation I had recorded between a two-month-old and her mother. He defined the dimensions of 'pulse', 'quality' and narrative in the 'communicative musicality' of their cooperation. These are the essential elements of Maturana *et al.*'s 'autopoesis' or 'self-making' of control for the forces of body movement of any animal, which must be measured in time, with regulation of energy and with prospective control for the completion of imagined projects. In engagement with environmental affordances, and in communication to establish cooperation or 'consensuality' of any kind, they must be controlled to make effective action possible.

The contributors to this volume, between them, have many years of experience of working and managing services in health, education and the voluntary sector. Many of them are qualified practitioners of creative therapies combining art, dance, music and dramatic story-making, and who record their experiences here with detailed descriptions of case studies in which expressive actions and explanations of a person engaged in therapy are related to those of family members. Together they create services to establish and strengthen family relationships of affection and trust, and integrate work with adoptive parents, foster and kinship carers and teachers and health professionals. By helping troubled individuals find self-confidence and pleasure in relationships they strengthen the community.

Further reading

Conkbayir, M. (2017) *Early Childhood and Neuroscience: Theory, Research and Implications for Practice.* London: Bloomsbury Academic.

Daniel, S. and Trevarthen, C. (eds) (2017) *Rhythms of Relating in Children's Therapies.* London: Jessica Kingsley Publishers.

Edwards, J. (2011) *Music Therapy and Parent-Infant Bonding.* Oxford: Oxford University Press.

Goodrich, B. (2010) 'We do, therefore we think: Time, motility, and consciousness.' *Reviews in the Neurosciences,* 21, 331–361.

Maturana, H., Mpodozis, J., and C. Letelier, J. (1995) 'Brain, language and the origin of human mental functions.' *Biological Research,* 28, 1, 15–26.

Meares, R. (2016) *The Poet's Voice in the Making of Mind.* London/New York: Routledge.

Panksepp, J. (2007) 'Emotional feelings originate below the neocortex: Toward a neurobiology of the soul.' *Behavioral and Brain Sciences,* 30, 1, 101–103.

Porges, S. W. (2011) *The Polyvagal Theory: Neurophysiological Foundations of Emotions, Attachment, Communication, and Self-regulation.* New York: WW Norton.

Stern, D. N. (2000) *The Interpersonal World of the Infant.* New York: Basic Books.

Stern, D. N. (2010) *Forms of Vitality: Exploring Dynamic Experience in Psychology, the Arts, Psychotherapy and Development.* Oxford: Oxford University Press.

Trevarthen, C. (2004) 'Brain development.' In R.L. Gregory (ed.) *Oxford Companion to the Mind.* Oxford, New York: Oxford University Press, pp. 116–127.

Trevarthen, C. (2004) 'Infancy, mind in.' In R.L. Gregory (ed.) *Oxford Companion to the Mind.* Oxford & New York: Oxford University Press, pp. 455–464.

Trevarthen, C. (2015) 'Infant Semiosis: The psycho-biology of action and shared experience from birth.' *Cognitive Development,* 36, 130–141.

ACKNOWLEDGEMENTS

We would like to thank the following people for generously giving their time to read and comment on drafts of chapters at different stages of the writing of this book: Dr Leslie Bunt, Dr Ruth Bullivant, Kate Cairns, Michael Daniels, Jane Kitson, Helen Oakwater, Tom Pyne, Dean Reddick and Jane Vincent. We would like to thank the following contributors to chapters in the book for reading and commenting on drafts of other chapters: Franca Brenninkmeyer, Dr Renée Potgieter Marks and Dr Elizabeth Taylor Buck.

We would like to thank all members of the executive group of Attachment in Action (the UK Association for the Advancement of Attachment Therapies), of which we were both founding and executive members, for the generous sharing of ideas and practice during the years 2002–2011.

We would like to thank all the many children and families we and other contributors to the creative practices described in this book have worked with over many years. All the vignettes in the book are composites of these families and all have been completely anonymized.

Anthea Hendry and Joy Hasler

INTRODUCTION

ANTHEA HENDRY AND JOY HASLER

The inspiration for this book comes from a group of therapists around the UK who have learned and explored together how to provide strong research-based therapies for working with the effects of trauma on families. This book encompasses both familiar and innovative therapy models and we hope that it will inspire others. The title is deliberately inclusive. There is no exclusive group of therapies known as 'creative therapies'. In the UK the Health and Care Professions Council (HCPC) registering body for the arts therapies currently includes art therapy, music therapy and dramatherapy. Dance and movement therapy and play therapy are approved through different bodies but are included in our understanding of creative therapies and are represented here.

Who the book is about and who it is written for

This book aims to provide information about therapy for families living with traumatized children who are not able to live with their birth parents. It describes different support and therapy for their children whilst respecting them as part of the healing process. In the UK these families include foster carers, kinship carers, Special Guardians and adoptive families. Kinship care in the UK is an arrangement whereby the statutory local authority maintains some legal responsibility for a child who is placed with a family member or friend. Special Guardianship Orders are increasingly being used in these situations. This is a formal court order that allows parental control over a child by a person or persons other than the parent. This may be a grandparent, close relative or even a family friend.

Adoption is changing in the UK as more children come into Social Care. Children who are permanently removed from their birth families, after a period in foster care, may be moved to live with adoptive families. Since May 2015 more support is available for adoptive families through the government's Adoption Support Fund. Because of the increased availability of social media and accessible training courses, parents, Special Guardians and carers are much more aware of the needs of their children and are better informed about research about the effect of trauma on the infant brain.

It has become increasingly understood that the whole community around a child needs to have a common understanding of the issues related to difficulties around attachment and trauma. This community should include school staff, extended family and friends, other groups such as scouting or outdoor pursuits and anyone who looks after the child for any length of time. This book is for anybody in this position, to help them understand how to be supportive when a family is involved with therapeutic services and when parents need direct support from a calm, confident companion. These children are back to front. They may not trust praise, and punitive actions can reinforce their feelings of worthlessness, so they need opportunities to help them feel safe, to be accepted for who they are and to be encouraged to explore and play.

Therapists qualified in any of the creative therapies are adapting their therapeutic models to meet the needs of this special group of children and young people. We hope this book will open the door to all qualified professionals, and those in training or considering training, to look at this developing field of therapeutic work.

Origins in Attachment in Action

The seeds of content for this book were sown 20 years ago at the Rainbow of Adoption conferences, which took place under the auspices of Adoption UK from the mid-1990s. They were a valuable opportunity for therapists in the UK, working specifically with adopted children who had experienced early trauma, to come together and share their practice. Amongst the participants at these events were a number of arts therapists who were specialists in working with adoptive families and who were beginning to incorporate the emerging evidence from attachment and neurobiological research into their work. It was clear to us that the difficulties the families were presenting with were often misunderstood by statutory services, and many of these families resorted to the voluntary and private sector for support and therapy.

At the final Rainbow of Adoption Therapies Conference in September 2001 the participants agreed that the time had come to form a professional body for this group of therapists and therapeutic approaches. *Attachment in Action – the UK Association for the Advancement of Attachment Therapies* was born at a follow-up meeting in February 2002. A steering group was formed and over the next two years a constitution, mission statement, training programme and membership criteria were drawn up. We were all working full-time with different organizations and agencies and were scattered around the country, which meant that sometimes progress seemed frustratingly slow. There were representatives from the public sector (Child and Adolescent Mental Health Service and Social Services), private practitioners and specialist voluntary agencies on the steering group. This was to be one of Attachment in Action's great strengths: bringing together therapists working in this wide range of settings, all with a common purpose of providing better services for adopted children and their families. Between 2004 and 2011 we held an annual conference with keynote presenters including David Howe, Colwyn Trevarthen, Kate Cairns, Fran Waters, Luiza Rangel and Richard McKenny. We ran two training seminars a year on subjects including sibling placements, trauma and dissociation, children with attachment difficulties and trauma histories in schools, preventing disruption and the adoptive parents' role in therapy, and days of sharing more general aspects of our developing therapeutic practice.

In 2011 we had the final meeting of Attachment in Action and closed the association as an official organization. We felt we had done our job and that the understanding of the effects of early trauma and attachment difficulties in children living in permanent new homes had moved on. The therapies we were developing in the 1990s have now become more accepted therapeutic approaches and are better understood. The National Institute for Health and Care Excellence (NICE) guideline *Children's Attachment: Attachment in Children and Young People Who are Adopted from Care, in Care or at High Risk of Going into Care* (NICE 2015) includes:

- developing attachment-focused interventions to treat attachment difficulties in children over 5 and young people who have been adopted or are in the care system

- supporting children with attachment difficulties at school

- supporting and training adoptive parents, foster carers and kinship carers

- researching the relationship between attachment difficulties and complex trauma.

The structure of the book

Part 1 of this book is the backdrop to the clinical chapters that follow. In Chapter 1 Franca Brenninkmeyer thoroughly traces the history of post-traumatic stress disorder, complex trauma and developmental trauma through the lens of diagnostic criteria and psychiatric disorders. This story is ongoing because complex trauma and developmental trauma in children are not officially recognized disorders despite the fact that both are commonly used descriptively amongst professionals. It is an important chapter that clearly establishes the group of children who are the subject of this book. In Chapter 2, Anthea Hendry draws from this theoretical base and looks at some of the broad implications for practice. This includes looking at some of the therapeutic frameworks and models that have been developed from this body of theory, and some implications for caregivers. Janet Smith follows this theme in Chapter 3 from the perspective of the caregiver. She emphasizes how challenging it is for parents and caregivers of children with a history of complex trauma. Although their task will have rewards, the demands are great and this needs understanding from all professionals supporting them. Both of these chapters emphasize the need to understand the strengths and difficulties of the individual child and his particular family situation, and the importance of the Team Around the Child working closely together. Vignettes are used in Janet's chapter and all the subsequent clinical chapters to bring alive both how these children have been affected by early abuse and neglect and what they need from their caregivers and from therapeutic services to help them recover.

Assessments are requested increasingly to advise on planning support for children with a history of complex trauma and their families. In Chapter 4 Joy Hasler follows the model used by Catchpoint to assess attachment difficulties and the effects of developmental trauma to inform which therapy programmes are suitable for a family. Through observations and reported behaviours in different settings the assessment draws together the patterns of behaviour that show what is going on for these children, how they view themselves and how they view the world. This is a window into the inner world of the child who is troubled by his traumatic past, so that parents, guardians and carers can increase their understanding of how their child's brain ticks and what the triggers are to his traumatic past.

Chapters 5–10 are clinical chapters with vignettes that paint vivid descriptions of therapeutic work with children who have complex trauma histories. In Chapter 5 Alan Burnell and Jay Vaughan describe how their work has developed over many years at Family Futures. The elaboration of their Neuro Physiological Psychotherapy approach is enhanced by diagrams, which are highly recommended for study by anybody who is unclear about what a neurosequential model of work means. This model is brought to life through description and case material. In Chapter 6 Anthea Hendry and Elizabeth Taylor Buck clearly outline the contribution that art psychotherapists can make to working with this group of children and families. The focus of their chapter is Dyadic Parent–Child Art Psychotherapy – a model of work they have researched, written about and developed training for over the last few years. They outline three different approaches to dyadic work, each one illustrated with a vignette.

In Chapter 7 on music therapy Joy Hasler explores the power of rhythms in our lives and then within therapy. There is a wealth of new research into music and the brain, and examining this and relating it to working with healing the effects of trauma are creating exciting opportunities for families to work in therapy together, and for therapists to use rhythm and music to gain a better understanding of what is happening in the family. Chapter 8 by Molly Holland and Joy Hasler is an interview with Molly, a dramatherapist, who works at Catchpoint. In the dialogue she tells her story from being a child interested in drama to becoming a therapist using drama to work with families. She draws on the processes in dramatherapy and on the power of storytelling which helps the child develop a shared narrative with his parents. The stories, developed between the parent and child, start the process of the child playing with the concepts of 'What happens next?' and the growing belief that he can change things and live in a world that is safe.

Play has long been known to be an essential element in the healthy development of a child. In Chapter 9 Renée Potgieter Marks looks at the value of conventional play therapy alongside the needs of the child suffering the effects of trauma, together with the newer therapy of Eye Movement Desensitization Reprocessing (EMDR). Renée puts them together in an exciting chapter that explores the possibilities that this combination offers to families caring for traumatized children. She believes in the need for a new approach to therapy for complex trauma, and by combining two powerful therapeutic media she is offering just that: a new approach based on ancient knowledge and new research.

In Chapter 10, dance movement therapists Hannah Guy and Sue Topalian both sensitively describe their work with families caring for a traumatized child or children. They show how multi-sensory sequential rhythmic activities can bring about emotional and social healing. They look at the dance of attachment and break it down into elements that can be used therapeutically for older children with permanent carers or adoptive parents who seek to build a positive attachment with their children. Dance movement therapy gives opportunities to bring together the theories of the trauma experts around the world, and put these theories into practice.

The third and final part of the book contains two chapters describing innovative work in different educational settings. Marion Allen is an educational consultant to schools working for Family Futures. She has the advantage of that organization's multi-disciplinary team and assessment process providing a guide to understanding why a particular child is struggling in school. In Chapter 11 Marion offers practical ways to support the child, other children in the school and the school staff to make school a safer and happier learning environment for children who often do not feel this because of their histories of complex trauma. The importance of school staff being trained and supported in managing children with attachment difficulties is a key recommendation in the NICE guideline referred to previously (NICE 2015). The final chapter, Chapter 12, by Sarah Ayache and Martin Gibson, is a fascinating description of their innovative work developing a therapeutic service in a boys' residential school over the last ten years. They emphasize the importance of the therapy team developing close links with the school and care staff, but at the same time they have a dedicated therapy building, which has become an important neutral space both for the boys and the therapy team. Their multi-disciplinary team has developed creative working practices for boys who may be in the school for six or seven years and therefore have the benefit of specialist therapeutic support throughout their time in the school.

Reference

NICE (National Institute for Health and Care Excellence) (2015) *Children's Attachment: Attachment in Children and Young People Who Are Adopted from Care, in Care or at High Risk of Going into Care.* NICE guideline 26. Available at www.nice.org.uk/guidance/ng26, accessed on 7 October 2016.

— PART 1 —

MAPPING OUT
THE TERRITORY

Chapter 1

COMPLEX TRAUMA IN CHILDREN

An Overview of Theoretical Developments

———————— FRANCA BRENNINKMEYER ————————

Trauma really does confront you with the best and the worst. You see the horrendous things that people do to each other, but you also see resiliency, the power of love, the power of caring, the power of commitment, the power of commitment to oneself, the knowledge that there are things that are larger than our individual survival.

Bessel van der Kolk

This chapter will give an overview of the theoretical developments with regard to the concept of 'complex trauma' in children. By way of introduction a summary of where this concept has emerged from will be presented.

Trauma, post-traumatic stress disorder and the *DSM*

'That was awful, really traumatic…' – a spontaneous expression that can often be heard in relation to taxing events in everyday life. Thankfully, many of these exclamations will not relate to psychological trauma in a clinical sense, but they indicate that there is a popular understanding of 'trauma' referring to psychological upset following distressing events.

The word 'trauma' stems from the Greek language and means 'injury' or 'wound'. The use of the word 'trauma' for a 'psychological injury/wound' only appeared at the end of 19th century (Weisaeth 2014). However, it was not until the late 1970s that an official consensus emerged around what a 'psychological trauma' consisted of. This led to the diagnostic category of 'post-traumatic stress disorder' (PTSD), which was first included in the third edition of the American Psychiatric Association's *Diagnostic and Statistical Manual of Mental Disorders* (*DSM-III*) (APA 1981). The enormous number of Vietnam War veterans who were struggling with severe psychological distress helped to advance this development in considerable measure (Friedman, Resick and Keane 2014; Turnbull 1998).

The *DSM* generally defines mental health conditions by their symptoms and not their causes. In an exception to this, the *DSM* defines PTSD explicitly with regard to both *cause* and *effect* (Greenberg, Brooks and Dunn 2015). The cause of the disorder is a traumatic event and the effects are the ensuing PTSD symptoms. The *traumatic event* is termed the 'stressor criterion' or criterion A. After some revisions, criterion A was defined in the *DSM-IV* (APA 1994) as having two parts: criterion A1 is specified as 'the person experienced, witnessed, or was confronted with an event or events that involved actual or threatened death or serious injury, or a threat to the physical integrity of self or others'; criterion A2 became 'the person's response involved intense fear, helplessness, or horror' (APA 1994). The subsequent possible *effects* of such a traumatic event were defined in the *DSM-IV* (APA 1994) as three symptom categories or criteria: criterion B describes recurrent and intrusive *re-experiencing* symptoms (such as dreams, flashbacks), criterion C describes *avoidance* symptoms (including numbing, detachment) and criterion D describes *arousal* symptoms (such as hypervigilance, increased startle). Two further criteria, E and F, respectively stipulated that the symptoms had to last for at least one month and that the distress or 'functional impairment' had to be significant (Friedman *et al.* 2014).

The symptom categories B, C and D each had a subset of symptoms of which a specified minimal number had to be present for PTSD to be diagnosed. Criterion D (arousal symptoms) would, for example, be met if at least two of the following were present: 1) difficulty falling or staying asleep; 2) irritability or outbursts of anger; 3) difficulty concentrating; 4) hypervigilance; 5) exaggerated startle response; and 6) 'physiological activity upon exposure to events that symbolize or resemble an aspect of the traumatic event' (APA 1994). The details regarding the three symptom categories highlight the potentially varying PTSD presentations. These are further added to by the *DSM-IV*

(APA 1994) describing 'specifiers' (acute, chronic and delayed-onset PTSD) as well as possible 'associated features' (e.g. survival guilt, marital problems, loss of job) and 'associated disorders' (e.g. panic disorder, phobias, depression). PTSD was initially classified under the broader category of 'Anxiety Disorders', but this changed in the *DSM-5* (see below).

PTSD in the *ICD*

The International Classification of Diseases (*ICD*) is published by the World Health Organization (WHO). It covers all known medical diseases and includes mental health conditions. PTSD was added in 1992 and defined in a similar manner to how it appeared in the *DSM* (Turnbull 1998).

PTSD and children

The initial *DSM-III* criteria for PTSD in adults were also meant to be used for children and adolescents. It soon appeared, however, that PTSD presented differently in children and therefore the criteria needed to be adjusted. This led to a small number of age-specific features gradually being included (Cohen 1998). With regard to criterion A, the *DSM-IV* specifies that children may react with 'disorganized or agitated behavior' when first exposed to the traumatic event. Criterion B, event re-experiencing, could be expressed through 'trauma related repetitive play', 're-enactment' and 'frightening dreams that may have non-recognizable contents'. Criterion C remained the same as for adults. It was furthermore mentioned that children may express having physical ills (e.g. stomach pains and headaches) and that there may be 'omen formation' (a belief that warning signs must have preceded the trauma and need to be looked out for to prevent future traumas). As it is difficult for children to verbalize their symptoms, the *DSM-IV* stated that the evaluation of symptoms in children must include reports from parents, teachers and other observers (APA 1994).

Traumatized children, especially very young children, continued to be under-diagnosed with PTSD, however, resulting in a number of researchers voicing that the criteria for children needed to be more 'behaviourally anchored' and 'developmentally sensitive' (Friedman and Resick 2014, location no.1084). Kaminer, Seedat and Stein (2005) drew renewed attention to the issue that 'eight of the eighteen PTSD criteria require a verbal description of internal states and experiences, a task beyond the cognitive and expressive language of young children' (p.121–122). PTSD symptoms in young children could therefore easily be missed. Instead, the focus could end up on a co-morbid disorder, such as oppositional defiant disorder and separation anxiety disorder, when these may in fact be 'part and parcel of the PTSD' (Cohen and Scheeringa 2009, p.93). It was advocated to move away from the concept of frequency of a certain number of symptoms, towards considering intensity of symptoms and the ensuing level of impact on the child's functioning and development. It was also pointed out that a number of trauma-related manifestations in children were not included in the criteria, such as regressive behaviours, new fears or re-emergence of old fears, increased carelessness, attention deficit hyperactivity disorder-like (ADHD) behaviours, depression and complex grief symptoms (Cohen 1998, 2010; Frem 2013; Kaminer et al. 2005). However, Cohen and Scheeringa (2009) concluded that although in need of revision, PTSD was 'a well-validated disorder and the most useful construct of child and adolescent post-trauma psychopathology for research and clinical purposes' (p.98). These authors stressed that professionals must improve their knowledge of PTSD, as well as their assessment skills, before arguing that PTSD criteria are not suitable for children, especially chronically traumatized children.

Complex trauma

The concept of 'PTSD' was undoubtedly groundbreaking when first formalized in 1980. Voices questioning it could soon be heard though. Judith Herman, in her seminal book *Trauma and Recovery* (1997, first published 1992), argued that the PTSD criteria were based too much on the experiences and symptoms of war veterans. Traumatic experiences were actually happening closer to home and in significant numbers, especially with regard to domestic and sexual violence. Herman also argued that extreme forms of psychological traumatization were not sufficiently covered by the PTSD criteria. These severe psychological traumas typically occurred in situations where the victim was held in physical or emotional captivity whilst under the permanent, harsh or cruel control of another human being (such as in concentration/prisoner-of-war camps, brothels, long-term domestic violence and in various forms of child abuse). It was thought that the personal, repeated and prolonged nature of these traumas resulted in chronic helplessness (inability to escape), chronic dissociation (detachment from events/ others/self in order to survive), as well as a chronic loss of trust and sense of self. The most significant consequences of functioning in this highly compromised manner were a fragmented self and an inability to relate to others. In addition, there was a heightened chance of being re-victimized and thus a consolidation of symptoms. It was for this altogether more complex and deeper-seated presentation that Herman proposed a new diagnosis of 'complex PTSD'.

Rather than a variation of PTSD, Herman thought of complex PTSD as a separate disorder with its own (seven) diagnostic criteria. The first, stressor criterion (1) was defined as prolonged (months' to years') exposure to 'totalitarian control' that often includes physical and/or sexual abuse/exploitation. The ensuing symptoms were clustered into six criteria defined as 'alterations' in: 2) affect regulation; 3) consciousness; 4) self-perception; 5) perceptions of the perpetrator; 6) relations with others; and 7) systems of meaning. Each of these clusters had two to five symptoms, some of which were traditionally associated with borderline personality disorder (Herman 1997, p.121).

The concept of 'complex PTSD' seemed to resonate with clinicians and researchers, who recognized the symptoms in many of their traumatized clients/study subjects. Bessel van der Kolk (2001), for example, describes how 'over the years, it has become clear that in clinical settings the majority of traumatized treatment seeking patients suffer from a variety of psychological problems that are not included in the diagnoses of PTSD' (p.2).

Research results with regard to complex PTSD – temporarily also known as 'disorders of extreme stress not otherwise specified' (DESNOS) – led to proposals for complex PTSD to be included in the *DSM-IV* and the *DSM-5* as a separate disorder to PTSD (van der Kolk *et al.* 2005). Although to date the proposals have not been successful, the symptoms of complex PTSD were included under the previously mentioned 'associated features' of PTSD in the *DSM-IV*, and a long list of symptoms it is (APA 1994).

Emerging recognition of complex trauma in children

Already in 1991 Terr suggested two subtypes of PTSD in children. The first subtype (I) related to one-off, sudden traumas that resulted in PTSD symptoms as per the *DSM-III*. The second type (II) related to chronic, multiple traumas (e.g. physical or sexual abuse) that led to symptoms of 'denial and numbing, self-hypnosis and dissociation, and rage'; 'considerable sadness' could also occur. Terr notes that 'crossover conditions' (a combination of type I and type II) were possible too (Terr 1991, p.10). It would take a few years before these ideas were progressed (by others). The growing research with regard to complex PTSD in adults advanced this development as it increasingly pointed to the significance of early childhood trauma such as ongoing sexual, physical and emotional abuse (van der Kolk *et al.* 2005). One of the important, large-scale studies (17,337 participants) in this regard is the 'Adverse Childhood Experiences' (ACE) study, which showed strong correlations between the extent of prolonged childhood trauma and the extent of both physical and mental health problems in adulthood (Anda *et al.* 2005; Felitti *et al.* 1998).

Other studies focused on the significant effects of complex trauma on children themselves: persistent difficulties in the children's relational, emotional and educational functioning and further development were repeatedly found – even after the children had been removed from the traumatizing relationships. Professionals increasingly observed that the diagnosis of PTSD only covered limited aspects of these children's multi-faceted and complex presentation. This could on the one hand lead to children being given a combination of seemingly unrelated diagnoses, including PTSD, depression, ADHD, oppositional defiant disorder, anxiety disorder, reactive attachment disorder, etc., which were followed by piecemeal treatments. On the other hand, some children did not meet the thresholds for any of these disorders, in spite of presenting significant difficulties across various domains, which then led to 'no diagnoses' and 'no interventions' (Cook *et al.* 2003; van der Kolk *et al.* 2009).

It was also noted that many chronically traumatized children struggled with existential issues that were not captured by any of the *DSM* diagnoses. These issues related to the child's experience of a persistent, deep-seated lack of safety within his (often adoptive or other permanent substitute) family, as well as ongoing distress and confusion around reasons and sequence of life story events and thus a muddled or poor sense of identity (Hughes 1998; Levy and Orlans 1998).

The described difficulties have been affecting adoptive and other permanent parents/carers too. In the UK these parents more often than not end up parenting children that were chronically traumatized. How often do practitioners hear desperate parents say, 'We thought our child needed safety, love and guidance – after all he had been through – but he keeps reacting with rejection and defiance; why is this and how do we deal with it? We are at our wits' end!' In addition the parents'/carers' own issues are likely to be triggered, especially if they have unresolved loss and trauma experiences themselves (Levy and Orlans 1998; Schooler, Smalley and Callahan 2009).

All of the above galvanized further research and theory formation with regard to complex trauma in children. The National Child Traumatic Stress Network (NCTSN), which was established in 2000 by the US Congress as part of the Children's Health Act, has played an important role in this, as have the Trauma Center at the Justice Resource Institute (van der Kolk and colleagues) and the 'Child Trauma Academy' (Bruce Perry and colleagues).

The NCTSN has since provided evidence to show that high numbers of children referred to mental health clinics for trauma-related concerns have in fact experienced multiple, chronic, interpersonal traumas. The NCTSN's studies also concluded that the *DSM-IV* criteria for PTSD are not sufficient for these children as their symptoms spanned a much wider range (Briggs *et al.* 2012).

According to some child mental health experts, the number of children, families and communities who are grappling with the effects of chronic, interpersonal trauma are on the increase (in Western societies) – to the extent of identifying it as a major public health concern (D'Andrea *et al.* 2012; Shaw and De Jong 2012; Tarren-Sweeney and Vetere 2014).

A possible definition of complex trauma in children

In 2003 the NCTSN published its *White Paper on Complex Trauma in Children and Adolescents* (Cook *et al.* 2003). Prior to setting out their definition, the authors clarify that similar to the term 'trauma', the term 'complex trauma' is often used to refer to both exposure to trauma as well as the ensuing immediate and longer-term impact (Cook *et al.* 2003).

The NCTSN's definition of complex trauma in children and adolescents can be summarized as follows: complex trauma in children is the exposure to multiple forms of chronic, interpersonal maltreatment – such as emotional, physical and sexual abuse, emotional neglect, witnessing of domestic violence – that start in early childhood and that take place either simultaneously or sequentially within the child's caregiving system. The overall impact of this exposure is a loss of core capacities for self-regulation, for interpersonal relatedness and for the development of age-appropriate competencies, which often leads to long-term problems (i.e. into adulthood). These long-term problems include further victimization and cumulative impairments in physical and mental health, work, family life and with regard to the law (Cook *et al.* 2003; Kinniburgh *et al.* 2005).

The specific symptoms of complex trauma in children are classified into seven inter-related domains of impairment: 1) attachment; 2) biology; 3) affect/emotional regulation; 4) dissociation; 5) behavioural regulation; 6) cognition; 7) self-concept. These impairments affect the child at the time of exposure, as well as during his subsequent developmental trajectory. The authors note that the seven domains are phenomenologically classified domains, i.e. as they clinically appear, rather than being derived from formally approved epidemiological research (Cook *et al.* 2003). Each of the seven domains of impairment will be briefly elaborated on below (whereby the order of the domains was slightly changed to enhance fluency: 'affect regulation' will be commented on before 'biology').

Attachment

An attachment between infant and parent (which includes regular or permanent caregivers) begins to form when the parent appropriately reads and responds to the infant's cues for protection, nurture and connection, whilst providing emotional and physical regulation when the child is uncomfortable or upset. As the infant develops, the parent also provides permission and stimulation, as well as safe boundaries, for the child's natural instinct to explore the world. If over time the parent is consistently available and sensitive to the young child's needs for safety, connection and exploration, the parent will become a source of safety, a 'secure base' for the child. The child will want to stay close to/return to the parent, especially when distressed, as the child 'knows' that the parent will regulate him and keep him safe, loved and validated. Thus a 'secure attachment' to his parent develops. This will gradually be internalized by the child, who learns to trust that others and the world are (basically) safe, and that life is manageable, including a certain amount of (dis)stress.

Numerous studies have shown that important aspects of a child's development, in particular his capacity to self-regulate, communicate, trust and have close relationships, as well as his curiosity and sense of agency, are positively related to a secure attachment in early childhood (Bowlby 1965, first published 1953; Grossmann, Grossmann and Waters 2005; Karen 1998).

Considering the definition of complex trauma, it becomes clear why a compromised attachment is both part of the exposure to complex trauma as well as a subsequent 'domain of impairment'. A child exposed to complex trauma (i.e. 'to chronic, interpersonal maltreatment that takes place within the child's caregiving system') is often a child whose experience of attachment constitutes a trauma in itself. The ensuing 'impairment' with regard to attachment is an insecure attachment pattern that will affect the child even if removed from the traumatizing parent. The insecure attachment pattern will often be of the 'disorganized' type (Cook *et al.* 2003). This means that, when distressed, the child will not seek out the much-needed security from the parent – as he has learnt that the parent is a source of distress – but become highly anxious, confused, chaotic and possibly aggressive; attempts at self-soothing and dissociating/zoning out can be observed too. A disorganized attachment pattern leaves the child in the paradoxical situation of both desperately needing and intensely fearing attachment security (Karen 1998; Lyons-Ruth *et al.* 1991).

When a parent is 'merely' inconsistent or dismissive (rather than traumatic), the ensuing anxious or avoidant attachment patterns will nonetheless contribute to complex trauma exposure because the child has a less than secure base to turn to during/between episodes of trauma. (It is important to note that in a child's caregiving environment there may be more than one attachment figure; therefore, even in a child exposed to complex trauma, attachment patterns may vary.) Research has shown that having at least one safe, attuned, consistent and protective caregiver can provide a significant buffer against the most devastating effects of the exposure to complex trauma (NSCDC 2015).

However, over 80 per cent of children exposed to complex trauma do not have any secure attachments (Cook *et al.* 2003).

The centrality of a compromised attachment in children with complex trauma (both with regard to cause and effect) can be linked to the popularity of the concepts of 'attachment disorder' and 'severe attachment difficulties' in the late 1970s to the late 1990s (Levy and Orlans 1998).

Affect regulation

Affect regulation in this context includes sensory regulation. Normally when an infant or a child is distressed, the parent will help the child to regulate his physiological and internal states by sensory soothing, emotional calming and by 'making safe' and 'making sense'. Such a pattern of regulatory support is associated with the development of a secure attachment. In time the child will internalize the parent's modulating support and make it his own: he becomes more and more self-regulated (though many young and not so young people will maintain the need for regulation by others, especially at times of high distress). For this progress to take place, the parent needs to be aware of the co-regulation process that occurs when he regulates his child: the child will inadvertently feed off the parent's own sensory and affect regulation (Bronson 2000; Gerhardt 2006).

Affect regulation also involves being able to identify and express feelings with words, gestures and facial expressions, so as to facilitate communication about emotions. As parents soothe and regulate their young child, many will naturally identify and verbalize their child's feelings as well as their own (appropriately). In this process the young child will gradually learn to identify and name emotions, recognize them in himself and others and start empathizing with others (Bronson 2000; Gerhardt 2006).

If the child is left with limited or no regulatory support from caregivers when distressed, or the caregivers become the source of distress, the child may respond with confusion, helplessness, rage and withdrawal. He is likely to remain emotionally young and/ or illiterate and his attachment pattern is likely to become (highly) insecure. Rather than modulated, his emotional responses will generally become dysregulated, hyper-aroused (fight/flight) or dissociative, hypo-aroused (freeze/submit). A certain alternation between hyper- and hypo-reactivity is observed in most normally functioning children and adults. In children (and adults) with histories of complex trauma, however, these alternations can be more intense and faster, but also slower due to 'getting stuck' in either a hyper- or hypo-aroused state. In time, hyper- and hypo-aroused responses can become the default responses to any, even minor, (dis)stress. The capacity to regulate internal states thus becomes impaired (Blaustein and Kinniburgh 2010; Cook *et al.* 2003).

Biology

The most significant biological impairments in children that follow exposure to complex trauma relate to their neurobiological development. Studies have shown that complex trauma in childhood alters some aspects of normal brain formation and functioning, which results in a vulnerability to mental health problems long after the complex trauma has ceased. These findings are explained by the young child's brain being exposed to excessive amounts of stress-related substances that overwhelm and negatively affect the stress-regulating parts of the brain. Consequently the child is likely to be both highly susceptible to stress and less able to manage stress. The visible symptoms of this are emotional, behavioural and cognitive dysregulation/hyper-reactivity that alternate with dissociative responses and hypo-reactivity (Anda *et al.* 2005; Perry 2008).

The *Journal of Child Psychology and Psychiatry* (2016) published an annual research review regarding the 'enduring neurobiological effects of childhood abuse and neglect'. The conclusion was that 'structural and functional abnormalities initially attributed to psychiatric illness may be a more direct consequence of abuse. Childhood maltreatment exerts a prepotent influence on brain development and has been an unrecognized confound in almost all psychiatric neuroimaging studies' (Teicher and Samson 2016, p.241). The authors further state that the observed changes in the brain are 'best understood as adaptive responses to facilitate survival and reproduction in the face of adversity' (p.241). Remarkably, these changes were also observed in resilient individuals who had been exposed to maltreatment histories. The relationship between structural and functional changes in the brain and psychopathology therefore left many more questions to answer.

Dissociation

Dissociation can be considered an adaptive mechanism to cope with the chronic exposure to interpersonal trauma: the child learns to disconnect from the world and himself in order to minimize distress. In the long run this can lead to sensations, emotions, memories, thinking and behaviour not being associated with each other, nor integrated into meaningful wholes; instead they become compartmentalized and 'operate on their own' or outside the conscious awareness of the child. Connecting to these compartmentalized aspects of functioning may only be possible separately, in part, or not at all. The child may therefore be prone to a lack of conscious sensory and emotional awareness (e.g. simply not sensing when he has eaten enough, not feeling that he has emotionally hurt someone). He can also display automatic behaviours and genuinely 'not know' about them later on. In addition there can be regular or constant aloofness. Dissociation in chronically traumatized children can go as far as resulting in a vague or fragmented sense of self, or even a multiple sense of self. The child may develop an internal awareness of different self-states, sometimes referred to as 'imaginary others' or 'invisible friends' – for example, Joey is strong and mean, he wants to hurt people; Mitzi is the clever one, she knows what people think (Cook *et al.* 2003; Wieland 2011).

The capacity to process, associate and integrate sensory, emotional and cognitive information into cohesive wholes is essential with regard to the child's overall development and 'integrity'. Impairments in this domain (i.e. dissociation) can increase children's vulnerability to re-victimization and to remaining stuck in old patterns with regard to various aspects of their functioning, including attachment and challenging behaviours. Dissociation is likely to play a role in children who themselves become perpetrators of chronic interpersonal trauma (Cook *et al.* 2003; Wieland 2011).

Behavioural regulation

The effect of complex trauma on children also manifests itself as a lack of behavioural regulation. Hyperactive, reactive and impulsive behaviour ensues and often manifests itself together with an intense need for control. This can lead to relentless defiance, aggression, destruction, sexual acting out and a seeming disregard of norms around respecting others' space, belongings and feelings. The need for control can be most prominent in potentially close relationships (i.e. with parents, siblings and peers). Conversely, there can be rigid behaviours, with a great need for routines and predictability, which are set and maintained by others. Changes and transitions are not tolerated well.

Some children do not present with obviously dysregulated behaviour, but as withdrawn, regressed or compulsively compliant. This may change in early adolescence, however, when their behaviours can suddenly become extremely challenging. Self-harm and risk-taking behaviours (especially with regard to online activities, gangs, drugs and alcohol) may start to appear. The carers/parents are often dismayed at this development in their previously seemingly well-adjusted child (Blaustein and Kinniburgh 2010; Cook *et al.* 2003; Gerhardt 2006).

Some of the dysregulated behaviours can be understood as automatic reactions to reminders of previous traumas, or as re-enactments of experiences. Yet others are function of a neurobiologically related lack of self-regulation/stress management combined with an intense yet immature need for mastery, recognition, intimacy and protection (against perceived threats and unmanageable feelings). One way or another, these behaviours are likely to interfere with relationships, with learning, with leisure pursuits and even with engaging in activities that could potentially be regulating (Blaustein and Kinniburgh 2010; Cook *et al.* 2003).

Cognition

Children exposed to complex trauma are likely to have some cognitive impairments compared to peers who were not exposed to complex trauma. Expressive and receptive language development is often delayed in young children, and their overall IQ scores tend to be lower too. As they progress though primary school it becomes clear that their attention, flexibility and creativity are not as strong as in their non-traumatized peers, and neither are their executive functioning and emerging abstract reasoning. This is reflected in lower educational achievements, which may in turn affect their already low self-esteem as well as future chances with regard to jobs and careers (Blaustein and Kinniburgh 2010; Cook *et al.* 2003; Gerhardt 2006).

Self-concept

Unlike the positive self-concept that usually develops in non-traumatized and securely attached children, exposure to complex trauma often leads to a deep-seated sense of self that is unworthy, unlovable, helpless and incompetent; this may, however, be masked by excessive bravado and displays of power and control. Blaming themselves for matters that they were not in any way responsible for occurs too. These children are prone to an entrenched sense of shame that is related to having internalized the way they were treated by chronically maltreating caregivers. This can become more pronounced from the age of around 8 years, as awareness of the meaning of their own history, and how others might think of it, increases. Their sense of identity in relation to their birth family is often pained, confused and/or dissociated from. It is common for children with negative self-concepts to have difficulties engaging with others for mutual social enjoyment and support (Blaustein and Kinniburgh 2010; Brodzinsky and Schechter 1990; Hughes 1998).

Developmental trauma disorder

To distinguish the specificity of the effects of complex trauma on children, in that there are pervasive effects on children's *development* which then reverberate throughout the child's life and into adulthood, Bessel van der Kolk proposed a new diagnosis of 'developmental trauma disorder' (DTD). The proposal was formally published in the article 'Developmental trauma disorder: A new, rational diagnosis for children with complex trauma histories' in the May 2005 issue of the *Psychiatric Annals*, which had 'complex trauma' as its specific focus (van der Kolk 2005).

In the following years the NCTSN worked on a 'consensus of proposed criteria for Developmental Trauma Disorder'. These criteria for DTD were presented in a formal proposal to include DTD into the *DSM-5* which was submitted to the working parties of the DSM in 2009 (van der Kolk *et al.* 2009). The criteria for DTD were organized in *DSM* style and are therefore not a straightforward 'translation' of the seven aforementioned domains of impairment in children exposed to complex trauma. However, on closer reading, the seven domains of impairment are included in the six proposed clusters of symptoms (of which a certain number have to be present for a diagnosis to be made).

As for PTSD, criterion A relates to 'exposure' and has two parts. Criterion A1 refers to the child or the adolescent having directly experienced or witnessed 'repeated and severe episodes of interpersonal violence' for at least 'one year'. In addition, for criterion A2, the child or the adolescent must have experienced 'significant disruptions of protective caregiving' due to recurring changes in, and separations from, his primary caregiver and/or 'severe and persistent emotional abuse' (van der Kolk *et al.* 2009).

Criteria B, C and D correspond to 'affective and physiological dysregulation', 'attentional and behavioural dysregulation' and 'self- and relational dysregulation', which respectively have four, five and six symptoms each. The symptoms are likely to be familiar to many a practitioner who works with adopted and fostered children. Criterion D, 'self- and relational dysregulation', for example, includes: 1) difficult reunions with caregiver after separations; 2) a sense of self that is essentially negative; 3) relationships with peers and adults that are persistently marked by distrust, defiance and lack of reciprocity; 4) verbal and physical aggression; 5) inappropriate, disproportionate ways of trying to make intimate contact; and finally, 6) a lack of empathy or over-responsiveness to others' distress.

Criterion E refers to 'posttraumatic spectrum symptoms' (of which a minimum of two have to be present). Criteria F and G are respectively defined as symptoms having to be 'present for at least 6 months' and leading to 'functional impairment' in at least two domains of family, school, peer group, vocation, the law and health (van der Kolk *et al.* 2009).

The proposal for this new diagnostic category of DTD included numerous references to supporting empirical data (van der Kolk *et al.* 2009). However, in spite of diligent efforts (D'Andrea *et al.* 2012), DTD was not accepted into the *DSM-5* (APA 2013a). The reasons for this are intricate, involving at least in part ideology and politics (Bremness and Polzin 2014; Schmid, Petermann and Fegert 2013). Still, the definition of PTSD in the *DSM-5* saw its most significant revision since its inception in 1980 (APA 2013a).

PTSD in the *DSM-5*

The debates around PTSD in children, complex trauma in adults and children, as well as DTD, appear to have influenced the latest, *DSM-5* criteria of PTSD. These are now more inclusive of developmental considerations as well as symptoms associated with complex trauma. Also, PTSD has become part of a new overall category of 'trauma and stressor-related disorders' (rather than anxiety disorders as before).

With regard to the stressor criterion A1, 'exposure to sexual violence' and 'repeated exposure to traumatic materials' are explicitly mentioned. Former criterion A2 (i.e. 'the person's response involved intense fear, helplessness, or horror') has been removed in the *DSM-5* because research has shown that this criterion was not valid (Friedman and Resick 2014; Greenberg *et al.* 2015). Some of the PTSD symptoms have been reworded and reorganized into four rather than three symptom clusters or criteria. These criteria are now 'intrusion', 'avoidance', 'negative alterations in cognitions and mood' and 'alterations in arousal and reactivity' and between them they comprise three altogether new symptoms: 1) persistent inaccurate blame with regard to self or others for being the cause of the traumatic event or its consequences; 2) enduring negative emotions related to the trauma (such as fear, horror, anger and shame); and 3) behaviours that are self-destructive or reckless (APA 2013b; Friedman and Resick 2014).

The *DSM-5* also specifies a 'dissociative subtype of PTSD', which includes symptoms of derealization or depersonalization in addition to the other PTSD symptoms. This subtype is assumed to be typically more prevalent in 'complex' children/adults (i.e. those who have a history of multiple, chronic trauma and/or severe childhood adversity, and who are more challenging to treat) (Friedman and Resick 2014; Greenberg *et al.* 2015).

A new PTSD subtype for children of 6 years and younger

The *DSM-5* criteria for PTSD are still to be used for children of seven years and older. The changes together with the age-specific features of the *DSM–IV* seem to have made the criteria more appropriate for this age group of children, even for those with complex trauma.

For children of six years and younger, however, a new developmental subtype of PTSD – post-traumatic stress disorder in pre-school children

– is included in the *DSM-5*. For this age group, criterion A includes 'loss, injury, or death of a parent or caregiver' (Friedman and Resick 2014). The remainder of the criteria differ in that some of them have been reworded (e.g. 'irritable/aggressive behavior' has been extended to include 'extreme temper tantrums'). Also, the necessary number of symptoms has been reduced, and some have been deleted, especially those that cannot be derived from behaviours (i.e. amnesia, negative cognitions and self-blame). The new symptom of 'reckless behavior' is also not included (APA 2013b; Friedman and Resick 2014).

ICD-11

Interestingly, it seems that 'complex PTSD' will be included as a new diagnosis in the *ICD-11*, which will be published in 2017 or 2018. The *ICD-11 Beta Draft* (WHO 2016) describes the stressor criterion as 'an event or series of events of an extreme and prolonged or repetitive nature that is experienced as extremely threatening or horrific and from which escape is difficult or impossible'. The ensuing symptoms are clustered into the three PTSD criteria of 'event re-experiencing', 'avoidance' and 'arousal', and into three further criteria specific to complex PTSD: 1) affect regulation problems that are severe and pervasive; 2) persistent negative, diminishing beliefs about self, with deep-seated feelings of shame, guilt or failure (related to the traumatic events); and 3) enduring relationship problems especially in close relationships. The criterion of 'significant impairment in personal, family, social, educational, occupational or other important areas of functioning' will need to be met too (WHO 2016).

Conclusion

Children who have experienced chronic, interpersonal trauma often present a wide array of difficulties that are exceedingly challenging to live with – for the children as well as their families, peers, schools and communities. To study and therapeutically support these children, some researchers and practitioners will work within the conceptual framework of PTSD according to the *DSM-5*. It seems promising that aspects relating to child development and complex trauma have seen increased inclusion in the latest *DSM* criteria for PTSD.

Some researchers and practitioners (and organizations) will, however, (continue to) find that the concepts of complex trauma according to the NCTSN and/or the upcoming *ICD-11*, and even the unofficial 'developmental trauma disorder', are more accurate with regard to capturing these children's issues and thinking about effective support. The latter has led to some specific and innovative approaches to assessment and intervention, which include the use of creative arts. A number of these approaches will be elaborated on in the following chapters.

Acknowledgement

The writing of this chapter was made possible in part by a Lottery fund grant, which generously supported various aspects of PAC-UK's work between 2011 and 2016. PAC-UK is a registered adoption support agency in the UK; the author of the chapter heads their Child and Family Service in London.

References

Anda, R., Felitti, V., Bremner, J., Walker, J. *et al.* (2005) 'The enduring effects of abuse and related adverse experiences in childhood: A convergence of evidence from neurobiology and epidemiology.' *European Archives of Psychiatry and Clinical Neuroscience 256*, 3, 174–186.

APA (American Psychiatric Association) (1981) *Diagnostic and Statistical Manual of Mental Disorders (DSM-III)*. Washington, DC: American Psychiatric Association.

APA (American Psychiatric Association) (1994) 'Posttraumatic Stress Disorder.' *Diagnostic and Statistical Manual of Mental Disorders (DSM-IV)*. Washington, DC: American Psychiatric Association. Available at www.cirp.org/library/psych/ptsd2, accessed on 10 October 2016.

APA (American Psychiatric Association) (2013a) *Diagnostic and Statistical Manual of Mental Disorders (DSM-5)*. Washington, DC: American Psychiatric Association.

APA (American Psychiatric Association) (2013b) 'Posttraumatic Stress Disorder.' Available at www.dsm5.org/Documents/PTSD Fact Sheet.pdf, accessed on 10 October 2016.

Blaustein, M. and Kinniburgh, K. (2010) *Treating Traumatic Stress in Children and Adolescents*. New York, NY: Guilford Press.

Bowlby, J. (1965, first published 1953) *Child Care and the Growth of Love*. London: Penguin.

Bremness, A. and Polzin, W. (2014) 'Commentary: Developmental trauma disorder. A missed opportunity in DSM.' *Journal of the Canadian Academy of Child and Adolescent Psychiatry 23*, 2, 144–147.

Briggs, E., Fairbank, J., Greeson, J., Layne, C. *et al.* (2012) 'Links between child and adolescent trauma exposure and service use histories in a national clinic-referred sample.' *Psychological Trauma: Theory, Research, Practice and Policy 5*, 2, 101–109.

Brodzinsky, D. M. and Schechter, M. D. (eds) (1990) *The Psychology of Adoption*. Oxford: Oxford University Press.

Bronson, M. (2000) *Self-Regulation in Early Childhood.* New York, NY: Guilford Press.

Cohen, J. (1998) 'Practice parameters for the assessment and treatment of children and adolescents with posttraumatic stress disorder.' *Journal of the American Academy of Child and Adolescent Psychiatry 37* (suppl.), 4S–26S.

Cohen, J. (2010) 'Practice parameter for the assessment and treatment of children and adolescents with posttraumatic stress disorder.' *Journal of the American Academy of Child and Adolescent Psychiatry 49*, 4, 414–430.

Cohen, J. A. and Scheeringa, M. S. (2009) 'Post-traumatic stress disorder diagnosis in children: Challenges and promises.' *Dialogues in Clinical Neuroscience 11*, 1, 91–99.

Cook, A., Blaustein, M., Spinazzola, J. and van der Kolk, B. (2003) *Complex Trauma in Children and Adolescents.* White Paper. National Child Traumatic Stress Network. Complex Trauma Task Force. Available at www.nctsnet.org/nctsn_assets/pdfs/edu_materials/ComplexTrauma_All.pdf, accessed on 10 October 2016.

D'Andrea, W., Ford, J., Stolbach, B., Spinazzola, J. and van der Kolk, B. (2012) 'Understanding interpersonal trauma in children: Why we need a developmentally appropriate trauma diagnosis.' *American Journal of Orthopsychiatry 82*, 2, 187–200.

Felitti, V., Anda, R., Nordenberg, D., Williamson, D. *et al.* (1998) 'Relationship of childhood abuse and household dysfunction to many of the leading causes of death in adults. The Adverse Childhood Experiences (ACE) study.' *American Journal of Preventative Medicine 14*, 4, 245–258.

Frem, T. (2013) 'PTSD in pre-school children: A review and synthesis of research on the need for a separate DSM category.' *Concept 36.* Available at https://concept.journals. villanova.edu/article/view/1529, accessed on 10 October 2016.

Friedman, M. and Resick, P. (2014) 'DSM-5 Criteria for PTSD.' In M. Friedman, T. Keane and P. Resick (eds) *Handbook of PTSD: Science and Practice* (2nd edn). New York, NY: Guilford Press. (Kindle version, retrieved from Amazon.co.uk)

Friedman, M., Resick, P. and Keane T. (2014) 'PTSD from DSM-III to DSM-5: Progress and Challenges.' In M. Friedman, T. Keane and P. Resick (eds) *Handbook of PTSD: Science and Practice* (2nd edn). New York, NY: Guilford Press.

Gerhardt, S. (2006) *Why Love Matters: How Affection Shapes a Baby's Brain.* London: Routledge.

Greenberg, N., Brooks, S. and Dunn, R. (2015) 'Latest developments in post-traumatic stress disorder: Diagnosis and treatment.' *British Medical Bulletin 114*, 1, 147–155.

Grossmann, K., Grossmann, K. and Waters, E. (2005) *Attachment from Infancy to Adulthood.* New York, NY: Guilford Press.

Herman, J. (1997) *Trauma and Recovery. The Aftermath of Violence from Domestic Abuse to Political Terror.* New York, NY: Basic Books.

Hughes, D. (1998) *Building the Bonds of Attachment.* Northvale, NJ: Jason Aronson.

Kaminer, D., Seedat, S. and Stein, D. (2005) 'Post-traumatic stress disorder in children.' *World Psychiatry 4*, 2, 121–125.

Karen, R. (1998) *Becoming Attached.* New York, NY: Oxford University Press.

Kinniburgh, K., Blaustein, M., Spinazzola, J. and van der Kolk, B. (2005) 'Attachment, self-regulation and competency.' *Psychiatric Annals 35*, 5, 424–430.

Levy, T. and Orlans, M. (1998) *Attachment, Trauma and Healing. Understanding and Treating Attachment Disorder in Children and Families.* Washington, DC: Child Welfare League of America.

Lyons-Ruth, K., Repacholi, B., McLeod, S. and Silva, E. (1991) 'Disorganized attachment behavior in infancy: Short-term stability, maternal and infant correlates, and risk-related subtypes.' *Development and Psychopathology 3*, 4, 377.

NSCDC (National Scientific Council on the Developing Child) (2015) *Supportive Relationships and Active Skill-Building Strengthen the Foundations of Resilience.* Center on the Developing Child – Harvard University, working paper 13. Available at http://developingchild.harvard.edu/wp-content/uploads/2015/05/The-Science-of-Resilience1.pdf, accessed on 11 November 2016.

Perry, B. (2008) 'Child Maltreatment: A Neurodevelopmental Perspective on the Role of Trauma and Neglect in Psychopathology.' In T. Beauchaine and S. Hinshaw (eds) *Child and Adolescent Psychopathology.* Hoboken, NJ: John Wiley & Sons.

Schmid, M., Petermann, F. and Fegert, J. (2013) 'Developmental trauma disorder: Pros and cons of including formal criteria in the psychiatric diagnostic systems.' *BMC Psychiatry 13*, 3. Available at www.biomedcentral.com/1471-244X/13/3, accessed on 11 November 2016.

Schooler, J., Smalley, B. and Callahan, T. (2009) *Wounded Children, Healing Homes.* Colorado Springs, CO: NavPress.

Shaw, M. and De Jong, M. (2012) 'Child abuse and neglect: A major public health issue and the role of child and adolescent mental health services.' *The Psychiatrist, 36*, 9, 321–325.

Tarren-Sweeney, M. and Vetere, A. (2014) *Mental Health Services for Vulnerable Children and Young People.* Abingdon: Routledge.

Teicher, M. and Samson, J. (2016) 'Annual research review: Enduring neurobiological effects of childhood abuse and neglect.' *Journal of Child Psychology and Psychiatry 57*, 3, 241–266.

Terr, L. (1991) 'Childhood traumas: An outline and overview.' *American Journal of Psychiatry 148*, 1, 10–20.

Turnbull, G. (1998) 'A review of post-traumatic stress disorder. Part I: Historical development and classification.' *Injury 29*, 2, 87–91.

van der Kolk, B. (2001) 'The Assessment and Treatment of Complex PTSD.' In R. Jehuda (ed.) *Treating Trauma Survivors with PTSD.* Washington, DC: American Psychiatric Press. Available at www.traumacenter.org/products/pdf_files/Complex_PTSD.pdf, accessed on 10 October 2016.

van der Kolk, B. (2005) 'Developmental trauma disorder. A new, rational diagnosis for children with complex trauma histories.' *Psychiatric Annals 35*, 5, 401–408.

van der Kolk, B., Pynoos, R., Cicchetti, D., Cloitre, M. *et al.* (2009) *Proposal to Include a Developmental Trauma Disorder Diagnosis for Children and Adolescents in the DSM-5.* Available at www.traumacenter.org/announcements/DTD_papers_Oct_09.pdf, accessed on 10 October 2016.

van der Kolk, B., Roth, S., Pelcovitz, D., Sunday, S. and Spinazzola, J. (2005) 'Disorders of extreme stress: The empirical foundation of a complex adaptation to trauma.' *Journal of Traumatic Stress 18*, 5, 389–399.

Weisaeth, L. (2014) 'The History of Psychic Trauma.' In M. Friedman, T. Keane and P. Resick (eds) *Handbook of PTSD: Science and Practice* (2nd edn). New York, NY: Guilford Press.

WHO (World Health Organization) (2016) *ICD-11 Beta Draft (Foundation).* Available at http://apps.who.int/classifications/icd11/browse/f/en#!/http://id.who.int/icd/entity/585833559, accessed on 10 October 2016.

Wieland, S. (2011) *Dissociation in Traumatized Children and Adolescents.* New York, NY: Routledge.

Chapter 2

CREATIVE THERAPIES FOR COMPLEX TRAUMA

Theory into Practice

───────────── ANTHEA HENDRY ─────────────

Introduction

The evolution and definitions of complex trauma and developmental trauma in children are described in Chapter 1. In essence they both involve a child being exposed to repeated forms of chronic, interpersonal maltreatment that take place within the child's caregiving system (Cook *et al.* 2005; van der Kolk 2005). The indicators include emotional, behavioural and physiological dysregulation and impaired attachment relationships. The terms 'complex trauma' and 'developmental trauma' are used interchangeably in this book although in future there may be greater clarity on distinguishing features. The neurobiology of maltreatment research is complex and fast moving (Woolgar 2013), but a consensus of evidence is beginning to emerge that can give guidance to professionals. This chapter is about some of this guidance for practice developed from key researchers. It is divided into three main sections.

The first is an outline of the work of key researchers who have influenced our understanding of the neurodevelopmental impact of complex trauma. Each has indicated the implications of their work for practitioners and models, and frameworks of therapy have been developed from their work. Three of these are described: 'Dyadic Developmental Psychotherapy', the 'Neurosequential Model of Therapeutics' and the 'Attachment, Regulation and Competencies' model.

The second section is a description of some implications for caregivers, particularly the concept of 'developmental re-parenting' and its importance for caregivers and professionals working with children with complex trauma histories. This section also describes why there is a risk of secondary trauma for caregivers, and contains references to models of parenting based on the concept of developmental re-parenting and reasons for involving parents directly in the therapy with the child.

The third section gives an indication of the need for a holistic approach to the complexities and challenges in working with children with complex trauma and how creative therapists can contribute to this.

Implications for practice from key researchers

Allan Schore

Attachment theory has been central to working with adopted and fostered children since the 1980s (Fahlberg 1991). It has absorbed and integrated other major schools of thought with regard to human development and can now be considered an essential developmental theory and part of our understanding of the effects of maltreatment (Howe 2005). Schore has synthesized 'findings from psychoanalytic theory and attachment theory with neuroscience research to highlight the pivotal role of favourable early attachments in the proper development of the right hemisphere of the brain, which in turn critically influences the development of emotion regulation' (Crenshaw 2014, p.22). Schore continues to develop his model of the brain development and the biological disruptions that are affected by relational trauma (Schore 2013). He describes relational trauma as the quintessential expression of complex trauma. Using recent research evidence he examines relational trauma and its impact on stress regulation and dissociative defensive functions. He concludes that the implications for psychotherapy are the need to recognize 'the survival strategy of dissociation' (p.17), the early formation of which requires therapeutic approaches that aid the processing of unconscious emotions, especially negative ones.

Dan Siegel

Dan Siegel has integrated this understanding of attachment theory and how the brain knows and remembers into his 'Interpersonal Neurobiology of the Developing Mind'. He reviewed findings, including the work of Schore, from a range of disciplines, and concluded that collaborative interpersonal interaction is 'the key to healthy development' (Siegel 2001, p.72) and that 'the mind may continue to develop in response to emotional relationships throughout the life span' (p.90). This means that we all continue to benefit from the experience of living with the basic elements of secure attachments, which Siegel suggests consists of five components:

- Collaborative, contingent communication – including non-verbal attunement through eye contact, tone of voice, bodily gestures, timing and intensity.

- Reflective dialogue, including in infancy a caregiver making sense of a child's signals in her own mind and communicating this sense in a way that is meaningful to the child.

- Interactive repair to re-establish connection after an attunement disruption.

- Coherent narratives connecting past, present and future.

- Emotional communication so that both positive and negative emotions are accepted, recognized and shared.

These five components in infancy and early childhood are described by Siegel as major contributory factors in a child's ability to develop a sense of emotional well-being and psychological resilience. He combined the findings from attachment research and psychotherapy research and 'added the contributions of neuroscience to our understanding of how attachment and psychotherapy change the structure of the brain' (Crenshaw 2014, p.22).

Dyadic Developmental Psychotherapy

The implications of Siegel's work for therapy with traumatized children have most notably been utilized by Dan Hughes, who for the last 20 years has integrated these components into his attachment-based treatment, Dyadic Developmental Psychotherapy (DDP) (Hughes 2004, 2007, 2014). He gives particular weight to what works in the therapeutic relationship. 'A therapeutic relationship that is modelled on the principles of attachment and intersubjective relationships is likely to be a good formulation for meeting the therapeutic needs of these children' (Hughes 2014, p.4). The aims of DDP are to help both the child and the caregiver to feel safe enough to enter into interactions with the therapist and each other that offer a different intersubjective experience. This enhances attachment security whilst helping the child to process, connect and make sense (cognitively and emotionally) of present, past and future.

Bruce Perry

Perry (2009) integrates core concepts of neurodevelopment into a practical clinical approach. He describes four main principles that come from neurodevelopmental research and that have particular implications for therapists. First, the brain undergoes a sequential development from the bottom (brainstem area) to the top (limbic and cortical area), whereby development of the higher parts of the brain depend on successful development of the lower parts. Second, the brain is user-dependent, which means that if a child's stress response is activated repeatedly the brain will adapt and develop in response to this. Third, the brain has sensitive periods of development, particularly during infancy and young childhood, during which the brain has high plasticity. Fourth, the influence of relationships on the developing brain in infancy is particularly important for modulating stress.

From these key principles Perry suggests the following implications for therapists:

- The timing of childhood trauma is significant. In-utero and infant trauma has a more fundamental impact than trauma experiences in an older child. To overcome early negative neurodevelopmental experiences, therapeutic input needs to focus first on the regulation of anxiety and impulsivity. Perry suggests that 'therapeutic massage, yoga, balancing exercises, and music and movement, as well as similar somatosensory interventions that provide patterned, repetitive, neural input to the brainstem...would be organising and regulating input that would diminish anxiety, impulsivity, and other trauma related systems' (Perry 2009, p.243).

- Patterned, repetitive activity is also effective, given the brain's use-dependence, but one hour a week of therapy will not be sufficient to alter the impact of early trauma. It is essential to get a child into a stable environment and understand that the caregiving relationship is the major mechanism through which change will happen. It is in this relationship that the patterned repetitive activity will be most beneficial.

- Following work on self-regulation, the focus can turn to relational-related problems for which creative therapies are very appropriate. There is a 'recommendation for co-therapeutic activities where parent and child can engage in services together' (Perry 2009, p.255). After this, verbal or insight-orientated therapies can be considered. The therapeutic process therefore follows the sequential process of brain development.

The Neurosequential Model of Therapeutics

Perry has developed the Neurosequential Model of Therapeutics (NMT), which incorporates these principles. NMT is 'not a specific therapeutic technique; it is a multidimensional assessment "lens" designed to guide clinical problem solving and outcome monitoring by providing a useful "picture" of the client's current strengths and vulnerabilities in the context of his or her developmental history' (Perry and Dobson 2013, p.250). The data gathered in either quantitative or qualitative form is 'organised into a neuroscience "map"...which provides the clinical team with an approximation of the current functional organisation of the client's brain' (p.250).

Perry and Dobson make some specific recommendations for professionals working with children who have been exposed to complex trauma (Perry and Dobson 2013). These include:

- The importance of the *therapeutic web*: the collective of healthy, invested adults and peers who provide the relational milieu of the child' (p.256, original emphasis).

- The importance of the child's family being 'trauma-informed' (p.257), which means providing psycho-education not just to the adults parenting the child but also to any siblings in the household.

- The need for activities for the child that can provide 'patterned, repetitive and rewarding experiences' (p.257).

Bessel van der Kolk

Bessel van der Kolk (2005) highlights three areas that professionals involved in helping traumatized children need to focus on. First, he emphasizes the importance of encouraging the child to 'react differently from his habitual fight/flight/freeze reaction' (p.7). Only then can he feel safe to explore, which allows him to play, have fun, enjoy activities with others and gain a sense of competency and mastery. Second, traumatized children tend to react fearfully and aggressively to anything new, including parents and teachers who introduce rules or anything perceived by the child as controlling or demanding, even when it is an attempt to keep the child safe. It is important for therapists to understand this need for control, and focus on helping the child realize he is often repeating early negative experiences that are no longer helpful as he is now in a safe environment even if internally he does not feel safe. Third, these children frequently cannot focus on learning and enjoying because they do not know how to relax. They are either hyper- or hypo-aroused but never truly calm and relaxed in their bodies; activities that calm and soothe are therefore essential. 'The challenge of recovery is to re-establish ownership of the body and mind – of yourself. This means feeling free to know what you know and to feel what you feel without becoming overwhelmed, enraged, ashamed or collapsed' (van der Kolk 2014, p.203).

The Attachment Regulation and Competencies model

Developed from the work of van der Kolk (2014), an intervention called the 'Attachment Regulation and Competencies' (ARC) model was proposed (Kinniburgh *et al.* 2005). This model is based on the three core areas: 'Attachment', 'Regulation' and 'Competencies'. Kinniburgh and colleagues emphasize that there is no one therapeutic approach to suit all children with complex trauma but there are overarching principles that can guide assessments and interventions for children and their families. The ARC model has been developed further by Blaustein and Kinniburgh (2010). The authors emphasize that they are not replacing any of the current treatment interventions but are aiming to 'organise, encompass and facilitate their use' (p.vii). The model can therefore help guide creative therapists in making modifications for working with children with complex trauma. The 'Attachment' work in this model targets two primary areas: '(1) the building of a "safe-enough", "healthy-enough" relationship between the child and his or her caregiving system, which requires felt safety within the system itself; and (2) the building of skills and a context that the care-giving system will use to support the child's healthy development' (Blaustein and Kinniburgh 2010, p.36). There is an emphasis in the model of the important role the caregiver has as a mechanism of change. The management of affect, attunement and being consistent in his responses, whilst providing routines and rituals, is regarded as central to the 'Attachment' part of the work. The 'Regulation' aspect in this model has three aspects that target children's '(1) awareness and understanding of their internal experience, (2) ability to modulate that experience, and (3) ability to safely share that experience with others' (p.38). These dimensions of 'Attachment' and 'Regulation' have to be the focus first. Only then can the attention move to developing 'Competencies' through executive functioning and addressing self-concept and identity, which are frequently impaired. The final target of the ARC model is 'Trauma Experience Integration', which requires all the skills acquired in the 'Attachment', 'Regulation' and 'Competency' stages.

ARC is one of four models incorporating the learning from developmental trauma that have been designated as evidence-based or promising by the National Child Traumatic Stress Network (Ford *et al.* 2013). The other three are: 'Trauma Affect Regulation: Guide for Education and Therapy' (TARGET); 'Structured Psychotherapy for Adolescents Responding to Chronic Stress' (SPARCS); and 'Real Life for Heroes'. Each of these models 'offers a relational foundation informed by attachment research and theory, and teaches skills to help youth and their caregivers and adult mentors/role models recognise stress reactions and self-regulate their bodies, emotions, thinking and behaviour' (Ford *et al.* 2013, p.272). The models do not require detailed disclosure of the traumatic events but offer structures to help children and young people and their caregivers create coherent narratives about the past, present and future. Some of the vignettes in Chapters 5 and 6 using arts and play therapy models reflect this way of working with trauma.

Implications for caregivers

Developmental re-parenting

The research and models of therapy just described all emphasize the importance of the caregiving system around the child. As a response to this, the concept of developmental re-parenting was conceived in the UK adoption literature (Archer 1999a, 1999b, 1999c). This came from the combined understanding and knowledge of adoptive parents who shared their difficulties and management of living with children with complex trauma. This was developed into the training course designed and run by Adoption UK-trained adoptive parents that started in 2000 called 'A Piece of Cake' (Selwyn, del Tufo and Frazer 2009). A main aim of the training was to enhance the adopter's parenting skills, unlike many other parenting programmes that are designed to change poor parenting (Rushton *et al.* 2006).

Developmental re-parenting aims to provide experiences an infant and toddler would normally have with good enough parents for children and young people who missed out on these crucial learning experiences in the early years. The focus is specifically on addressing the developmental deficits caused by early abusive and neglectful care. These deficits will be specific to each child's adaptation to early abuse, but the main principle is to respond to a child's emotional development rather than his chronological age. Adoptive and foster parents often need help to make the links between a child's behaviour and what deficits this may indicate, for example, learning about the connection between internal and external sensory experiences: 'feeling hungry, taking in the appropriate food and experiencing gratification' (Archer 1999a, p.20). As Siegel (2001), van der Kolk (2005) and Perry (2009) emphasize, the best place for this developmental repair to happen is in the context of the primary attachment relationship of the child, where newer and healthier neural connections can be made through repetitive and relational experience.

Sydney and Price (2011) suggest that caregivers of children with complex trauma need to change the trajectory of their parenting. For some new parents this may include giving up ideas of the 'wished for' family and child and living with the actual family reality. Reflecting on their own attachment history and considering the fact that they are living with a child with a disability who is likely to need support well into their early adulthood is also part of developmental re-parenting.

To succeed at this, parents need a team around them, all of whom understand this style of parenting in order to support and sustain them during the inevitable hard times.

Secondary trauma

Developmental re-parenting requires the parents or caregivers to understand why love is not enough and why conventional parenting strategies may not work. Quite ordinary events can provoke a significant stress response in these children, which can lead to either aggression (fight response), fear (flight response) or becoming overwhelmed (freeze response). 'A key challenge of developmental re-parenting is to ensure that they (the caregivers) can both self-regulate (self-calm or soothe) and co-regulate (be a calming presence) for the child' (Sydney and Price 2011, p.23). If these parents do not get the support and understanding they need, they will often lose these capacities as a result of experiencing secondary trauma. One of the first things that an assessment for therapeutic help relating to any child who has experienced complex trauma needs to address is the possibility that the caregivers are suffering from this most debilitating state. Secondary traumatic stress is 'the cost of caring for others' emotional pain' (Figley 1995, p.9) and is regarded as natural and treatable, but only if it is recognized. Caregivers suffering from it will experience some of the symptoms of their traumatized child, such as hypervigilance, feelings of fear and an inability to think and act normally. This clearly impairs their capacity to parent, which is explored further in Chapter 3.

Developmental re-parenting strategies

Caroline Archer and Christine Gordon devised a parenting mentor scheme to help adoptive and foster parents develop appropriate strategies to help their particular child (Archer and Gordon 2006). Dan Hughes recommends parenting with Playfulness, Acceptance, Curiosity and Empathy (PACE) (Hughes 2009). These models are based on the understanding that adoptive parents and caregivers providing permanent new families to children who have been exposed to complex trauma need help to interpret and respond to their child's behaviour. The parent's aim is to help his child begin to live in a state of felt security and dependency on adults being understanding and empathetic and consistent. To do this is extremely hard work requiring specialist understanding, resourcefulness, resilience and determination by the caregiver, which will often necessitate professional support.

Involving parents in the therapy

Early models of involving parents directly in the therapy to help children with developmental and attachment difficulties began around the same time as Bowlby's major exposition of attachment theory; for example, Filial Play (Topham, VanFleet and Sniscak 2014) was initiated in the 1950s and Theraplay (Booth, Lindaman and Winstead 2014) in the 1970s. Both these models, in which the presence of the parents in the therapy is central, have adapted their methods for use with children with relational trauma. Some models of family therapy have included attachment considerations into their work (Bentovim 2007) and these have been used in relation to thinking about the needs of adoptive families (Bingley Miller and Bentovim 2007). However, the systemic perspective of family therapy has a different rationale and theory base from models of therapy that use attachment research as central to their work, especially with regard to the significance of caregiver sensitivity. Mary Ainsworth's research indicated that caregiver sensitivity towards an infant was central to attachment security (Ainsworth, Bell and Stayton 1974). A meta-analysis of 51 randomized controlled studies (Bakermans-Kraneneburg, van IJzendoorn and Juffer 2003) concluded that relatively brief dyadic parent–child interventions that focus on increasing maternal sensitivity are successful in reducing a disorganized attachment pattern in a child. However, this was less effective when parents had a history of unresolved trauma (Moran, Pederson and Krupa 2005).

Caregivers and adoptive parents of children with complex trauma will therefore need help to address any unresolved loss or trauma because Dyadic Parent–Child Therapy often triggers the parent's own trauma responses. Nonetheless, it is often difficult in the early stages of working with a family to determine whether there is unresolved trauma in the parent's past or whether he is affected by secondary trauma. The two can become inextricably entwined. In the early stages of working with a family the widely accepted first phase in trauma recovery work – that of 'stabilization' – needs to be the initial focus; gradually efforts are then made to disentangle whether it is unresolved trauma or secondary trauma that dominates the caregiver's responses to the child. Some interventions have proved to be more effective if they include discussions of the parent's childhood attachment experiences with regard to the particular child he is parenting (Velderman *et al.* 2006).

Hughes (2004) suggests that the active presence of the caregiver greatly enhances interventions aimed at non-verbal attunement, affective/reflective dialogue and repairing disturbances within a relationship. Not only is it more effective for the therapist to observe these live interactions, but also it makes it easier 'for children to incorporate these transforming experiences into their daily lives' (Hughes 2004, p.274).

> The caregiver, too, may intersubjectively enter into the shame/ terror experiences of the child's past, allow it to have an impact on him/her, and give expression of his/her subjective experience of it which the child can also now hold along with his/her own and the therapist's. (Hughes 2004, p.274)

The caregiver needs some capacity for affective and reflective relating to engage in the therapy with the child. He needs to be able to stay engaged with the child at times when the child is distressed or unregulated. Hughes (2004) calls this the adult's continuing subjective presence. If he is not able to do this, the therapist will need to reduce the intensity of the work. In creative therapies that want the caregiver to participate in an activity, as well as remaining actively present for his child, parents will need preparation for this dyadic parent–child work. Some parents may get anxious about being able to be creative (Hanney and Kozlowska 2004) and fear, for example, that their art-making may be interpreted. There are different approaches to Dyadic Parent–Child Psychotherapy that will involve the parents in different ways. These are explored further in Chapter 6.

The need for a holistic approach
Multi-disciplinary, multi-agency and multi-systemic working

The focus of mental health services for children and young people in the UK is usually based on the assessment and diagnosis of a difficulty or disorder followed by an evidence-based intervention. This is a problem for creative therapists working with children with a history of complex trauma. First, because complex and developmental trauma are not currently recognized as a psychiatric disorder; and second, creative therapies do not yet have the evidence base to be recommended by the National Institute for Health and Care Excellence (NICE) in relation to trauma work with children and young people. However, arts and play therapists working with these children need to be part of a Team Around the Child. Children with a history of complex trauma are likely to have deficits in multiple domains and so need access to a range of knowledge, skills, perspectives and therapies from different disciplines and different agencies. The professionals most likely to be providing specialist interventions to these children are social workers, clinical or educational psychologists, child psychiatrists, occupational therapists, family and child psychotherapists, and arts and play therapists. Multi-disciplinary team work is challenging enough in settings with a long history of this way of working, such as Child and Adolescent Mental Health Services (Worrall-Davies and Cottrell 2009), but will be additionally so when the different disciplines work in different agencies. This will frequently be the case with children who are permanently removed from their birth parents. The mutual trust and respect needed between different professional disciplines and different agencies to achieve good outcomes for these children can be hard to achieve. Barriers to effectively working together can include competitive relationships between services, interdisciplinary power struggles, lack of accountability and lack of a common language (Worrall-Davies and Cottrell 2009). These barriers can be challenging and need to be acknowledged in order to provide services that will be in the best interests of the child and family.

Differential susceptibility

A holistic approach includes understanding the limitations of our current knowledge of the neurobiological consequences of early maltreatment. Development is complex and the effects of maltreatment on the brain are related to other factors in a child, including biological, psychological and social factors (Woolgar 2013). 'The interrelatedness between these factors also needs to take into account the way in which maltreated children are more or less susceptible to different outcomes, depending on their experience and their biology' (Woolgar 2013, p.248). Some children can be very sensitive to environmental factors and will not thrive if they are in a sub-optimal context; others are constitutionally more resilient and their development will be more even across negative or positive environments (Woolgar 2013). It is not possible to predict how an individual child's experience of maltreatment will influence his development, but some will have complex neurodevelopmental problems. This is evidenced by the high number of children in care with such problems (Woolgar 2013), and it supports the need for comprehensive multi-disciplinary assessments.

The contribution of arts and play therapies

Creative therapies can make a very positive contribution to a holistic approach to working with children with complex trauma and their families. The arts therapies are beginning to develop frameworks to incorporate elements of the attachment, psychoanalytic, trauma and neuroscience research. Vija Lusebrink's 'Expressive Therapies Continuum' is one such attempt (Lusebrink and Hinz 2014). Malchiodi has developed a 'Trauma-Informed Expressive Arts Therapy' model which 'integrates neurodevelopmental knowledge and the sensory qualities of all the arts in trauma interventions' (Malchiodi 2012). These models utilize findings from neuroscience and suggest that:

- 'Traumatic sensory-motor memories are stored nonverbally and are accessible primarily through expressions involving the body as the main point of entry' (Lusebrink and Hinz 2014, pp.42–43).

- 'Non-verbal and verbal memories of trauma remain disjointed segments without temporal narrative organisation' (Lusebrink and Hinz 2014, p.43). Expressive arts can help create and integrate trauma narrative (Gantt and Tinnin 2009).

- 'The creative therapies are "brain-wise" interventions. When used in purposeful ways, these approaches are compatible with what we currently understand about the brain and attachment; they capitalize on nonverbal and right hemisphere communication, active participation, and the self soothing nature of creative expression through images, sound, movement, and enactment' (Malchiodi and Crenshaw 2014, p.16).

Conclusions

- Developmental trauma and complex trauma are the best current descriptions of the range of difficulties frequently displayed by children with a history of early abuse or neglect who are frequently placed in foster care, kinship care, with Special Guardians or are adopted.

- Adoptive parents and permanent caregivers are essential in helping children with complex trauma develop healthier responses. It is vital that they are provided with the necessary therapy, support and psycho-education so that the children they are caring for learn to trust, relax, play and learn.

- The concept of developmental re-parenting usefully describes the type of parenting usually appropriate for adoptive parents and caregivers of children displaying behaviours that fit the description of complex trauma or developmental trauma.

- The risk of secondary trauma for these parents and caregivers is high and needs to be recognized.

- Because of the complex range of difficulties these children often have, they are likely to have multi-disciplinary and multi-agency needs that introduce a particular set of challenges. These need to be recognized and processed by professionals working together.

- Creative therapists can make a significant contribution to therapeutic work with these children and their families.

- Involving the parents/caregivers directly in the therapy is an approach that needs to be considered whenever possible.

References

Ainsworth, M. D. S., Bell, S. M. and Stayton, D. J. (1974) 'Infant-mother attachment and social development: Socialisation as a product of reciprocal responsiveness signals.' In M. Richards (ed.) *The Integration of a Child into a Social World.* London: Cambridge University Press.

Archer, C. (1999a) 'Re-parenting the traumatised child: A developmental process.' *Young Minds Magazine 42,* 19–20.

Archer, C. (1999b) *First Steps in Parenting the Child Who Hurts: Tiddlers and Toddlers.* London: Jessica Kingsley Publishers.

Archer, C. (1999c) *Next Steps in Parenting the Child Who Hurts: Tykes and Teens*. London: Jessica Kingsley Publishers.

Archer, C. and Gordon, C. (2006) *New Families, Old Scripts: A Guide to the Language of Trauma and Attachment in Adoptive Families*. London: Jessica Kingsley Publishers.

Bakermans-Kranenburg, M. J., van IJzendoorn, M. H. and Juffer, F. (2003) 'Less is more: Meta-analyses of sensitivity and attachment interventions in early childhood.' *Psychological Bulletin 129*, 2, 195–215.

Bentovim, A. (2007) 'Attachment, trauma and systemic thinking.' *Context 90*, April, 25–28.

Bingley Miller, L. and Bentovim, A. (2007) *Assessing the Support Needs of Adopted Children and their Families*. London: Routledge.

Blaustein, M. E. and Kinniburgh, K. M. (2010) *Treating Traumatic Stress in Children and Adolescents: How to Foster Resilience through Attachment, Self-Regulation, and Competency*. New York, NY: Guilford Press.

Booth, P., Lindaman, S. and Winstead, M. (2014) 'Theraplay in Reunification following Relational Trauma.' In C. Malchiodi and D. Cranshaw (eds) *Creative Arts and Play Therapy for Attachment Problems*. New York, NY: Guilford Press.

Cook, A., Spinazzola, J., Ford, J., Lanktree, C. *et al.* (2005) 'Complex trauma in children and adolescents.' *Psychiatric Annals 35*, 5, 390–398.

Crenshaw, D. (2014) 'Play Therapy Approaches to Attachment Issues.' In C. Malchiodi and D. Crenshaw (eds) *Creative Arts and Play Therapy for Attachment Problems*. New York, NY: Guilford Press.

Fahlberg, V. (1991) *A Child's Journey through Placement*. Indianapolis, IN: Perspective Press.

Figley C. R. (ed.) (1995) *Compassion Fatigue: Secondary Traumatic Stress Disorder from Treating the Traumatized*. New York, NY: Brunner Mazel.

Ford, J., Blaustein, M., Habib, M. and Kagan, R. (2013) 'Developmental Trauma Therapy Models.' In *Treating Complex Stress Disorder in Children and Adolescents*. New York, NY: Guilford Press.

Gantt, L. and Tinnin, L. (2009) 'Support for a neurobiological view of trauma with implications for art therapy.' *The Arts in Psychotherapy 3*, 3, 148–153.

Hanney, L. and Kozlowska, K. (2004) 'Healing traumatised children: Creating illustrated story books in family therapy.' *Family Process 41*, 1, 37–65.

Howe, D. (2005) *Child Abuse and Neglect: Attachment, Development and Intervention*. Basingstoke: Palgrave Macmillan.

Hughes, D. (2004) 'An attachment-based treatment of maltreated children and young people.' *Attachment and Human Development 6*, 3, 263–278.

Hughes, D.A. (2007) *Attachment-Focused Family Therapy*. New York, NY: W. W. Norton.

Hughes, D.A. (2009) *Attachment-Focused Parenting* New York, NY: W. W. Norton.

Hughes, D. (2014) *Dyadic Developmental Psychotherapy: Toward a Comprehensive, Trauma-Informed Treatment for Developmental Trauma*. DDP Network. Avaialable at http://ddpnetwork.org/backend/wp-content/uploads/2014/03/DDP-Toward-a-Comprehensive-Treatment-Dan-Hughes.pdf, accessed on 11 November 2016.

Kinniburgh, K., Blaustein, M., Spinnazzola, J. and van der Kolk, B. (2005) 'Attachment, self-regulation, and competencies: A comprehensive intervention framework for children with complex trauma.' *Psychiatric Annals 35*, 5, 424–430.

Lusebrink, V. and Hinz, L. (2014) 'The Expressive Therapies Continuum as a Framework in the Treatment of Trauma.' In J. L. King (ed.) *Art Therapy, Trauma and Neuroscience: Theoretical and Practical Perspectives*. New York, NY: Routledge.

Malchiodi, C. (2012) 'Developmental Art Therapy.' In C. Malchiodi (ed.) *Handbook of Art Therapy* (2nd edn). New York, NY: Guilford Press.

Malchiodi, C. and Crenshaw, D. (2014) *Creative Arts and Play Therapy for Attachment Problems.* New York, NY: Guilford Press.

Moran, G., Pederson, D. and Krupa, A. (2005) 'Maternal unresolved attachment status impedes the effectiveness of interventions with adolescent mothers.' *Infant Mental Health Journal 26,* 231–249.

Perry, B. (2009) 'Examining child maltreatment through a neurodevelopmental lens: Clinical applications of the neurosequential model of therapeutics.' *Journal of Loss and Trauma 14,* 240–255.

Perry, B. and Dobson, C. (2013) 'The Neurosequential Model of Therapeutics.' In J. Ford and C. Courtois (eds) *Treating Complex Stress Disorders in Children and Adolescents.* New York, NY: Guilford Press.

Rushton, A., Monck, E., Upright, H. and Davidson, M. (2006) 'Enhancing adoptive parenting: Devising promising interventions.' *Child and Adolescent Mental Health 11,* 1, 25–31.

Schore, A. (2013) 'Relational Trauma, Brain Development and Dissociation.' In J. Ford and C. Courtois (eds) *Treating Complex Traumatic Stress Disorder in Children and Adolescents.* New York, NY: Guilford Press.

Selwyn, J., del Tufo, S. and Frazer, L. (2009) 'It's a piece of cake? An evaluation of an adopter training programme.' *Adoption and Fostering 33,* 1, 30–43.

Siegel, D. (2001) 'Towards an interpersonal neurobiology of the developing mind: Attachment relationships, "mindsight", and neural integration.' *Infant Mental Health Journal 22,* 1–2, 67–94.

Sydney, L. and Price, E. (2011) 'Developmental reparenting.' *Adoption Today,* April, 22–23.

Topham, G., VanFleet, R. and Sniscak, C. (2014) 'Overcoming Complex Trauma with Filial Therapy.' In C. Malchiodi and D. Crenshaw (eds) *Creative Arts and Play Therapy for Attachment Problems.* New York, NY: Guilford Press.

van der Kolk, B. (2005) 'Developmental trauma disorder: A new rational diagnosis for children with complex trauma histories.' *Psychiatric Annals 35,* 5, 401–408.

van der Kolk, B. (2014) *The Body Keeps the Score: Brain, Mind and Body in the Healing of Trauma.* New York, NY: Viking.

Velderman, K., Bakermans-Krannburg, M., Juffer, F. and van IJzendoorn, M. (2006) 'Effects of attachment-based interventions on maternal sensitivity and infant attachment: Differential susceptibility in highly reactive children.' *Journal of Family Psychology 20,* 266–274.

Woolgar, M. (2013) 'The practical implications of the emerging findings in the neurobiology of maltreatment for looked after and adopted children: Recognizing the diversity of outcomes.' *Adoption and Fostering 37,* October, 237–253.

Worrall-Davies, A. and Cottrell, D. (2009) 'Outcome research and interagency work with children: What does it tell us about what the CAMHS contribution should look like?' *Children and Society 23,* 5, 336–346.

Chapter 3

PUTTING THEORY INTO PRACTICE

Implications for Caregivers

JANET SMITH

It is not possible to access the brain's 'joy juice' naturally without emotional connection with others.

Sunderland (2007, p.90)

Introduction

In the last 20 years the understanding of the impact of complex trauma on children has been well documented (van der Kolk 2005; Perry and Szalavitz 2006). There is increasing recognition amongst therapists and other professionals that children who have experienced early, repeated interpersonal trauma come with a complex range of needs that can prove exceedingly challenging for their caregivers (Hughes and Baylin 2012; Sunderland 2007). To meet this challenge caregivers need 'to develop knowledge and understanding of the impact of the children's earlier experiences on their development and behaviour and to acquire new and specific parenting skills' (Lindsey 2006, p.11). This view has gained momentum over the last decade with the caregivers and their parenting approach seen as central to helping children heal from early trauma. Caregivers are now being tasked with providing developmental re-parenting, often described as 'therapeutic parenting', which requires understanding of complex psychological and physiological theory on developmental trauma. To do this caregivers need support to become and remain emotionally and physically healthy themselves (Golding and Hughes 2012; Hughes 2009; Hughes and Baylin 2012; Hughes *et al.* 2012). This shift in the expectations placed on caregivers also means they need to be treated as central members of any professional Team Around the Child (TAC) (CWDC 2009).

During my many years as Director of Adoption Support for Adoption UK and in my present role on the frontline as Practice Manager in Adoption Support with Families for Children, I have become increasingly aware of how these demands impact on caregivers. This chapter will explore the most significant consequences of these new demands. Composite vignettes, drawn from my work experience, are used to illustrate some of the complexities for this group of parents and caregivers: foster carers, kinship carers, Special Guardians and adoptive parents.

No one size fits all

Caregivers will be at different points along the parenting journey with the child. Some will have only recently become caregivers whilst others will have been looking after the child for a number of years. Some will have a greater understanding of developmental trauma and the need to be 'therapeutic' parents whilst others may never have heard of these concepts and may be very confused, frightened, exhausted, angry, disappointed or at their wits' end, with little hope for the future. The thought of being a 'therapeutic parent' or being a key member of any TAC will be daunting and overwhelming for some, whilst others will have been 'fighting' for this status for years and be angry and disheartened by the lack of understanding amongst some professionals and agencies. All these caregivers will have gone through an approval process. Adopters may have spent many months or years going through the adoption process before becoming a parent, whereas kinship carers may have found themselves looking after a child out of necessity for a long time before being officially recognized as the caregiver. Their journey, legal status, motivation and background will be diverse, as will be their gender, culture, sexual orientation and family structure. Kinship carers, for example, often already know the children when they take over their care, and there can be themes in these families related to the ties that bind, in particular, loyalties to the birth parents (Barratt and Granville 2006) which need navigating.

DORIS AND HER GRANDSON

Doris is the kinship carer of her grandson who is 8. He has been mainly in her care since he was born, owing to her daughter's learning difficulties and her vulnerability to exploitation by violent males. Doris had to face the most difficult decision of her life five years ago in order to maintain care of her grandson. The courts decided that continued contact between her daughter and grandson was not in his best interest and in order to show she could keep her grandson safe she had to cut all ties with her daughter. Doris lives with this grief every day.

Conversely, adopters quite often choose adoption because of infertility issues and they and their children have 'nominal opportunity of choosing each other and no previous experience of living together' (Tollemache 2006, p.129). Furthermore, some foster carers and their families are tasked with committing to a close and meaningful relationship with a child and have to tolerate the pain of letting him go at any time. Foster carers differ too because their familial and legal relationship to the child is different from that of adoptive parents or kinship carers. Granville and Antrobus (2006, p.185) note that 'it is significant to consider the extent to which they experience themselves as "parenting" as opposed to "caring", the meaning of these to them, and what this signifies in terms of the personal and professional identities and relationships, that are thereby constructed'. Consequently, when working with these families, there needs to be an awareness of the complexities and challenges of the different client groups, and each family needs to be seen as unique and supported accordingly.

The importance of a secure base for the caregivers

Caregivers tasked with parenting children with complex trauma are quite often stressed and exhausted and confused by the children's behaviours, which impacts on their belief about their effectiveness and abilities as a parent. Before any attempt is made to provide them with different parenting strategies or therapeutic approaches, they need acceptance and empathy for their situation.

MARY, TED AND THEIR
THREE ADOPTED CHILDREN

Mary and Ted are adoptive parents of three siblings: a son aged 14 and daughters who are 12 and 8. They became adoptive parents because of their infertility. The two older children have been with the couple since they were 4 and 2 and the youngest child was placed when she was a few months old. The elder two children experienced neglect, domestic violence and drug abuse, and the youngest child experienced pre-birth trauma because of her birth mother's drug addiction and poor maternal care during pregnancy. Mary and Ted were exhausted and not coping with the complex behaviour of all their children. There were high levels of aggression towards the parents from the eldest child and between the middle and eldest child. All the children were struggling in school. For both parents there was a great sense of failure and disbelief. They had expected some problems in the early period but not the ongoing issues, which seemed to increase rather than diminish over time. They had minimal understanding of developmental trauma, and their expectation was that because the children were placed at an early age, things would be fine. Ted was at the point where he was not sure he wanted to be in the family any longer. The family was in such a fragile state that it was evident that they would need a lot of support to get them to a point where they could see hope for the future. A plan of support was agreed with them for therapeutic parent training, therapeutic support for all the family and work with school. Funding was applied for from the Adoption Support Fund (ASF).

The ASF has been available since May 2015 for adoptive families. It was recognized by the Department for Education (DfE) that many families need some kind of therapeutic support following adoption, and the fund is to enable them to access the services they need more easily. As of April 2016 the fund is also available to Special Guardians and Overseas Adopters. The fund is available for children living in England up to and including the age of 21 (or 25 with a Statement of Special Educational Needs or Education, Health and Care Plan).[1]

---

1   For further details, please visit www.first4adoption.org.uk/adoption-support/adoption-support-fund, accessed on 8 October 2016.

Many caregivers take on children with minimal understanding of the complexity of the full range of issues caused by developmental trauma. They usually have some understanding of attachment issues and think consistent loving care and 'normal' parenting will be sufficient to overcome the children's early experiences. In Ted and Mary's case the role of the support worker in the first instance was not to judge or criticize but to listen to their experience of parenting their children and the impact on them so they felt listened to and understood. It is very important to build a trusting relationship and to give caregivers the opportunity to explore their experience of parenting rather than be tempted to offer reassurances or solutions (Golding and Hughes 2012). The latter scenario would not acknowledge the reality of the fact that there are no quick fixes or easy solutions and would ignore the enormity of the challenges of loving and living with these children. Those supporting caregivers in such circumstances need to give time to helping them address the emotional aspects of caring for these children, giving them the opportunity to talk about their journey, their hopes, dreams and disappointments.

The painful realities of the caregivers' experiences are very evident when talking about the gaps between their hopes and expectations (Tollemache 2006). Most expect just to get on with the job of parenting and do not believe they will need psychological support for themselves and their family – any suggestion of this may be interpreted as a sign of failure or criticism of their parenting (Lindsey 2006). Ted and Mary felt that their children rejected their love. Their level of loss was significant as they felt that despite all the love and care offered, they were not helping the children and believed they were failing as parents. A recent study found that foster carers need to experience mutual attachment and receive love or recognition from the children they parent (Bunday et al. 2015). One foster carer expresses it thus: 'Very often he just ignores me. I get a bit upset sometimes, when I tuck him into bed he won't say goodnight, I know I should get used to it after all these years, but it does hurt' (Bunday et al. 2015, p.153). Hirst (2009, p.65) acknowledges how parents move to 'an acceptance of the situation as it really is and for some this has meant a considerable revision of the hopes, dreams and aspirations of all concerned'. For caregivers to 'keep their mind and heart open to the child so that they can remain engaged' (Hughes et al. 2012, p.23), they need others who engage with them whom they trust to be empathic, who understand the challenges they have endured over months or years, and who can appreciate why they have lost hope, warmth, compassion and joy and that caring for the child may have just become a job.

The impact of the caregiver's own history

When working with families, it is necessary to help them understand not only their child's attachment history but also their own. A theory of attachment, 'a way of conceptualizing the propensity of human beings to make strong affectional bonds to particular others' (Bowlby 1999, p.127), was developed by Bowlby and Ainsworth in the 1960s, 70s and 80s. Research focused on how children's attachment develops and suggests that children who grow up in a safe and secure environment form inner representations of trustworthy and dependable caregivers, whereas a child who suffers trauma in childhood will be unable to form inner representations of safe, consistent caregivers (Erikson 1995; Herman 1992). Later studies have concentrated on the attachment styles of caregivers. The study by Steele and colleagues in 2003 investigated the influence of the adoptive mother's state of mind on the attachments, as expressed in narrative story completions, of a sample of older adopted and previously maltreated children (Prior and Glaser 2006; Steele 2006). Maternal states of mind were assessed using the Adult Attachment Interview (AAI), and the children's expectations and perceptions of family roles, attachments and relationships were assessed using the Story Stem Assessment Profile (SSAP). The study found that when unresolved loss or trauma in the parent was paired with vulnerability in the child, the vulnerability in both is heightened (Prior and Glaser 2006).

Research by Bunday and colleagues (2015), on foster carers' reflective functioning (RF), identified a lack of awareness of how their own internal states or histories could interplay within, or crucially misrepresent, their current relationships. A caregiver's understanding of the effect of his own history on his parenting is significant because his child's behaviour or feelings may activate unresolved issues for him. When this happens the carer and/or child will have a poor sense of safety in the relationship. It is therefore important that caregivers recognize the triggers in their own attachment history and how a child's emotional state, such as anger, fear, sadness and shame, can create a similar dysregulating emotional state in the caregiver, bringing up the carer's own fears (Hughes 2009). Few individuals or marriages are perfect or without some level of dysfunction and 'sub-clinical' emotional issues. These usually insignificant or non-interfering issues can come to the surface when under adverse stressful situations such as when caring for traumatized children (Delaney and Kunstal 1997). An adoptive parent describes how her daughter brought out such extreme emotions in her that she did not recognize the 'demented screeching hag that she could suddenly become with seemingly little provocation' (Hirst 2009, p.40). She goes on to explain how unhappy and guilty she felt until it was explained that her daughter found it hard to express her own emotions so she got others to express them for her. If caregivers are unable to manage their own emotions, this can escalate children's distress.

This was true for Ted and Mary, who needed help to understand how their own attachment histories can be triggered when parenting children and particularly those with complex trauma. It was highly relevant for Ted, who had become quite depressed since the death of his father 18 months earlier. This had brought up a lot of feelings about his lack of closeness to his father, whom he described as a deeply angry man. He had hoped to be a very different father but now characterized himself as just the same. He spoke of the lack of connection to his son, his increasing anger and how he did not recognize himself as a person he liked anymore. He was overwhelmed with shame, guilt and failure. He felt his presence made things worse and the best solution was for him to leave. Working through these strong emotions helped him to understand where the feelings were coming from, which enabled him to take ownership and manage them better. Ted and Mary were helped with this process by giving them more understanding of the 'intersubjective' or mutual influence of attachment – their own and their children's – and how this influences our sense of self and the world (Golding and Hughes 2012).

Reflecting in this way may not be easy for some parents or caregivers and does not happen overnight. It may take months before a 'shift' in thinking about themselves and the children can allow them to see the crucial role they can and do play in the psychological recovery of their children. Accepting that it takes a long time to build a new relationship that repairs the old imprint and that there is no magic wand or quick fix may take time too. Caregivers may need help in moving from 'What is my child trying to do to me?' to 'What is my child trying to say to me?' and see the child's behaviour as a message for the real issues, which are a lack of trust: a disbelief that adults can keep him safe and will be there permanently for him. Once they have made this shift, they feel less persecuted by the child and more readily accept the need for psychological support for the whole family. Getting some caregivers to this point of understanding and acceptance that the empathic daily 'caregiver' is pivotal in helping children recover from complex trauma can be a long, painful and emotional journey.

Secondary trauma

Professionals working with caregivers of children with complex trauma need to be vigilant for signs of secondary trauma or 'the stress and personal damage caused by helping or wanting to help a traumatised person' (Conrad 2011, cited in NSPCC 2013, p.2). Cairns (2008, p.21) notes: 'Secondary traumatic stress (linked to a particular care-giving experience) and burnout (stress disorder arising from emotional exhaustion after prolonged duress), are probably as common in adoptive families as in professional disciplines providing care and services for traumatised children.' This is because they are exposed to the child's trauma on a daily basis. Secondary trauma is not unusual but is often overlooked (Cairns 2008). If professionals or caregivers are not aware of secondary trauma or the symptoms, it cannot be treated and the caregivers will not get the help that they need.

ANNETTE AND DANNY

Danny is three. He was placed with Annette five weeks ago. Annette is a single foster carer and an experienced parent with three grown-up children. This is her first experience of fostering but it is something she has wanted to do for a long time. Annette is ringing Danny's social worker because she is really struggling to care for Danny. She tells the social worker she is exhausted, feeling anxious and completely out of her depth. She cannot connect with Danny; he screams and kicks her at the slightest provocation; he will not sit down to eat and she dare not take him out because he will not sit in a pushchair and she fears he will run off. She understands some of the reasons for these behaviours. She knows he lived with a chaotic, unpredictable, alcoholic mother and a series of her violent partners. What she did not anticipate was the impact this little boy would have on her. She feels completely unlike her usual self: out of control, confused and angry.

Annette is showing signs of secondary trauma. Indications of this in caregivers are anxiety, sleep difficulties, poor eating habits, tension or being easily overwhelmed and having difficulty with emotion regulation (Marshall 2014). Caregivers with secondary trauma talk about a sense of loss and not recognizing the person they have become. They may describe how they avoid the child by staying at work rather than coming home, or how they feel like they are walking on 'egg shells' a lot of the time and that their thoughts are dominated by the child, reliving events over and over again in their mind and worrying about what might happen next. They may present as agitated, depressed or exhausted. There will be no sense of joy, not only in parenting but also in life itself. Children with complex trauma have often felt very little joy because of circumstances in their birth families, and the frustration, fear, anger and hopelessness felt by their new caregivers can once again make family life a 'joyless' experience. 'In the brain there is a foundational genetic system for joy, but how it unfolds depends on the interaction of those genes with social experiences. By and large, it is not possible to access the brain's "joy juice" naturally without emotional connection with others. It is possible to feel pleasure, but not real joy' (Sunderland 2007, p.90).

Caregivers suffering from secondary trauma may find it difficult to maintain empathy for the child, doing only what they have to do in a functional way. This can create immense feelings of guilt, confusion and disappointment. This was not the way it was supposed to be! This can result in what Hughes and Baylin (2012, p.6) term 'blocked care', when a caregiver continues to do what is necessary to care for a child but is no longer able to sustain loving feelings and empathy towards the child. Annette needs immediate professional help to understand what is happening to her. If this does not happen, Annette's own state of mind may deteriorate to the point of Danny needing to be moved and Annette not fostering again.

Secondary trauma is not an uncommon experience when caring for traumatized children and it can be very distressing for the caregiver. Donovan (2015) talks about what happens as a parent of a traumatized child if you do not take care of yourself and how trauma is catching, particularly when you spend a lot of time with someone with trauma: 'Trauma is in the air and catches in the hair, is breathed in the lungs and clings to the skin. It invades the brain and hijacks the emotions. It feels like something has stolen your identity, like a horrible parasite' (p.202). She says it was the worst experience of her life: she became hypersensitive to noise, was pumped full of adrenaline and constantly braced for action, felt restless, lacked concentration, was worried about the future and felt hopeless.

Another adoptive parent talks about the impact of parenting a child who communicates her internal turmoil and hurt through her behaviours, some of which are violent: 'Hello, my name is Dave, and I am a traumatised parent. I am still coming to terms with those words. It's taken a while for the penny to drop; even though on one level I've known it for some time' (Collins (pseudonym) 2015, p.22). He describes how living with trauma changed life dramatically for everyone in his home. Julie Selwyn (Selwyn *et al.* 2014), in her research on life beyond the Adoption Order, identified a high level of child-on-parent violence, which has promoted a flurry of training for professionals and caregivers to support and help them deal with the violence. One such programme is 'Non Violent Resistance' (NVR), a short-term intervention that complements other therapies. NVR was introduced in the UK in 2006 by Peter Jakob. He adapted NVR to be used with adoptive families and children who are looked after in foster care or residential services. Peter says that 'NVR is a highly effective, innovative systemic approach to the violent, harmful and self-destructive behaviour in young people' (Jakob 2016).

Therapists and other professionals will need to help caregivers understand what is going on, the importance of addressing their own state of mind and how to stay emotionally and physically well. It is vital that they implement self-care into their daily routines and understand the necessity of using support networks such as extended family, friends and peer-to-peer support. The use of relaxation techniques, massage, exercise and making time for their own interests can be helpful too (Cairns 2008; Perry 2014). The benefits of yoga and mindfulness as ways of reducing stress have been particularly stressed by van der Kolk (2014) and are recognized as beneficial by many agencies. Some agencies are now offering yoga and/or mindfulness training and activities to caregivers and children.

Foster carers, kinship carers, Special Guardians and adoptive parents are generally highly committed, develop a bond with the children they care for and feel a high level of responsibility for their welfare. They recognize the benefits and rewards for both themselves and the children. Providing a stable loving home, feeling good about helping a child recover from trauma, loving and being connected to a child, and not losing a child into the care system can make the experience feel positive, but this can get lost when life feels like a struggle. With good support that helps parents gain confidence in their parenting and moves them to a better place both physically and psychologically, and with good self-care strategies that help to reduce and manage stress and build resilience, they can and do feel pleasure in parenting the children, and the experience of joy can return to the whole family.

The importance of extended family and/or friends

All of us need good support networks to encourage and help us when we are in need. We usually turn to our family, friends and local communities, and research suggests that support can enhance resilience to stress (Ozbay *et al.* 2007; Sippel *et al.* 2015). However, for foster carers, adopters and kinship carers, finding the right support is not always easy because of the behaviours the children present or because they need to adopt different parenting styles and strategies that others do not understand. This can bring them into conflict with grandparents, other family members and friends who advocate traditional techniques (Tucker 2012). Trying to join groups of young mothers who became friends shortly after giving birth can be difficult, particularly for adoptive parents when talk of birth experiences and who their child looks like are so common. People can ask all sorts of personal information about a child when they know he is fostered, adopted or in kinship care. This can make caregivers of these children feel different and they may also feel the need to protect the children and themselves from others who may not understand the complexities, confidentiality issues and challenges of parenting them. Supportive action can include:

- Provision of family and friend training sessions to help parents have a better understanding of what life has been like for these children, why they behave the way they do, the need for a different parenting style, and looking at how family members and friends can support the child and caregivers.

- Training groups for adopters, foster carers and kinship carers help them come together with people in similar circumstances. There are particular relationship dilemmas relevant to all these families as their experience of parenting is very different. This can affect the sense of entitlement to parent, as well as the meaning of relationships they are building in their family. Coming together helps them share experiences, strengths and concerns with others and helps develop their skills alongside others in a supportive environment (Granville and Antrobus 2006).

- Many caregivers join a support network like Fostering Network, Grandparent Groups for Kinship Carers or Adoption UK (a peer-to-peer support organization for adopters) so they have opportunities to talk to others 'walking the same walk'. Many of these caregivers voice that their best supporters are those whom you do not have to explain your child or parenting to.

- Opportunities for adoptive, foster and kinship families to come together for family days and activities help provide mutual support but also give the children and young people the opportunity to not feel different.

The carer as part of the Team Around the Child (TAC)

The complexities that these children bring mean that their families generally need support from professionals across several disciplines, such as education, health, social care, youth services and police. It is stressful enough having to manage everyday life, but this can be made worse when caregivers find themselves dealing with many different professionals who do not communicate with them or each other and who have little understanding of the complexities of complex trauma.

BARBARA AND GEORGE
AND THEIR GRANDCHILDREN

Barbara and George, a couple in their late 50s, have been caring for their two grandchildren aged 12 and 14 for the last six years because of their daughter's drug and alcohol abuse. Their main support is another daughter, but she has her own young family. They are frequently called up to school because of the disruptive behaviour of the youngest, who has Attention Deficit Disorder (ADD) and is under the care of Child and Adolescent Mental Health Services (CAMHS). The eldest child is linked to youth services via the local police because of some minor offending. Neither grandparent is in good health. Both are highly anxious and stressed because of the years of worry created by their daughter's issues and caring for their grandchildren. Nobody has helped them with all the loss, guilt and confusion they have experienced. They have been given no understanding of developmental trauma or 'therapeutic' parenting approaches. They feel very misunderstood and blamed for their daughter's and grandchildren's behaviour, and have been shown little empathy with regard to the challenges they face. The professionals involved are not communicating with each other and nobody has thought of calling a TAC meeting to assess the needs of the family. The breaking point comes when George is rushed to hospital with breathing problems. Barbara contacts the local children's services to say they can no longer continue to look after their grandchildren without support.

It is crucial to communicate with the essential people in the lives of vulnerable children; also because 'when these children see "their" adults working together, it instils in them some trust and faith in those adults' (Marshall 2014, p.129). TAC meetings are a key element of the process of successfully working with children and young people. The purpose of a TAC is to prevent the fragmentation and confusion that families often experience when the people supporting and working with the family keep their work separate from each other. A TAC approach brings all professionals and caregivers together, to assess, plan and support the needs of the child and family. Such meetings ideally involve professionals and family members who:

- are directly and relevantly involved with the child or young person

- are able to offer support services to the family

- have relevant information to share.

A TAC meeting can be called by any agency that has concerns about a child or young person with additional needs that they feel may require a response from more than one agency but without requiring statutory intervention. They are usually convened by the practitioner who has initially identified unmet needs following an initial assessment. This practitioner identifies those who need to be invited and may take responsibility, at least at the first meeting, to act as Chair. However, he may not necessarily continue to be the lead (as he may not always be the most appropriate person to be the lead professional going forward). It is, however, very important to identify and appoint a lead professional for the following reasons:

- to act as a single point of contact for the family

- to co-ordinate the delivery of the actions agreed

- to reduce overlap and inconsistency in the services received.

The lead professional is not accountable or responsible for the actions of other professionals and services. Any member of the TAC can be the lead professional; it is for the TAC team to decide and agree this role (CWDC 2009).

Good practice suggests that the family should be involved in all stages of the process, unless it chooses not to be. The child or young person's needs and rights must come first, though the rights of caregivers are also considered. There are times when it is not possible to involve the caregivers (e.g. the young person objects to caregiver involvement). If for any reason it is necessary to convene a meeting to discuss concerns without inviting or notifying the child or young person's caregiver, this should be recorded and the meeting becomes a 'Professionals' Meeting'. However, generally caregivers need to be treated as a key member of the team and as allies. They hold valuable information about the child and are fundamental in providing a child with a secure base. They may need help in understanding the policies, politics and processes within the education, health and social care systems (as well as their limitations), but if the plan is for the child to live with them long term, they are the child's best resource and therefore they need to be at the heart of any plans or arrangements and fully engaged, supported and consulted at every stage. Additionally, to build trust, caregivers need to feel confident that the professionals working with them understand complex trauma and the challenges that the children and the caregivers both face.

An example of good practice is the 'Team Parenting®' approach developed by Foster Care Associates:[2]

> Central to 'Team Parenting®' is the move from the child and young person as the 'client' in any therapeutic work, to the 'child in placement' as the 'client'. This shift acknowledges the critical role of the foster carer as the predominant agent of therapeutic change in the child's life, and as such recognises the primacy of the daily caregiving dynamic between foster carer and child. However, the phrase 'child in placement' encompasses all those involved in the placement. Whilst the relationship between the carer and the child and young person is central, given the foster carer's potential as an attachment figure, all the other relationships and roles are seen to be important to the overall wellbeing of the child and young person. Everyone involved in the child's placement holds different information and experiences of that child, and when brought together can hold the child together and create a cohesive full picture of the child, their strengths and their needs. In the Team Parenting® model the therapists play a central role to ensure that other professionals, foster carer, [and] social worker understand how traumatic and abusive experiences can affect a young person, before educating them on how to respond therapeutically. They also see the foster carer's feedback as crucial as this can lead to a much better understanding of the child's internal world which is seen as at the heart of Team Parenting®. (Foster Care Associates 2016)

---

2   For more information about Foster Care Associates *Team Parenting®*, please visit www.
thefca.co.uk/why-choose-us/team-parenting

Conclusion

Foster carers, kinship carers, Special Guardians and adoptive parents do offer children who cannot live with their birth family a very positive alternative experience of family life. There is no question that along with the challenges there are rewards and benefits for both caregivers and children. However, for the caregivers to meet the needs of children with complex trauma it has to be accepted that parenting them is no easy task. In all trauma recovery models, safety comes first. The support offered needs to be given with empathy, acceptance, encouragement and patience in order to build a trusting and safe relationship. Caregivers need an opportunity to explore their relationship with the child, their disappointments, fears and anger, along with the successes and joys. They need support in understanding their own relationships (past and present) values and belief systems, and how these help or hinder their responses to the challenges of parenting therapeutically. Provision of training in understanding complex trauma, developmental re-parenting, secondary trauma, self-care and the importance of support networks are essential. The high level of complexity evident in many of these families means they will often require a multi-disciplinary approach and multi-agency support. Involvement with the family may need to continue over a long period of time or at different stages of a child's development. As all families and children are unique, any therapeutic or support package offered needs to show flexibility and creativity. All professionals and agencies involved need to have a comprehensive understanding of complex trauma and attend regular TAC, or equivalent, meetings which include the caregiver as a central member of the team where appropriate.

References

Barratt, S. and Granville, J. (2006) 'Kinship Care: Family Stories, Loyalties, and Binds.' In J. Kendrick, C. Lindsey and L. Tollemache, L. (eds) (2006) *Creating New Families: Therapeutic Approaches to Fostering, Adoption, and Kinship Care.* London: Karnac Books.

Bowlby, J. (1999) *The Making and Breaking of Affectional Bonds.* London: Routledge.

Bunday, L., Dallos, R., Morgan, K. and McKenzie, R. (2015) 'Fostercarers' reflective understandings of parenting looked after children: An exploratory study.' *Adoption & Fostering 39,* 2, 145–158.

Cairns, K. (2008) 'Caring for those who care.' *Adoption Now 2,* 20–23.

Collins, D. (2015) 'Living with your child's violence.' *Therapy Today 26,* 8, 22–26.

CWDC (Children's Workforce Development Council) (2009) *Coordinating and Delivering Integrated Services for Children and Young People. The Team Around the Child (TAC) and the Lead Professional Guide for Managers.* Available at http://webarchive.nationalarchives. gov.uk/20130401151715/http://www.education.gov.uk/publications/eOrdering Download/LeadPro_Managers-Guide.pdf, accessed on 11 October 2016.

Delaney, R. and Kunstal, F. (1997) *Troubled Transplants: Unconventional Strategies for Helping Disturbed Foster and Adoptive Children* (2nd edn). Oklahoma City, OK: Wood 'N' Barnes Publishing.

Donovan, S. (2015) *The Unofficial Guide to Adoptive Parenting: The Small Stuff, the Big Stuff and the Stuff In Between.* London: Jessica Kingsley Publishers.

Erikson, E. (1995) *Childhood and Society.* London: Vintage.

Golding, K. and Hughes, D. (2012) *Creating Loving Attachments: Parenting with PACE to Nurture Confidence and Security in the Troubled Child.* London: Jessica Kingsley Publishers.

Granville, J. and Antrobus, L. (2006) 'From Tired and Emotional to Praise and Pleasure: Parenting Groups for Adoptive, Foster, and Kinship Carers.' In J. Kendrick, C. Lindsey and L. Tollemache (eds) *Creating New Families: Therapeutic Approaches to Fostering, Adoption, and Kinship Care.* London: Karnac Books.

Herman, J. (1992) *Trauma and Recovery: The Aftermath of Violence – From Domestic Abuse to Political Error.* London: Harper Collins Publishers.

Hirst, M. (2009) *Loving and Living with Traumatised Children: Reflections by Adoptive Parents.* London: BAAF Adoption & Fostering.

Hughes, D. A. (2009) *Attachment-Focused Parenting: Effective Strategies to Care for Children.* New York, NY: W. W. Norton.

Hughes, D. and Baylin, J. (2012) *Brain-Based Parenting: The Neuroscience of Caregiving for Healthy Attachment.* New York, NY: W. W. Norton.

Hughes, D., Miles, L., Gethin, J. and Gethin, P. (2012) *Emotional and Behavioural Difficulties.* London: BAAF Adoption & Fostering.

Jakob, P. (2016) *Non Violent Resistance (NVR).* Available at www.partnershipprojectsuk. com/people/dr-peter-jakob, accessed on 11 October 2016.

Lindsey, C. (2006) 'Theoretical Considerations.' In J. Kendrick, C. Lindsey and L. Tollemache (eds) *Creating New Families: Therapeutic Approaches to Fostering, Adoption, and Kinship Care.* London: Karnac Books.

Marshall, N. (2014) *The Teacher's Introduction to ATTACHMENT: Practical Essentials for Teachers, Carers and School Support Staff.* London: Jessica Kingsley Publishers.

NSPCC (National Society for the Prevention of Cruelty to Children) (2013) *Vicarious Trauma: The Consequences of Working with Abuse.* Research briefing. Available at www. nspcc.org.uk/globalassets/documents/information-service/research-briefing-vicarious-trauma-consequences-working-with-abuse.pdf, accessed on 11 November 2016.

Ozbay, F., Johnson, D., Dimoulas, E., Morgan, C., Charney, D. and Southwick, S. (2007) 'Social support and resilience to stress: From neurobiology to clinical practice.' *Psychiatry 4*, 5, 35–40. Available at www.ncbi.nlm.nih.gov/pmc/articles/ PMC2921311, accessed on 11 October 2016.

Perry, B. (2014) *The Cost of Caring: Secondary Traumatic Stress and the Impact of Working with High-Risk Children and Families.* Houston, TX: Child Trauma Academy.

Perry, B. and Szalavitz, M. (2006) *The Boy Who Was Raised as a Dog and Other Stories from a Child Psychiatrist's Notebook: What Traumatized Children Can Teach Us about Loss, Love and Healing.* New York, NY: Basic Books.

Prior, V. and Glaser, D. (2006) *Understanding Attachment and Attachment Disorders: Theory, Evidence and Practice.* London: Jessica Kingsley Publishers.

Selwyn, J., Wijedasa, D. and Meakings, S. (2014) *Beyond the Adoption Order: Challenges, Interventions and Adoption Disruptions.* Research report. London: Department for Education.

Sippel, L., Pietrzak, R., Charney, D., Mayes, L. and Southwick, S. (2015) 'How does social support enhance resilience in the trauma-exposed individual?' *Ecology and Society 20,* 4. Available at http://dx.doi.org/10.5751/ES-07832-200410, accessed on 11 October 2016.

Steele, M. (2006) 'The "Added Value" of Attachment Theory and Research for Clinical Work in Adoption and Foster Care.' In J. Kendrick, C. Lindsey and L. Tollemache (eds) *Creating New Families: Therapeutic Approaches to Fostering, Adoption, and Kinship Care.* London: Karnac Books.

Sunderland, M. (2007) *What Every Parent Needs to Know: The Remarkable Effects of Love, Nurture and Play on your Child's Development.* London: Dorling Kindersley.

Tollemache, L. (2006) 'Minding the Gap: Reconciling the Gaps between Expectation and Reality in Working with Adoptive Families.' In J. Kendrick, C. Lindsey and L. Tollemache (eds) (2006) *Creating New Families: Therapeutic Approaches to Fostering, Adoption, and Kinship Care.* London: Karnac Books.

Tucker, S. (2012) 'A different kind of parenting.' *Education Now,* 10–11.

van der Kolk, B. (2005) 'Developmental trauma disorder: Toward a rational diagnosis for children with complex trauma histories.' *Psychiatric Annals 35,* 5, 401–408.

van der Kolk, B. (2014) *The Body Keeps the Score: Brain, Mind, and Body in the Healing of Trauma.* New York, NY: Viking.

------------------- PART 2 -------------------

CLINICAL APPLICATIONS OF CREATIVE THERAPIES FOR COMPLEX TRAUMA

Chapter 4

HOW DOES TRAUMA AFFECT THE WHOLE FAMILY?

Assessments of the Effect of Trauma on Attachment Relationships

———————————— JOY HASLER ————————————

There are many researched models and tools of assessment of attachment available that can be used on their own or as part of a more comprehensive model. This chapter will describe a comprehensive model of assessment developed at Catchpoint. Catchpoint is a registered Adoption Support Agency in the UK that offers support and creative therapies for permanent families caring for children who have been removed from their birth family owing to early trauma. We developed our own Collaborative Assessment to assess the attachment patterns and the effects of trauma in children with known experiences of abuse and neglect who are living in adoptive families or other permanent family placements. Our assessment model includes how a child's trauma-triggered behaviours can be observed within the family, at school and within a clinical setting.

The chapter will draw on the assessments of more than one child and does not contain a complete example of an assessment. Names and identifying details in vignettes have been changed to protect confidentiality.

THE SMITH FAMILY

The Smith family arrived at our centre, and from watching them approach the entrance we could observe behaviours that matched with the patterns of a child affected by early trauma and attachment difficulties. Jason, aged 8, came up to the front door ahead of his parents, and when invited in, walked with a pseudo-confidence as if he had been there many times before. He walked across the room and did not wait for instructions but started to investigate what was in the room. When invited to sit down, he complied but sat on his own. He was polite and co-operative throughout the session. For the first 10 minutes he did exactly what we asked, and then started to disrupt in subtle ways – doing almost what was asked but not quite (e.g. when invited to choose an instrument, he chose two, and when asked to let someone else have a turn with banging a drum, he continued to play for a few seconds and then stopped). He did things that he knew would irritate his parents: chewing his clothes or tapping his feet and watching them to see if they were going to respond. His parents said nothing but spoke to the therapists after the session. The session was being videoed so we could look back and pick up on minute details that we might have missed when running the session. The parents said to us when we spoke after the session: 'You're not seeing any of the behaviours we get at home so how can you make this assessment?' Our reply was that Jason had been very co-operative and polite to hide any difficulties from us, but he did not know what we were looking for. From the small, subtle behaviours that we had seen, we were aware that there were likely to be many more difficulties at home.

What is the purpose of an assessment?

An assessment is a piece of research requiring the same discipline as any dissertation and the same process in order to inform a plan or programme of work to enable recovery from specific disorders. An assessment requires expertise in the areas and issues of concern. It requires a familiarity and access to relevant research and an ability to communicate with children and young people without raising anxiety. It requires an understanding that whatever is observed or reported will only be part of the picture and that the assessment will contribute to existing knowledge and not necessarily stand alone. There needs to be an openness that the suggested difficulties – in this case attachment difficulties – may not be the root cause of the behaviours the parents are struggling with and that further assessments may be necessary.

The purpose of an assessment is to inform planning and practice. For Catchpoint, our assessments are to inform the inter-agency planning for supporting a family with a traumatized child. They are to offer authoritative advice to help the child or young person recover from the negative effects of developmental trauma, which may include attachment difficulties but could also include other difficulties such as anxiety disorders, executive function disorder or dissociative disorders.

Catchpoint Comprehensive Assessment format

1. Preparation

- Naming the research and theory that informs the assessment: How do we know what we are looking for?

- Identifying the expertise that qualifies us to be doing this assessment.

- Listing the tools and methodology used for collecting the evidence.

- Collecting and listing background information related to the particular case.

2. Collecting evidence

- Reading background information and previous reports.

- Meeting relevant people connected to the case – parents or carers, social workers, school staff and anyone else professionally involved.

- Observing behaviours in three different settings: home, school and clinical.

- Completing any standardized tests (e.g. Trauma Symptom Checklist for Children (TSCC)).

- Feedback from people involved – other observers, parents, teachers, professionals involved in any setting.

- Reviewing recordings of clinical sessions with the family.

3. Analysis

- Comparing observations.

- Looking for patterns.

- Analysis of questionnaire responses.

- Analysis of evidence.

- Writing the assessment report.

- Identifying needs in response to analysis.

4. Recommendations based on evidence and analysis

- Proposals for therapy and support programmes.

- Recommendations of any further assessments needed.

- Plans for reflection and review.

Collaborative Assessments require:

- good observational skills – avoiding mixing observations with assumptions

- understanding the impact of early trauma on the development of the brain

- respect for the opinions and perceptions of other people around the child

- recognition of the effects of the child's behaviours on the family and community

- expertise in communicating with children without unduly raising anxiety levels

- an understanding of secondary trauma and compassion fatigue.

To document the degree of debate around attachment and trauma would be beyond the limits of this chapter, but we do lean on generally accepted tenets about attachment theory and the global effects of developmental trauma.

Background research and theory is addressed in Chapter 2, but we will look at a few specifics that informed the choice of our observations:

- The Strange Situation Assessment Tool, which was devised by Ainsworth in 1969, has been incorporated into many attachment assessments that have developed since (Prior and Glaser 2006). Observing children's response to strangers when they are with their parents/carers or separated, either in familiar surroundings at home or in a strange place, enables us to see behaviours that could be categorized as disinhibited or inhibited attachment patterns. Some children are superficially charming and indiscriminate about their attention to strangers, while others will be socially withdrawn and avoid contact with strangers. Some indiscriminate behaviours emanate from a child's lack of trust that he will be kept safe by his key attachment figures, so he has to befriend the stranger in order to feel safe.

- Exploration is part of the child's means of discovering his world, and a secure child has an automatic assumption that his carers will be interested in what he is exploring. An insecurely attached child has no such assumption. Prior and Glaser (2006, p.25) describe how a secure infant 'is quickly soothed…and within a few minutes returns to exploration and play'. Secure children give their attention to attachment or exploration, depending on the circumstances. Children with avoidant patterns focus their attention on exploration rather than attachment (i.e. 'I don't need help'). Children with resistant (also called ambivalent) patterns focus towards attachment and away from exploration (i.e. 'I can't do it and I can't ask for help') (Prior and Glaser 2006). This matches the patterns we have observed when presenting children with opportunities to explore.

- The Strange Situation is not exactly replicated, but we are interested in how the child responds to a parent leaving the room and how he responds to reunion. There are times when working with a single parent and child that we judge that a child could become too distressed to be left with strangers and so we observe how the child behaves if the parent's attention is distracted away from the child. We have to be sure that parents and children leave safely (not with a child in a distressed state). The Strange Situation gives an indication about how the child explores, which is a key feature of our assessment.

- Internal Working Models (IWMs) are much written about and give an indication of a child's sense of self (Bowlby 1979). Schore (1994, p.540) says that 'attachment patterns are understood to be imprinted into internal working models that encode programs of affect regulation and guide the individual's future interpersonal interactions'. Siegel says that IWMs are not only unconscious but that once established they are also highly resistant to change after infancy. He comments about the relationship between insecurely attached children and their adoptive parents: 'The more emotionally significant and demanding the current relationship, the more earlier relationships and the inner working models developed to represent and cope with them will be brought into play' (Siegel 2003, p.43) We look to understand how children perceive themselves and their relationships with others as an indicator of their IWM.

- Another aspect of the IWM can be observed in how a child perceives praise. Children with low self-worth can find it hard to accept praise that contradicts their Inner Working Model that they are not worth being cared for. We observe how the child at home or at school responds to praise, or how he may try to avoid it. Disorganized attachment patterns can lead the child to actually destroy or rubbish things that have been praised. It can also be a symptom of dissociation when one part of the child seeks praise and another part disrupts it (Silberg 1996). Whether a child is chaotic or ordered can also indicate a child's IWM. Some children with disorganized attachment behaviours are very chaotic; however, we are also interested in those children who can create a feeling of chaos in the adults who work or care for them but without creating obvious chaos.

- Turn taking (reciprocity) is at the heart of communication from birth onwards. Colwyn Trevarthen's research (2005) into parent–child interactions showed that when parents talk to their children, they leave a gap for the baby's response and this gap comes at regular intervals so the infant very quickly picks up the rhythm and joins the conversation by filling the gap.

- Children who need to be in control find transition between activities very difficult. This is because there is always an element of the unknown or possible unexpectedness that creates anxiety until the child feels safe. These children develop a series of behaviours to protect themselves. If a child cannot self-regulate, then moving from structured activity to unstructured activity and back again creates difficulties. If the unstructured play time raises his excitement level, he finds it very difficult to return to a classroom and sit down quietly. We have observed many strategies for avoiding this, including the child being helpful to a teacher, which gives the child an excuse for being late turning up to the classroom and yet still being praised.

- 'Everyone who has raised anxiety for whatever reason becomes hypervigilant, which is the direction of a significant proportion of energy, attention and thinking towards monitoring the external environment' (Smith 2009). Children who live with a higher state of anxiety are hypervigilant. This causes them to have a low concentration span and to be easily distracted – in some cases they cannot focus on a page in front of them because their eyes have a wide focus to take in as much of what is going on around them as possible. These children notice noises outside the session room and are distracted by other objects in the room.

- We do not attempt to diagnose a dissociative disorder but we look for any evidence that this may be worth further assessment. Dissociation is a spectrum from causal daydreaming, through fiddling, rocking and tapping, to spacing out and then to switches in emotional states and presenting as very different personalities – one moment speaking in a baby voice and the next with a clear age-appropriate voice, and many more variations that exceed normal playfulness and changes of mood. Dissociation is the child's protective system from repeated trauma and 'is a way of keeping overwhelming events, feelings, sensations and thoughts away from the core self' (Wieland 2011, p.6).

Any one issue never stands alone. It is rare that evidence that might indicate a particular issue will not be affected by other issues – when looking for the traits of developmental trauma this may also be affected by inherited syndromes, pre-birth environment, hospitalization of the child, mental health of the parent, autism spectrum disorder (ASD), foetal alcohol spectrum disorder (FASD), obsessive compulsive disorder (OCD), dyslexia, dyspraxia and many more. Any of these factors can combine to affect the child in a way that is similar to some of the effects of trauma. For example, there are known overlaps between ASD and attachment disorders. There are known effects of foetal alcohol syndrome that affect a child's attachment but are different from the effects of early trauma. Many children have been misdiagnosed because one disorder has been assessed without taking others into account. At Catchpoint we look for patterns of behaviour that indicate potential disorders and then follow some of these up with a specific standardized test, such as the Trauma Symptom Checklist for Children (Briere 1996), or the Child Dissociative Checklist (Putnam 1997) or ASD on the NHS website.[1] These are not diagnostic tests but are intended to ascertain if a further specialist assessment is needed.

Questionnaires as an assessment tool

We have not found a suitable standardized test that adequately measures relational dynamics and therefore attachment, so we have devised our own group of questionnaires for parents and children with multiple choice answers. Here is an example of some questions for children:

- If you are pleased with something you have done, do you:

    a. Show it to your teacher or parents?

    b. Spoil it?

    c. Leave it for someone to find?

- When you are asked to line up, do you:

    a. Stand with your friends?

    b. Try to be at the front of the line?

    c. Go to the back of the line?

---

1   Available at www.nhs.uk/conditions/Autistic-spectrum-disorder/Pages/Introduction.aspx, accessed on 11 November 2016.

Another questionnaire includes questions such as whether the child experiences 'switching off' or being blamed for things he did not do. We then ask parents to answer the same questions to see if they have the same perception as their child. This is not to mark them down if they are different but to be able to note that there is a difference in perception. We are also aware that some children will reply to questions with answers that they think we want to hear, so a parent questionnaire could illustrate this difference. This does not disqualify the child's responses but illustrates the child's attempt to please us, which is in itself a symptom of attachment difficulties.

We have a questionnaire for each parent that measures the effects of living with a traumatized child, including the effect on the relationship. This is adapted from Megan Hirst's questionnaire (Hirst 2005). The questions are divided into four areas: 1) Organizational Effects; 2) Mental Effects; 3) Physical Effects; and 4) Relational Effects. This gives us a broad picture of what is happening for each of the parents and their relationships. It is also a questionnaire we can use to reassess parents' progress for a review.

The written assessment report

Our report is divided into five sections:

1. Information

2. Observations

3. Key Points

4. Discussion and Summary

5. Recommendations.

Information

This section explains who we are, what reports we have read, who we have spoken to and what we have set up to collect the evidence. It also involves the history of the child including previous therapeutic interventions.

Observations

The Catchpoint assessments are based on observations by two or more qualified people in three different settings as well as listening to the people around the child or young person. The three settings are:

- At home to observe how a child responds to a stranger coming into his home, and how the child responds to a stranger talking to his parents – a situation that could be reminiscent of social work visits before being placed for permanence.

- At school to observe the child in structured and unstructured situations, to see how he copes with transitions between the two, and to observe him with peers. We also speak to the relevant staff.

- In a clinical session where specific situations can be set up so that we can observe the child's reactions. This includes structured and unstructured activities, and at some point the parent is asked to leave and return to the room. A clinical session is always run by two therapists, at least one of whom has met the parents so that parents can introduce the therapist to the children. The session is always videoed so that therapists can look back at the session and check their observations.

These observations are then compared and grouped into 13 categories, as shown in Table 4.1.

Table 4.1 Catchpoint assessment observations

Element of attachment behaviour	What is being observed
Response to strange people and places	Stranger visiting home or child visiting strange place – is the child: • Charming and engaging? • Avoidant or dismissive?
Exploration	How the child explores unusual objects – does the child: • Share exploration with parents? • Ask questions about the instruments? • Avoid exploring at all?

cont.

Element of attachment behaviour	What is being observed
Reciprocity	Taking turns – is the child able to: • Take turns and wait for his turn? • Take part in a reciprocal conversation?
Emotional expression	Range of emotional expressions – does the child show: • Appropriate or inappropriate emotional expressions? • Flat emotional presentation?
Peer friendships	Different settings, structured and unstructured – how does the child: • Respond to working with peers in a classroom setting? • Respond to peers at play time?
Representation of family	The family are invited to draw a picture of what they do together – does the child: • Engage in discussion with parents about the picture? • Represent all or part of the family? • Use relationship terms?
Separation and reunion	Parent leaves the room without saying where he is going – does the child: • Enquire where the parent has gone? • Respond when the parent returns? • Show parent what he has been doing while separated?
Transition	Observing child moving between structured and unstructured activities – how does the child: • Respond to change of activity? • Move out to playground? • Respond to being asked to line up? • Come back into the classroom?
Chaos and order	How does the child organize himself: • Is he chaotic or over-ordered? • Does he create a feeling of chaos?

A sense of self	Inner Working Models – does the child: • Present as needing or not needing adults? • Show confidence or lack of confidence? • Accept or reject praise? • Celebrate achievement? • Have a sense of shared humour?
Control	Observations of the child's need to be in control – does the child: • Accept control from adults? • Listen to instructions? • Try to take control through subtle or overt means?
Hypervigilance	Observations of child's awareness of the immediate environment – does the child: • Appear to be watchful and aware? • Notice sounds outside the room? • Sit where he can see the rest of the room?
Dissociation	Indicators of dissociative behaviours – does the child show: • Repetitive behaviours such as rocking, fiddling, chewing? • Incessant chatting with no purpose? • Switching off? • Sudden changes of behaviour, voice or skills?

Key Points

Having collected our observations and other evidence from interviews, reports and documents, we select key points that we want to draw on in our 'Discussion and Summary'. Key Points are presented as bullet points that highlight the specific aspects of the evidence that illustrate a particular element of an attachment pattern. We always start by listing the positives that we have observed, such as politeness, imagination or a sense of shared humour. We then move on to the points that illustrate difficulties we have observed.

Discussion and Summary

This section is the analysis of the evidence. We look for patterns in the evidence that fit categories of attachment, and indicate possible disorders and difficulties. In this section we compare research and theory with what we have observed, to give a picture of the needs of the child and the family.

Recommendations

We make recommendations for a Therapy and Support Plan designed to meet the assessed needs of the child and family. This plan can include training or consultations for schools, and an informal support network around the family (i.e. trusted people chosen by the parents from their circle of friends and extended family).

SALLY AND HER ADOPTIVE PARENTS

Family: Sally and her adoptive parents, Tim and Marian

Catchpoint observers: Joy, Tom and Hannah

Information
Summary of history

Sally, aged 10, was born to a mother who was a drug addict. She was premature and spent her first two months in a Special Care Baby Unit. From the unit, she went with her mother to a Mother and Baby Unit, but this was not successful and at 4 months Sally was placed in foster care. Her mother was reported to have been in a violent relationship. Sally was placed with her adoptive family at 11 months old. Her brother, who is 2 years older, was also placed for adoption with a different family. The two families arrange contact visits twice a year and Sally looks forward to her time with her brother. It was reported to us that the brother has similar difficulties to Sally, so they are carefully monitored while together. There is no contact with their birth parents.

Home situation

Tim and Marian reported that Sally had always been a child who was difficult to calm and they had been told to expect this because of her mother's drug taking. They were advised to set firm boundaries and give her a lot of love. The main reported difficulties now are stealing, aggression – mainly targeting Mum – exclusions from school and difficulties getting Sally to do what she has been asked to do, especially getting ready to go to school in the morning. Her parents are also worried that she has no friends. Sally is aware that she will be moving to secondary school next year and says she is not worried about this.

Previous intervention

Sally had a Story Stem Assessment Profile which was developed by the Anna Freud Centre in 1990. This is an assessment tool that presents children with the start of 13 stories and the child is invited to complete each story. These responses are rated and used to form constructs: Security, Insecurity, Disorganization, Defensive-Avoidance, and/or Positive and Negative Adult and Child Representations. Sally's report from the previous year was shared with us along with other reports. This is a comparison of our observations with observations in her Story Stem Assessment Profile.

Story Stem Assessment Profile	Catchpoint
Checks time throughout the assessment	Constantly checking the clock at school
Appears to likes rules	Tells teacher when others break rules
Asks if Mum is OK	Checks that Mum is OK (clinical session)
Is competitive	Wants to win and says what she is good at
Notices sounds outside the room	Asks who is outside the room (clinical session)
Short concentration span	Is easily distracted and has a short focus
Tries to interrupt the activity	Interrupts music, telling Mum what to do
Tries to split parents and therapists	Asks Mum when therapist has asked her to wait

Observations
Reaction to strange people and places
Home visit: Sally came to open the door when Joy, the observer, arrived and then, without greeting her, disappeared into another room but with the door open. She came back in when Joy was talking to Mum but did not speak to her. Instead she asked Mum if she could have a drink. Marian said yes and asked her to come and talk to us but she moved to the other end of the room and occupied herself with her back to Joy and Mum. She made herself busy sorting newspapers and magazines as if she was looking for something.

School visit: Sally made eye contact with Tom, the observer, as soon as he entered the room but then appeared to ignore him. Later she took a pen to him that he had left on a desk. She did not speak to him.

Clinical session: Sally arrived with her parents and immediately went into the room and started exploring what was in there. When asked to sit down, she complied but refused to speak. Silence was accepted. She then said that Mum had told her she could have some snacks. She went to Mum's bag and took out some snacks intended for later. She was asked to put them back but ignored this and continued opening the crisp bag. Hannah invited everyone to have some snacks (that had been put out ready for the break). Sally joined in with everyone having a snack and then sat down and listened to what was being said.

Separation and reunion
Clinical session: Marian quietly left the room with Joy without saying anything. Sally looked up but did not ask where they were going. She then continued with the drawings they had been making. After a few minutes she said she wanted to go to the toilet. She was asked if she wanted to find out where Mum was. Sally asked where she was and was told that she was in the next room and that she was watching her through the video link. Sally immediately went to the video and said 'Hi, Mum'. Mum knocked on the wall. This set up a conversation between Mum and Sally, ending with Sally asking her if she was coming back in. As she heard a door open and Mum's footsteps coming towards the room,

she ran to the other side of the table and started drawing. When Mum came in, Sally ignored her. Mum went over to her and asked about her picture. Sally scribbled all over it and said it was rubbish. Mum returned quietly to her picture and they continued. Sally then asked Mum where she had been. Mum told her she was talking to Joy and that she had seen her on the TV. Sally laughed.

Chaos and order

Home visit: Sally occupied herself where she could hear what Mum and Joy were saying. She seemed to be tidying some magazines. Then she started throwing things around – at first just a magazine but then a toy, almost threatening to hurt Mum or Joy if they did not stop her. Mum tried to distract her and she threw a plate (plastic) on the floor and went out into the garden. She could be seen throwing a ball for the family pet dog. Mum was clearly anxious and asked Joy to move with her nearer the window so they could check on Sally.

School visit: Sally appeared to be calm and ordered at school. She told the teacher when some boys did something they were not supposed to. But each time the teacher asked for quiet, Sally picked up some paper and rustled it (although quietly so that it did not attract attention).

Clinical session: Sally started by being challenging and getting a snack from Mum's bag but then joined in the conversation about their journey and what was going to happen. She joined in playing music for a short while and then tried to say what instruments other people should choose. When her parents told her they liked what they were playing and basically ignored her attempts at control, she started throwing beaters around and saying that she wanted to play on her games console. She went to her bag and was asked to come back to the group. She came back and asked Dad for the drum he was playing. He gave it to her and she joined in again for a few minutes. She then changed her instrument and this time stayed with the group.

Peer friendships

School visit: Sally was observed in a small group with a Teaching Assistant. She moved in and out of giving the group attention. When focused, she made positive contributions, but when distracted she either ignored what the others were doing or annoyed other children, until she had to be removed from the group and work on her own. In the playground Sally mainly engaged with the adults on duty and then wandered around on the edge of groups of younger children. School reported that the main difficulty with Sally was with her peers both in class and at break time. She would be aggressive if they did not do what she wanted them to do, so she had few friends.

Key Points (examples)

- Articulate.
- Imaginative.
- Can be polite and co-operative.
- Shares things that excite her with her family.
- Shows raised anxiety with strangers.
- Could not explore when showing anxiety.
- Found following instructions difficult.
- Found taking turns or waiting for her turn difficult.
- Did not ask where Mum was when she left the room.
- Asked to leave the room when Mum was out of the room.
- Ignored Mum when she returned.
- Rubbished her work when she was praised.
- Was reported to have difficulties sustaining peer friendship.
- Drew herself as bigger than other people in her picture about her family.
- Created a feeling of chaos when she could not take control.
- Uses subtle and overt means of control including threat of aggression.
- Strong indicators of hypervigilance.

- Rocked on her chair and fidgeted.
- Used complaints about pains and aches to distract from an activity.

Discussion and Summary

This section considered the evidence and looked for patterns that gave indications of attachment difficulties without trying to make a specific diagnosis. The hope was to increase understanding of Sally's behaviours and her perception of the world in an attempt to inform a support plan for the family. We included in our discussion a summary of the trauma experienced and the known effects of drug taking and domestic violence before birth and the effect of having had several moves before being placed for adoption. In Sally's case we said that her pre-birth experience of her mother's drug taking and domestic violence would have caused significant damage to the developing brain, affecting her ability to regulate stress.

We felt that Sally had a disordered attachment pattern but that there were signs of positive bonds in the family. Sally had a strong sense of self in terms feeling powerful and not needing adults to keep her safe, but she also showed a feeling of worthlessness when she rubbished her picture and rejected praise. She could be ordered for short periods but also create a feeling of chaos. We observed her expression change when she felt anxious, from a soft look with appropriate smiles or interest in what was happening to a hard stare that was almost threatening. We became concerned about her distraction techniques (rocking and fidgeting) and her different personality presentations, so decided to do a further check using the Putnam Child Dissociative Checklist, again not to diagnose but to decide if we needed to recommend a further assessment. She scored 18, which is within the range of the children we work with who have experienced trauma. According to Putnam and colleagues, 'any score over 12 should be considered suspicious, and a score above 19 is an indicator of a serious dissociative disorder' (Putnam, Helmers and Trickett 1993).

We felt that Sally and her family would benefit from a Catchpoint Therapy and Support Programme, which uses a trauma recovery model – Stabilization, Integration, Adaptation (Hasler 2008) – with an attachment focus by working with the parent and child together. The programme includes consultations with parents, consultation with school, informal support network meetings, and fortnightly therapy with parents and children together with two therapists using creative therapies to help the child build trust in the key attachment people in her life, and increase her resilience.

We felt that one of the sources of Sally's anxiety was anticipation of separation from her parents, especially her mother, because it was her mother that she transferred this fear onto by attacking her. Some of her anxiety, which she tried to disguise, was around her inability to make and sustain friends, as observed at play time. This could be helped by her being able to engage at a much younger age level in therapy sessions, and work through the developmental stages alongside her parent by engaging in the shared creative activities.

Recommendations

A plan was drawn up to offer support to the parents, therapy for the parents and child together, advice for the school, consultations for the informal support network, and review meetings so that everyone is working together with a common understanding and an integrated approach to helping Sally enjoy living in her family with a sense of security and stability – a stable base from which to grow, encourage friendships and develop personal skills that will help her sense of worth. No other assessments were recommended.

Conclusion

In this chapter I have brought together the theory, the format and the practice of our assessments at Catchpoint to illustrate the way the behaviours of the child weave into patterns that give a picture of how the child has been affected by developmental trauma. The Assessment Report is a drawing-together of reported behaviours and observations, put into a frame of attachment theory and of developmental trauma disorder. The proposed therapy and support plan is structured according to a trauma recovery model with an attachment focus. This is flexible to match the varying needs of the family because there is no one size that fits all. There may need to be others involved rather than just the Adoption Support Agency, such as physiotherapy or a nurturing group at school.

The Assessment is the doorway to an integrated approach to working with the whole family and its community with a common understanding of the needs and hoped-for outcomes.

References

Bowlby, J. (1979) *The Making and Breaking of Affectionate Bonds*. London: Tavistock.

Briere, J. (1996) *Trauma Symptom Checklist for Children: Professional Manual*. Lutz, FL: Psychological Assessment Resources Inc.

Hasler, J. (2008) 'Table 9.1. Comparison of trauma recovery models.' In A. Oldfield and C. Flower (eds) *Music Therapy with Children and their Families*. London: Jessica Kingsley Publishers.

Hirst, M. (2005) *Loving and Living with Traumatised Children: Reflections by Adoptive Parents*. Sutton: BAAF.

Prior, V. and Glaser, D. (2006) *Understanding Attachment and Attachment Disorders: Theory, Evidence and Practice*. London: Jessica Kingsley Publishers.

Putnam, F. W. (1997) *Dissociation in Children and Adolescents*. New York, NY: Guilford Press.

Putnam, F. W., Helmers, K. and Trickett, P. K. (1993) 'Development, reliability and validity of a child dissociation scale.' *Child Abuse and Neglect 17*, 731–741.

Schore, A. (1994) *Affect Regulation and the Origin of Self: The Neurobiology of Emotional Development*. Hillsdale, NJ: Lawrence Erlbaum Associates.

Siegel, D. (2003) 'An Interpersonal Neurobiology of Psychotherapy: The Developing Mind and the Resolution of Trauma.' In M. Solomon and D. Siegel (eds) *Healing Trauma: Attachment, Mind, Body and Brain*. London: W. W. Norton.

Silberg, J. (1996) *The Dissociative Child: Diagnosis, Treatment and Management*. Brooklandville, MD: Sidran Press.

Smith, L. (2009) *Patterns of Functioning of the Child with Attachment Disorder*. Available at www.attachmentdisordermaryland.com/attachmentdisorder.htm, accessed on 11 November 2016.

Trevarthen, C. (2005) 'Assessing Attachment Difficulties.' Presentation at Attachment in Action Open Forum, London, 7 March 2005.

Wieland, S. (2011) *Dissociation in Traumatized Children and Adolescents: Theory and Clinical Interventions*. New York, NY: Routledge.

Chapter 5

BEYOND WORDS

Family Futures' Neuro Physiological
Psychotherapy Approach to the Assessment
and Treatment of Traumatized Children

——— ALAN BURNELL AND JAY VAUGHAN ———

Introduction

Family Futures CIC is an Independent Adoption Agency based in London, which specializes in the placement, assessment and treatment of traumatized children. In this chapter we describe our Neuro Physiological Psychotherapy (NPP) approach to the treatment of complex trauma in children who are fostered or have been adopted. Our work with traumatized children began nearly 20 years ago when the framework for our therapeutic work was attachment theory. Since then, advances in the field of neurodevelopmental biology, particularly the work of Bessel van der Kolk (2005) and Bruce Perry (2006), have helped us recognize that for children who have experienced multiple trauma and who also have had insecure attachment relationships, their whole development is impacted from birth through infancy by repeated 'relationship' or 'ambient' trauma. This phenomenon has subsequently been given the title of 'developmental trauma', which creates a more complex picture than attachment theory. It is not just the infant's attachment relationships that are distorted, but also his neurological, physiological and cognitive development is compromised. Developmental trauma is described in more detail in Chapter 1 of this book.

This reformulation of infant development broadened our psychological understanding of what was happening with the children in our treatment programmes, by putting it in a biological and neurological context. We realized that to help fostered or adopted children recover and heal effectively, we needed to develop integrated multi-disciplinary treatment programmes to address all aspects of a child's development. Most importantly, they needed to be implemented at the earliest opportunity.

Figure 5.1 is our visual representation of developmental trauma. We use it in our work with parents and children to help them understand how traumatic events that affect a child in infancy (the roots) continue to affect all branches of the child's development as he grows and develops.

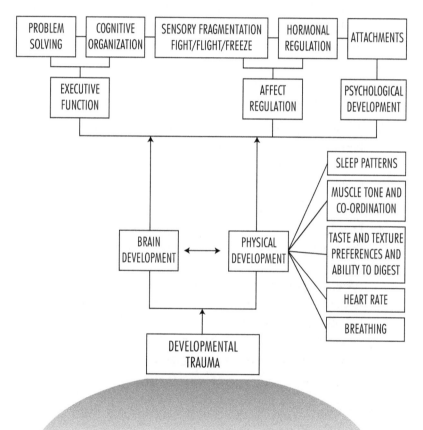

The Trauma Tree's roots are in the prolonged neglect, deprivation, loss, abuse, violence, upheaval or any combination of these that the child has experienced in his or her early childhood, fundamentally affecting the development of the brain, body and the relationship between them.

Trauma Tree devised by Family Futures (© Family Futures 2011)

FIGURE 5.1 THE NEURO PHYSIOLOGICAL PSYCHOTHERAPY APPROACH TO WORKING WITH CHILDREN WITH DEVELOPMENTAL TRAUMA

Family Futures' NPP assessment and treatment model is underpinned by four pillars:

1. Acceptance of the concept of developmental trauma as described above.

2. Recognition of the need for a multi-disciplinary assessment and treatment service. In our view, this flows as a logical consequence of acknowledging that trauma has a developmental impact that affects all aspects of a child's development – neurological, physiological and psychological. For this we have a multi-disciplinary team comprising social workers, child and adult psychotherapists specializing in creative arts, clinical psychologists, a paediatric occupational therapist specializing in sensory integration, an education consultant and education specialist, a neurodevelopmental psychologist, a child and adolescent psychiatrist and a paediatrician.

3. A neurosequential approach (Burnell and Vaughan 2006; Perry and Szalavitz 2006) to assessment and treatment. By neurosequential we mean an approach that follows the sequence of brain and central nervous system development in neonates and infants.

4. Developmental re-parenting, which works in tandem with the three previous pillars. This requires parents to understand the physiology of stress and how the brain and central nervous system respond to it. We have devised models of developmental re-parenting enabling foster and kinship carers and adoptive parents to interpret traumatized children's behaviour as emanating from fear (Forbes and Post 2006; Hughes 2009). Developmental re-parenting is described in more detail in Chapter 2.

Figure 5.2 describes the NPP model.

The level of the brain		
PRIMITIVE BRAIN	LIMBIC BRAIN	CORTICAL BRAIN

The focus		
TRAUMA	ATTACHMENT	IDENTITY

The themes		
FEAR AND STRESS REDUCTION CO-REGULATION AND ATTUNEMENT EMOTIONAL AND PHYSIOLOGICAL AWARENESS	DEVELOPING A MORE SECURE ATTACHMENT SHAME REDUCTION THE DEVELOPMENT OF CONSCIENCE AND EMPATHY	DEVELOPING A COHERENT NARRATIVE REFLECTIVE CAPACITY

and the form of intervention		
SOMATIC WORK AND SENSOIRMOTOR THERAPY TO CALM THE NERVOUS SYSTEM ALONG WITH SENSORY INTEGRATION THERAPY DEVELOPMENTAL RE-PARENTING AND ONE-ON-ONE TIME AT HOME FOOD SLEEP TOILETING MEDICATION WHERE APPROPRIATE SCHOOL-BASED INTERVENTION OR HOME SCHOOLING	DYADIC DEVELOPMENTAL PSYCHOTHERAPY AND NON-VERBAL CREATIVE ARTS THERAPY TO ADDRESS TRAUMA RE-ENACTMENT AND SUPPORT ATTACHMENT RELATIONSHIPS THERAPLAY TO ENHANCE ATTACHMENT DEVELOPMENTAL RE-PARENTING SCHOOL-BASED WORK WITH TEACHER AND PEERS MEDICATION WHERE APPROPRIATE	DYADIC DEVELOPMENTAL PSYCHOTHERAPY TO HELP THE DEVELOPMENTAL OF A COHERENT NARRATIVE AND IDENTITY ISSUES WITH A LIFE STORY WORK FOCUS FACILITATED CONTACT – REUNIONS WITH NON-THREATENING BIRTH RELATIVES AGE-APROPRIATE PARENTING SUPPORT ONGOING SCHOOL SUPPORT IDENTITY AND SELF-ESTEEM WORK INDIVIDUAL THERAPY MEDICATION WHERE APPROPRIATE

With parents the focus of intervention is		
ANXIETY REDUCTION UNRESOLVED PARENTAL TRAUMA REGULATION STRATEGIES EDUCATING SUPPORT NETWORKS	COUPLE RELATIONSHIP COUNSELLING AND INDIVIDUAL THERAPY INFERTILITY AND LOSS PARENT MENTORING NETWORK MAINTENANCE	AGE-APPROPRIATE PARENTING PREPARATION FOR ADULTHOOD SEXUALITY ISSUES PARENT INDIVIDUAL AND COUPLES WORK

Alan Burnell and Jay Vaughan 2006, revised 2012

FIGURE 5.2 HOW NEURO PHYSIOLOGICAL PSYCHOTHERAPY REFLECTS THE STRUCTURE OF THE BRAIN AND ITS DEVELOPMENT

The Neuro Physiological Psychotherapy model includes the following other facets of our programme:

- Psychiatric assessment.

- Paediatric assessment.

- Psychological assessment.

- Liaison with educational services. This is particularly important because we have found (Lansdown, Burnell and Allen 2007) a very strong connection between executive-functioning difficulties and children who have experienced complex trauma. This aspect of the work is explored in more detail in Chapter 11.

We will now describe the three broad phases of our work. Each description is followed by a brief case vignette.

Neuro Physiological Psychotherapy – working with the primitive brain

Although NPP is outlined as a *linear progressive programme* – working from the primitive brain to the limbic brain and then to the cortical brain – *it is not necessarily a linear process* (Vaughan, McCullough and Burnell 2016). Sometimes children will need to begin at a different point in the NPP programme and they will inevitably at times revert to more primitive brain responses. But the basic pattern of work is to move from primitive brain responses towards cortical brain responses. Foster and kinship carers, adoptive parents and professionals need to be aware of which part of the brain they are endeavouring to communicate with.

Traumatized children respond to many normal situations with primitive brain responses – fight, flight or freeze. As a consequence, it is hard for them to form secure attachments to primary carers. The focus of initial interventions with traumatized children needs to be on regulating the primitive brain responses to interpersonal interactions. This means understanding the various triggers (of the fear response) and focusing on developing a broader spectrum of ways in which the child can feel calm in his body and feel regulated and safe in all areas of life. This is slow and painstaking work and it led to our integration of more body-based and somatic therapeutic approaches. Although these approaches have been largely developed and shown to be successful in helping traumatized adults (Levine 1997), we apply these principles to our work with children. For traumatized adults and children, the impact of trauma inhibits the normal and effective discharge of stress, which becomes somatized in the body. We have learnt from Levine (2006, 2010) and Ogden, Minton and Pain (2006) how this somatic embodiment of trauma should be addressed.

Another important aspect of this work is sensory integration and functional paediatric occupational therapy work with the child. Occupational therapy is integrated into the overall NPP therapy programme and focuses on regulation of sensory processing and supporting the child and parent in understanding how the body processes sensory information. Sensory processing and sensory integration as a facet of normal child development has been highlighted by Ayres (2005). Normal sensory motor development and regulation is adversely impacted by insecure attachments and poor parenting. Occupational therapists have developed this original work with children and are now applying it to children with developmental trauma (Koomar 2009).

If a child is dysregulated in any of his senses, this will impair his ability to make sense of the world and interact meaningfully with primary caregivers in a way that is conducive to forming secure attachments. For this reason, the collaboration and co-working between psychotherapists, paediatric occupational therapists (trained in sensory integration) and parents is an essential ingredient in helping a child to stabilize and to feel safe. The caregiver and child become 'sensory detectives' (Auer and Auer 2010), learning how to track the body and the central nervous system. This process very much mirrors mother and baby interactions in the first years of life.

Parenting traumatized children is highly stressful and is liable to trigger unresolved trauma responses in caregivers. The potential for secondary trauma in caregivers is discussed in Chapter 2. An integral part of our treatment programme is to include therapeutic support for the caregivers and to develop their capacity for reflective parenting. Therapeutic developmental re-parenting is about responding to the needs of children appropriately, not reacting to them. For us, Siegel and Hartzell's *Parenting from the Inside Out* (2004) encapsulates this approach.

Supporting the Team Around the Child and the caregivers to understand the impact of working with a traumatized child and caregiver is also an essential feature of our model. The implications of secondary trauma and its potential impact on the Team Around the Family are discussed in Chapter 2. It cannot be emphasized enough how important this recognition is.

Hence Family Futures' NPP begins back to front – that is, with the primitive reptilian brain, allowing the child to experience, via the parent, what happy babies experience: periods of 'quiet alert' (Klaus 1999). During such periods, babies take in their environment and learn from their parents, wiring up their neurological systems in a developmentally adaptive way.

The following vignette describes working with a child in a primitive brain state.

HENRY AND HIS MUM

Henry was wild, breathing loudly with his eyes blazing. He was red in the face and sweaty as he careered full pelt at the door, crashing wildly into the beanbags piled up there. He then rolled around in a frenzy, laughing. His adoptive mother looked on calmly and smiled. It was good to see him having fun and laughing. Henry then manoeuvred himself onto the scooty board once more, skilfully got up once again and scooted to the far end of the room, meandering close to his mother. He then began the whole crashing process all over again. Henry repeated this time after time, each time rolling skilfully to one end of the room and then rolling (as fast as his little legs would allow) to the beanbags. Each time he rolled either way, he took a little diversion via his mum and was encouraged by the therapy team to see if he could grab a kiss as he passed by. Kisses were passed and giggles exchanged as Henry swooped closer to his mum and gathered 'fly by' kisses. Everyone cheered as he gathered up his kisses and Henry's sweaty little face was soon covered in kisses and 'I love you' stickers that Mum had been given to award him with.

Eventually Henry was exhausted and his hot little body lay resting on the beanbags, unable to clamber anymore onto the scooty board. Mum and the therapists joined him on the beanbags. He huffed and puffed, exclaiming he was too hot to speak. The therapy team suggested cool swinging on the swing with Mum might be good. He closed his eyes, muttered a deep 'yes' and allowed himself to be carried to the swing and to be carefully placed in the hammock. Henry quietly mouthed 'thank you' and Mum planted another kiss on him. Henry sighed and the hammock swung back and forth. The therapist gradually moved away as Mum sang gently to him as she rocked him back and forth. Henry kept his eyes tightly shut although he did sneak a quick look from time to time, checking Mum was still there. Mum smiled as she rocked her boy and watched his little body, hot from the play, resting. A rare event.

Henry is 8 years old and has been placed with adoptive parents. He has a history of neglect and abuse and also has cerebral palsy. For Henry the cerebral palsy means he has to use a walker to get around although he prefers to crawl as this is still quicker for him. No one had thought he would find adoptive parents but luckily he was fallen in love with at an Activity Day. He had been with his adoptive parents for coming up to a year when he was referred to Family Futures for support. Henry can still be extremely aggressive and finds it hard to be still or to let anyone be close to him. For Henry the gym and sensory strategies were perfect to engage him and, little by little, he was allowing himself to be cared for and finding some joy in the relationship with his parents. Henry delighted in the freedom the gym gave him to move unheeded by his walker, so he took great delight in the swing and the scooty board, shooting all over the room at great speed. Henry was also very responsive to being rocked and this would calm him and enable him after the rocking to allow his adoptive parents to be close to him and soothe him.

Henry's adoptive parents are supporting Henry in developing stronger leg muscles and using his walking sticks rather than his preferred mode of crawling. The sensory integration assessment helped contribute ideas as to how to support Henry and what his vestibular system would respond well to. The session above happened in the first year of therapy as an initial phase of work (so in the first few months) designed to help Henry settle and feel calm enough to begin to move towards more attachment-based work.

Neuro Physiological Psychotherapy – working with the limbic brain

Whilst the first phase of treatment is essentially body-based fear reduction work with the parent and child dyad, the second stage of treatment moves more towards the model of Dyadic Developmental Psychotherapy (DDP) developed by Hughes (2004). This psychotherapeutic approach, which involves close co-working with the substitute parent, helps the child and the parent to begin to explore the origins of the child's feelings and how they manifest in the here and now. Family Futures employs arts therapy approaches in its DDP work. These provide a medium for communication, exploration and symbolic representation of the child's internal world. We use painting, puppetry, sand trays, clay and drama to help the child express his feelings and body states. Fuller accounts of Family Futures' use of the creative arts can be found in Archer and Burnell (2003), Vaughan (in Jones 2007) and Vaughan (in Jones 2010).

Secure attachment behaviour and affect enrichment is only possible when a child is not living in a state of constant traumatization. At Family Futures we often say that a traumatized child has two feet in the past, and his head looking backwards, whereas a securely attached child has one foot in the present and one foot in the past, but he is looking through the present to the future. To achieve this requires parent and child to engage in more attachment-focused therapies. In this way, along with its reliance on DDP and the creative arts therapies, Family Futures also integrates Theraplay (Booth and Jernberg 2009) into NPP.

Developmental re-parenting using this model needs to be systematic and consistent across the child's network, including other family members, school and peers. At Family Futures we carry out a programme that involves educating the network about developmental trauma and the specific developmental needs of the child it is relating to. This is particularly relevant to children who have been physically and sexually abused as they may continue to act out at home, at school or with peers.

The following case vignette describes working with a child in the limbic brain state.

Rebecca and her Daddy

Rebecca sat on her daddy's lap and explored his large hands. He wondered with the therapist about all the little hurts on her hands and gently put on some cream to each little hurt and dry bits of skin caused by her severe eczema. Rebecca explored her daddy's hands as he did this, seeing how her little hands fitted inside his large hand and how if he closed his hands tight her little hand nearly disappeared from view. She played hide and seek with his hands and giggled with delight each time her hand burst out of his grasp. She suddenly said: 'Why are your hands not the same colour as mine, Daddy? I want my hands to be like your hands!' And her smile melted from her lips. Her daddy looked sad and the therapist acknowledged their different skin colours and that she wanted to be like her daddy and that Daddy was sad about this too. Rebecca ignored this comment and returned to the safety of hand hide and seek. The cream was smothered on thicker and Rebecca slithered down her daddy's arms into a little bundle on the floor.

Rebecca enjoyed her daddy picking her up and swinging her gently round, and squealed with delight as he held her up high. The therapist encouraged Rebecca's daddy to talk about what he would have done if Rebecca had been born to him and been his little baby. Rebecca's daddy smiled broadly and held her up to his face saying how he would have loved and treasured her and always kept her safe. He spoke of cuddles and toe counting, of tickles and love. Rebecca cooed and gurgled, babbling like a little one. Suddenly she began to squirm and demanded to be put down by her daddy, who looked shocked and confused. Rebecca asserted that she did not like this game and it made her sad. The therapist said how hard it was to think about not having had this special time with her daddy. Rebecca turned her back, but as Daddy pulled her close and placed his large hand on her hand, she tucked her fingers between his fingers and sighed a loud sigh. Daddy rocked her and whispered into her ear, 'I love you, Sweet Pea, to the moon and back and always will', and Rebecca calmed and mumbled, 'my daddy'.

Rebecca is 5 years old (and has been in placement for a year) but loves to spend time with her daddy and to be little again. Shortly after being placed, she completely shut down and became mute so she was rapidly referred for an assessment and then for a therapy programme. Rebecca responded very well to the sensory integration phase of work and really relished finding out about how her body worked and what she enjoyed. This body-based work led to her once more becoming verbal and led to a phase of Theraplay work. Rebecca has now been attending Family Futures for a year and the plan is that she will continue.

Rebecca finds it easier at this point with her daddy than with her mummy but there are increasing Theraplay sessions with Mummy as she begins to find ways to enjoy being enjoyed. Rebecca had been abused by her birth mother and never had a relationship with her birth father so the adoptive parents have been thoughtful about how this has impacted their relationship with her. Theraplay alongside some creative arts techniques are helping Rebecca make the connection between her life story and what is so hard for her now. She is also beginning to make sense of her identity as a transracially placed child.

Neuro Physiological Psychotherapy – working with the cortical brain

When parents and children are able to achieve moments of calm and reflection, it is possible to help the child to begin to make sense of his early experience and the effect it has had on his feeling states, behaviours and relationships. In our NPP model at Family Futures, we enable the child to begin to address the trauma through a form of life story work using the DDP model. As a precursor, one of the therapy team will have done an exhaustive and forensic search of the adoptive child's file when he was living in his birth family and in foster care. The aim of this exercise is not just to get a 'coherent narrative' of the child's life with dates, times, people and places, but also to create as vivid a picture of the child's lifestyle and day-to-day experience at each developmental stage as is possible.

The actual life story work often focuses on using a large sheet of paper, paints, crayons and other creative media to depict, using the metaphor of a road or a river, the child's life course. The child is helped to understand his history by the therapist and parent painting, drawing and sticking pictures of significant events and relationships onto his time-line. This will be annotated by the child with his expression of feelings that he had then or that he has now, which he can represent using paint, pastels, colours and words. Through this process, the child's feelings and experiences are acknowledged, validated and empathized with. There are many creative ways of helping children make sense of their history (Rees 2009).

The child is also encouraged and empowered to express his feelings and to retrieve often unpleasant memories in the safe and accepting environment created by the parents and therapists working together. As and when the child inevitably becomes resistant, dissociative or dysregulated, the role of the therapist is to set the pace that the child can cope with and model for the parents how best to help their child process his feelings. This process of mapping the child's life story often starts in the here-and-now, acknowledging the safe, nurturing environment in which he now finds himself, and working backwards chronologically into less safe and more scary times. This process can take months and often needs to be revisited at different times throughout childhood as the child's ability to make sense of and process his past develops.

For children who have experienced early trauma, which leaves them with a negative self-image and a heightened level of fear, a secure attachment forms the basis for the development of a positive sense of self and optimism about other people's intentions and the future. At this stage in the therapeutic process, it is hoped that the child is freer of pathological fear, has a more positively internalized secure attachment with the parent figure and can now develop a positive sense of self and self-worth. From this position, with the carer/adoptive parent and therapist, the child can develop and use his reflective capacity and his cortical capacity for integrative left-brain logical and right-brain affective thinking to begin to think about himself, his current relationships and his past, without the distorting lens of trauma hampering him so much.

Unfortunately this is often where therapy with adopted children starts – with 'Life Story Books', chronologies and contacts with birth family members that traditionally have been seen as continuity with the past. For the contemporary adopted child, for whom chaos, neglect and abuse were his first experiences of life, it is arguable that such continuity can be seen more as contamination and re-traumatization if the phases, outlined above, have not been worked through first. However bad or traumatizing a child's early experience and history might have been, if he has processed these feelings and experiences, and has been helped to form secure attachments, then he can begin to reflect upon his past and his present, and think about his future, with a greater sense of hope and optimism. At this stage the child should be regulated and be forming secure attachments in order to be able to do the cognitive processing required to develop a positive sense of self, a problem-solving capacity and emotional intelligence.

The ultimate aim of therapeutic work with developmentally traumatized children is not just to give them information about their past, but most importantly to enable them to develop understanding and forgiveness. Such resolution is something that can only come from within, and cannot be imposed from without. Just as the child has been helped to understand himself in the context of his history, he needs to be helped to understand his birth parents' and his birth family's behaviour in the context of their history.

The following case vignette describes working with children from the primitive brain state to the cortical brain state.

TINA AND TIMMY AND THEIR FOSTER CARERS

Tina and Timmy were placed together in foster care aged 6 years and 3 years, having been removed from a neglectful birth family. Tina was a quiet, undemanding child. Timmy was a handful, constantly on the go at home and at school. Two years on, aged 5 years, Timmy was proving extremely challenging and his high-risk behaviour led to the local authority seeking help.

When Timmy was referred to Family Futures for an assessment, this was a family-based assessment, so Tina participated too. During the course of the assessment Tina shared a little bit about how hard it was for her to talk about her feelings. It was clear that Tina was more dissociative and when under stress she was triggered into a 'freeze' state. Timmy meanwhile raged and rampaged around the building, bursting into rooms. It was not possible to talk to Timmy about what was going on as he was clearly constantly in a 'flight and fight' state.

It was agreed following this assessment that both children needed help. Aside from family-based work and parent support Tina was offered dyadic therapy sessions to help begin to make sense of her history and how hard she found relationships. Tina, as part of this dyadic approach, did body-based work to help reduce her dissociative state. For Tina the heart rate monitor in sessions was a revelation and she learnt how cuddling up with her foster carers in sessions helped to calm her. Tina also responded well to arts-based therapy woven into the dyadic work. She discovered a passion for painting, creating bigger and bigger images of buildings, which grew taller and taller as each week the paper was rolled out further. Tina laughed and laughed as the room was splattered with images of tower blocks. Her foster carers wondered if this was helpful but at the same time could see the little moments of connection between them grow. For Tina the body work woven with the arts and some meaning making helped her make a connection with her foster carers and she became less stuck in a frozen state.

Timmy on the other hand needed a sensory assessment to devise sensory strategies to calm his level of dysregulation. In sessions, keeping Timmy safe was hard work and his foster carers and the therapist often came out exhausted from them. Timmy loved climbing and would climb anything. He loved best of all to climb where he was not meant to climb. He made slow progress, always needing a lengthy gym-based session to be regulated enough to manage any thinking in sessions.

Tina enjoyed using the gym too, and sometimes in sibling sessions Timmy would urge his sister to climb with him. Tina was cautious and careful, always ensuring she was safe and never easily trusting that the adults had set things up properly without checking herself. Tina and Timmy gradually became more regulated and less inclined to be triggered into 'fight, flight or freeze'.

One day in a sibling session the therapists and foster carers were all momentarily distracted. Meanwhile Timmy somehow quickly managed to climb on top of the swing in the gym. He sat balanced precariously on the top. He said he would not come down. Tina reached out and took her foster carer's hand, saying quietly, 'I am scared'. The therapists wondered out loud about all the times Timmy had been scared when he was little. Tina then said, 'Don't jump, Timmy', and Timmy just laughed a manic little laugh. He then said quietly, 'But she tried to jump, Tina, and she had me in her arms.' Tina burst into floods of silent tears, making strange little gulping sounds. Timmy looked at his sister with huge eyes and a single tear ran down his cheek.

Timmy suddenly began to look terrified so a pile of cushions was put in place and his foster carers and the therapists worked together to climb up to help him down. Timmy collapsed and clung to his foster carers, who held him in their arms and rocked him. Tina and Timmy spent the rest of the session talking eloquently about their memories of the time on top of the tower block with their birth mother.

In later dyadic sessions Tina talked about how many times her birth mother had tried to kill herself and threatened to take them too. No one had known that she had threatened this and no one but the children knew about the night she went to the top floor of their tower block with Timmy in her arms and threatened to jump. It was Tina who talked her down. Tina had been saying this with her paintings and Timmy with his climbing but it was a memory held between the two of them that needed to be shared. Tina and Timmy are still with their foster carers and the foster carers are talking about adoption. Tina increasingly sneaks up to her foster carers for a hug and Timmy is still active but he does not seem so fearless now and is more able to talk. So the 'acting in' Tina and the 'acting out' Timmy moved from two very different primitive brain states to high-brain cortical thinking.

Conclusion

Figure 5.3 describes Family Futures' NPP approach to working with traumatized children. When carrying out an assessment, we use psychometric and clinical tools to assess the three main developmental systems: the sensory, the affective and the cognitive. We know that developmentally traumatized children have had all three systems impacted by early life experiences. These three developmental systems operate neurosequentially at all three levels of the brain. The diagonal arrow in Figure 5.3 illustrates the normal path of developmental trajectory, and, in our view, the trajectory of the therapeutic process. For the sake of simplicity, the diagram starts at birth, but we know of course that these developmental systems are impacted in utero by stress and other transgenic influences such as drugs and alcohol.

The aim of the assessment is therefore to work out how the child's brain and nervous system is functioning in terms of brain levels and developmental systems. It is essentially a mapping exercise. This map informs our formulations with regard to the NPP treatment programmes.

This approach highlights the need for a multi-disciplinary team who need the specialist knowledge in relation to sensory integration, affect development and attachment, and cognitive processing and executive functioning.

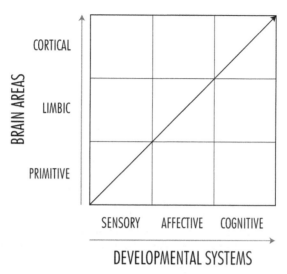

FIGURE 5.3 INTEGRATED APPROACH TO ASSESSMENT AND TREATMENT

Does the NPP model have an impact? Two papers have been recently published (McCullough *et al.* 2016; Vaughan *et al.* 2016) outlining Family Futures' NPP model. This evaluation of Family Futures' NPP treatment programme re-tested a significant percentage of the families who have received full treatment at Family Futures. This is one of the largest evaluations of a therapeutic model's treatment outcomes for adopted children and the results are very positive, with improved outcomes across a range of measures for children reported by both parents and teachers. These include improvements in parent–child, sibling and peer relationships. A high proportion of the children remained in education and did not have any involvement with the criminal justice system.

Family Futures provides this NPP service to children, usually at the point of crisis. Given the understanding we now have, some of these crises could have been averted had a multi-disciplinary assessment and treatment begun at the point of entry of the child into the public care system. We cannot wait for things to go wrong before children get help. Our awareness that child development is impaired by trauma needs to be the starting point for post-placement therapeutic intervention and decision making about the support these children and their families need.

We are only at the very beginning of being able to utilize neuroscience in our clinical work. However, all the science is of little value without the creative interpersonal therapy. Ultimately it is this that heals children and harnesses the plasticity of their brain and developmental systems.

References

Archer, C. and Burnell, A. (eds) (2003) *Trauma, Attachment and Family Permanence: Fear Can Stop You Loving.* London: Jessica Kingsley Publishers.

Auer, C. and Auer, M. (2010) *Making Sense of Your Senses: A Workbook for Children with Sensory Processing Disorder.* Oakland, CA: New Harbinger Publications.

Ayres, A. J. (2005) *Sensory Integration and the Child* (25th Anniversary edn). Los Angeles, CA: Western Psychological Services.

Booth, P. B. and Jernberg, A. M. (2009) *Theraplay: Helping Parents and Children Build Better Relationships Through Attachment-Based Play.* San Francisco, CA: Jossey Bass.

Burnell, A. and Vaughan, J. (2006) 'Working with an elephant in the room.' *Context, Family Therapy Journal,* 87, 46–50.

Forbes, H. T. and Post, B. B. (2006) *Beyond Consequences, Logic, and Control: A Love-Based Approach to Helping Children with Severe Behaviours.* Boulder, CO: Beyond Consequences Institute, LCC.

Hughes, D. A. (2004) 'An attachment-based treatment of maltreated children and young people.' *Attachment and Human Development* 6, 3, 263–278.

Hughes, D. A. (2009) *Principles of Attachment-Focused Parenting: Effective Strategies to Care for Children.* New York, NY: Norton Professional Books.

Jones, P. (2007) *Drama as Therapy, Vol. 1: Theory, Practice and Research.* London: Routledge.

Jones, P. (2010) *Drama as Therapy, Vol. 2: Clinical Work and Research into Practice.* London: Routledge.

Klaus, M. (1999) *Your Amazing Newborn.* Boston, MA: Da Capo Press Inc.

Koomar, J. (2009) 'Trauma- and attachment-informed sensory integration assessment and intervention.' *American Occupational Therapy Association* 32, 4, 1–4.

Lansdown, R., Burnell, A. and Allen, M. (2007) 'Is it that they won't do it or is it that they can't? Executive functioning and children who have been fostered and adopted.' *Adoption and Fostering 31,* 2, 44–53.

Levine, P. (1997) *Waking the Tiger: Healing Trauma – The Innate Capacity to Transform Overwhelming Experiences.* Berkeley, CA: North Atlantic Books.

Levine, P. (2006) *Trauma Through a Child's Eyes: Awakening the Ordinary Miracle of Healing.* Berkeley, CA: North Atlantic Books.

Levine, P. (2010) *In an Unspoken Voice.* Berkeley, CA: North Atlantic Books.

McCullough, E., Gordon-Jones, S., Last, A., Vaughan, J. and Burnell, A. (2016) 'An evaluation of Neuro-Physiological Psychotherapy: An integrative therapeutic approach to working with adopted children who have experienced early life trauma.' *Clinical Child Psychology and Psychiatry 21,* 4, 1–21.

Ogden, P., Minton, K. and Pain, C. (2006) *Trauma and the Body: A Sensorimotor Approach to Psychotherapy.* New York, NY: W. W. Norton.

Perry, B. D. (2006) 'Applying Principles of Neurodevelopment to Clinical Work with Maltreated and Traumatized Children: The Neurosequential Model of Therapeutics.' In N. B. Webb (ed.) *Working with Traumatized Youth in Child Welfare.* New York, NY: Guilford Press.

Perry, B. D. and Szalavitz, M. (2006) *The Boy Who Was Raised as a Dog and Other Stories from a Child Psychiatrist's Notebook: What Traumatized Children Can Teach Us about Loss, Love and Healing.* New York, NY: Basic Books.

Rees, J. (2009) *Life Storybooks for Adopted Children.* London: Jessica Kingsley Publishers.

Siegel, D. and Hartzell, M. (2004) *Parenting from the Inside Out: How a Deeper Self-Understanding Can Help You Raise Children Who Thrive.* New York, NY: Tarcher.

van der Kolk, B. (2005) 'Developmental trauma disorder: Toward a rational diagnosis for children with complex trauma histories.' *Psychiatric Annals 35,* 5, 401–408.

Vaughan, J., McCullough, E. and Burnell, A. (2016) 'Neurophysiological Psychotherapy (NPP): The development and application of an integrative, wrap-around service and treatment programme for maltreated children placed in adoptive and foster care placements.' *Clinical Child Psychology and Psychiatry 21,* 4, 568–581.

Further reading

APA (American Psychiatric Association) (2000) *Diagnostic and Statistical Manual of Mental Disorders (DSM-IV).* Washington, DC: APA.

Bowlby, J. (1997) *Attachment and Loss: Attachment* (Vol. 1). London: Pimlico.

Bowlby, J. (2005) *A Secure Base.* Abingdon: Routledge.

Howe, D. (2005) *Child Abuse and Neglect: Attachment, Development and Intervention.* Basingstoke: Palgrave Macmillan.

Hughes, D. A. (2006) *Building the Bonds of Attachment: Awakening Love in Deeply Troubled Children.* Lanham, MD: Jason Aronson.

Hughes, D. A. (2007) *Attachment-Focused Family Therapy.* New York, NY: W. W. Norton.

Hughes, D. A. and Baylin, J. (2012) *Brain-Based Parenting: The Neuroscience of Caregiving for Healthy Attachment.* New York, NY: W. W. Norton.

Main, M. and Solomon, J. (1986) 'Discovery of an Insecure Disorganized/Disoriented Attachment Pattern: Procedures, Findings and Implications for Classification of Behaviour.' In M. W. Yogman and T. B. Brazelton (eds) *Affective Development in Infancy.* New York, NY: Ablex.

O'Connor, T. G., Heron, J., Golding, J., Beveridge, M. and Glover, V. (2002) 'Maternal antenatal anxiety and children's behavioural/emotional problems at 4 years.' *British Journal of Psychiatry 180,* 502–508.

Perry, B. D. and Hambrick, E. P. (2008) 'The Neurosequential Model of Therapeutics.' *Reclaiming Children and Youth 17,* 3, 38–43.

Rothschild, B. (2000) *The Body Remembers: The Psychophysiology of Trauma and Trauma Treatment.* New York, NY: W. W. Norton.

Van den Bergh, B. R. H., Mulder, E. J. H., Mennes, M. and Glover, V. (2005) 'Antenatal maternal anxiety and stress and the neurobehavioural development of the fetus and child: Links and possible mechanisms: A review.' *Neuroscience and Biobehavioral Reviews 29,* 2, 237–258.

Volkers, N. (1991) 'Father's lifestyle can have fetal consequences.' *Journal of the National Cancer Institute 8,* 22, 1611–1612.

Chapter 6

DYADIC PARENT–CHILD ART PSYCHOTHERAPY WITH CHILDREN WHO HAVE BEEN EXPOSED TO COMPLEX TRAUMA

-ANTHEA HENDRY AND ELIZABETH TAYLOR BUCK-

Introduction

This chapter describes three different Dyadic Art Psychotherapy (DAP) approaches. We have named these three approaches to highlight the key differences between them, but they can be used flexibly and in combination. All three approaches include the parents or caregivers as participants in the art therapy in different ways. They are presented and illustrated through clinical vignettes. We will also outline the theoretical basis of this work and how it fits with the general practice of art psychotherapy with children and young people.

Background

Art therapy is a form of psychotherapy that uses art media as one of the primary modes of expression and communication. As a professional practice it can be found in many countries. There are parallel but distinct histories in the USA and the UK, with each having recognized pioneers and influences, which in turn have exerted influences on the global development of art therapy. To practise in the UK it is essential to be state registered with the Health and Care Professions Council (HCPC). The British Association of Art Therapy (BAAT) is the professional organization for art therapists in the UK. The titles 'art therapist' and 'art psychotherapist' are used synonymously and are protected in the UK so that they can be used only by those who have completed a postgraduate training in art therapy at Master's level.

Art psychotherapists working with children and families in the UK are employed in a wide range of settings, from National Health Service (NHS) Child and Adolescent Mental Health Services, mainstream and specialist schools and voluntary and charitable services for vulnerable or abused children, to services specifically designed to support fostered and adopted children. Although other professionals may use art materials in their work, a qualified art therapist will be familiar with a specialized body of art therapy literature which, alongside other research and his own experience of art making, will influence and inform his practice.

Over the last few years the authors have been supported by BAAT in developing a post-qualifying training in DAP. This grew from their experience of working with fostered and adopted children in various settings over many years and research into DAP (Taylor Buck, Dent-Brown and Parry 2012; Taylor Buck *et al.* 2014).

Theoretical influences on Dyadic Art Psychotherapy with children who have experienced complex trauma

Influences from the art therapy literature

In the UK the art therapy literature and training on working with children and young people have been significantly influenced by psychoanalytic theory (Case and Dalley 1990). The model of working individually with a child dominated the 1980s and 1990s, and case study accounts of art therapists' work with children who are in foster care, in kinship care or adopted are evident in this literature (Case 1990, 1995; Drucker 2001; Jefferies and Gillespie 1981). More recently, systemic and attachment-based influences are becoming more evident in art therapy practice (Waller 2006).

Art therapists have postulated a number of theories about the beneficial and therapeutic nature of art making. The theories most pertinent to the dyadic approaches we will describe in this chapter are:

- Art making as a means of non-verbal communication 'through which a person can achieve both conscious and unconscious expression' (Dalley 1984, p.xii).

- Art making as 'a bridge between inner and outer (and) towards a greater integration between the two' (Nowell-Hall 1987, p.157).

- Art making as a less threatening way of expressing difficult feelings and experiences (Dalley 1984).

- Art making as a way of processing memories (Lusebrink 2004), and expressing non-declarative memories (Hanney and Kozlowska 2002).

- Art making as an 'exposure and desensitization tool' – communicating intolerable feelings and unspeakable experiences in a concrete form that can then be reworked in the therapeutic process (Kozlowska and Hanney 2001, p.73).

- Art making stimulating 'new ways of articulating and thinking about experiences that break away from rigid thought patterns' with the potential for new neural pathways to be formed (Lobban 2012, p.10).

- The sensory nature of the art materials (e.g. sand, water or clay) stimulating the senses and acting as a route to somatic memory (Dalley 2008; Gillespie 2001; Meyerowitz-Katz 2003; O'Brien 2004; Sagar 1990).

Influences from attachment theory and neuroscience

Although the first tenets of attachment theory were set out by Bowlby (1969), much of its subsequent development was influenced by Mary Ainsworth and colleagues (1978), who reinforced basic concepts and introduced other key concepts and classifications. One of these concepts was maternal sensitivity. Ainsworth described four essential components to sensitivity: awareness of an infant's signals; accurate interpretation of them; appropriate responses to them (Ainsworth, Bell and Stayton 1974); prompt responses to them. Research has demonstrated a causal link between caregiver sensitivity and the child's attachment security (Bakermans-Kranenburg, van Ijzendoorn and Juffer 2003).

Research in the areas of the biological consequences of early maltreatment and neglect supports the view that infants and young children adapt to their caregiving environment. Woolgar (2013), in a review of findings, suggests this is one of the clearest findings in this complex area and emphasizes the inter-relatedness of the effects of maltreatment on brain development, physiology and genes:

> A biological adaptation in one context can be problematic in another when we make a radical change for the better, as in fostering and adoption. For carers, understanding that there is a sense behind self-defeating behaviours may help them to manage the rejection and hostility, and consider how their own responses might need to adapt to reduce the impact of these behaviours. (p.241)

Both attachment research and research into the neurobiology of maltreatment provide a rationale for dyadic therapies that seek to develop caregiver sensitivity. This is achieved by helping caregivers to:

- become more attuned and aware of behavioural signals

- develop an appropriate shared emotional language with their children

- develop or re-establish a connection with their children.

Accounts of parent–child psychotherapy come from the perspective of both attachment theory (Hughes 2004) and psychoanalytic theory (Acquarone 2004; Baradon 2005).

The development of Dyadic Art Psychotherapy

At the turn of the century, involving caregivers directly in the therapy was a treatment of choice in specialist services for adoptive families in the UK (Brenninkmeyer 2007; Burnell and Vaughan 2003), but a small study (Hendry 2005) found there was little evidence of this practice among British art therapists specializing in work with this population of children. More recent research indicates that a dyadic parent–child approach to art psychotherapy is being used by 60 per cent of British art psychotherapists working with children and young people with some degree of frequency (Taylor Buck *et al.* 2012).

There is now a growing body of literature relating to dyadic art therapy. A significant contribution to this literature has been made by Canadian art therapist Lucille Proulx (2003), whose book *Strengthening Emotional Ties through Parent–Child-Dyad Art Therapy* is a theoretical and practical guide to dyadic art therapy interventions primarily with infants and preschoolers. Additional accounts come from Landgarten (1975), Lachman, Stuntz and Jones (1975), Ambridge (2001), Schur (2001), Rubin (2005), Henley (2005, 2007), Malchiodi (2014), Regev and Snir (2015) and Hendry (2016). There are also good accounts of parent–infant art therapy group work (e.g. Hall 2008; Hosea 2006).

What follows is a description of the approaches to dyadic work that the authors have developed for use with children who have experienced complex relational trauma.

Three approaches to Dyadic Art Psychotherapy

DAP is a joined-up approach to art therapy involving children and their parents or caregivers in joint art therapy sessions at least some of the time. The make-up of the dyad varies with different children and different families but usually involves sessions with the child and an adult with whom the child has a significant and enduring relationship.

DAP is a needs-led flexible intervention that respects the diversity of family history, culture and individual experience (Taylor Buck, Dent-Brown and Parry 2012). An in-depth understanding of each dyad or family is needed to assess the feasibility and suitability of DAP. If dyadic work is indicated, it needs to be carefully planned to meet the needs and goals of each dyad. Not all dyads will benefit from the same approach, and the therapist will need to think about which is most appropriate. There are three key approaches we have identified, which are:

- child-led with caregiver as helper or witness

- joint engagement approach

- co-construction of a coherent narrative.

Depending on the identified needs and goals, the therapist may follow a single approach or combine more than one.

The key difference lies in the role taken by the caregiver. However, all three approaches include a significant element of relational engagement and attempt to develop the capacity for reflective functioning in both the caregiver and the child. They all embrace the need to enhance the child's self-worth and to encourage imagination and creativity.

There follows a brief description of each approach followed by a vignette to illustrate the approach. The vignettes are composites from many dyadic sessions with children who have experienced early trauma. The degree to which the sessions are structured varies. All the dyadic work described here follows a comprehensive assessment and careful preparation work with the caregiver before the start of the joint sessions.

Child-led art therapy with caregiver as helper or witness

The child-led approach is a way of working that keeps the focus on the child's self-directed art making. It is similar to traditional non-directive art therapy, but the caregiver is present and can witness the child's process at first-hand, and the therapist can model attuned responses for the caregiver. Following a period of child-led art making there may be time set aside for the dyad and therapist to reflect together on the art and the art-making process. There may also be discussions about emotion regulation, communication and understanding between the dyad. Often the focus in this approach is on enhancing the caregivers' sensitivity and understanding of their child.

MARINA: TOLERATING DIFFICULT FEELINGS

Marina (aged 12) has been with her foster carers, Ann and Colin, for six months. It is planned to be a long-term placement. She has been in care since she was 7 after years of living with domestic violence and the serious mental health problems of her birth mother. Previous placements with her younger siblings have been disrupted and she is now placed on her own. Ann and Colin have had support from their fostering agency but feel they want some more intense help with Marina. They have noticed that she seems to be very cut off from her feelings, and hypervigilant. An assessment has taken place, which included a consultation with Marina's social worker and her foster carers, some sessions with Ann and Colin on their own, and a family art therapy session including Marina. Following this, Ann, Colin and Marina agreed to try some dyadic art therapy sessions using a child-led approach with one carer present as witness and a reflecting presence.

Ann and Colin decided that due to work pressures and family circumstances it would be Colin who attended the sessions with Marina. The therapist then spent four sessions preparing Colin to understand the non-directive, reflective role he would take in sessions. The therapist also booked in sessions with both foster parents, interspersed between the dyadic sessions with Marina, so they could discuss the sessions from Colin's point of view, address any issues arising and include Ann in the reflective process.

In the first dyadic session Marina had found some polystyrene sheets and pressed a pencil into the sheets, creating deep grooves. She snipped some of the sheets up into smaller and smaller pieces. About halfway through the session Colin had become very involved, showing Marina how she could use a roller and ink to make prints from the polystyrene sheets and fragments. In the subsequent session with both foster carers Colin was able to acknowledge he had found Marina's destructive impulse to snip and scratch the polystyrene hard to bear and he had wanted to direct her to a more constructive activity. The therapist acknowledged how difficult the non-directive stance can be. They practised using reflective comments such as 'It looks satisfying to snip those sheets up' instead of directive comments or suggestions such as 'Why don't you make something nice out of this?'

Marina and Colin come to the second session looking hot and flustered. There had been some confusion about collecting Marina from school and they have only just made the session on time. The therapist reminds Marina of how the session will be structured, explaining that they will begin with some time during which Marina will take the lead and use the art materials in the way she chooses. This will be followed by a clearing-up time during which Colin will take the lead, and then there will be a short discussion time when they can talk about what Marina has made and about other things that seem important.

Marina seems distracted as she wanders round the room. She collects a range of materials and dumps them noisily onto the table. She picks up some masking tape and starts winding it tightly round her hand. It becomes like a tourniquet and the tips of her fingers redden. Colin says that it must be hurting, but she denies this. The therapist wonders aloud whether Marina finds it hard to let Colin know when she is hurting or feeling sad. Marina responds by saying that nothing ever hurts her. She rips the tape off and throws it into the bin.

Marina collects a large sheet of white paper and puts it on the table. She squirts a round spiral of paint, then another of a different colour, then another and so on. She seems immersed in this activity. The colours begin to merge in places, forming pools of varied colours, which Colin comments on. Marina starts moving the paint around with her index finger and eventually her whole hand becomes like a brush. The sheet turns a deep purple with a small edge of white paper remaining uncovered. She carefully pulls the paper to one side and repeats the same process on another sheet, using a lot of paint and covering the whole paper.

The therapist comments on the time and asks Marina and Colin to think about clearing up. Marina washes her hands, running both taps and taking a long time. With encouragement from Colin she helps put all the art materials she collected back where they came from. She asks if she can take the roll of masking tape away with her. The therapist explains that she can use the materials that are in the room but not take them away with her.

The following week when the foster carers and the therapist meet they reflect on the session. Colin says he felt unsure and uncomfortable in the session at times, wondering if Marina was using too much paint or if she should be given the tape she asked for. The therapist reassures him that it is her job to make decisions about boundaries and how the art materials are used.

They discuss how Marina seemed to enjoy the messiness of the paints and how this could be a way of communicating something about how she was feeling without using words. The therapist reflects that maybe she was communicating how messy she felt inside or was perhaps reconnecting with some very early sensory experiences. The therapist lets the foster parents know that they might not know at this stage, but it is important to tolerate the discomfort and the mess and accept this as Marina's way of communicating her feelings. There might be something important about witnessing in an accepting way the mess and the destructive feelings as well as the constructive ones.

Joint engagement

The joint engagement approach is a way of working that encourages the caregiver and child to jointly engage in art making. Following a period of joint engagement there may be time set aside for the dyad and therapist together to reflect on the art and the art-making process. In a joint engagement approach the dyad is encouraged from the outset to make art together. Researchers are looking at the developmental significance of joint parent–child engagement and in particular the importance of symbol-infused joint engagement (Adamson *et al.* 2004). Recent research has shown the impact that symbol-infused joint parent–child engagement has on the acquisition of theory of mind (Nelson, Adamson and Bakerman 2008). The study indicates that, when engaged in joint parent–child activities, toddlers can begin to compare their own feelings about an event with the adult partner's emotional reaction to it, and they can experience their adult partner as an intentional being. Although this research focuses on the joint engagement of parent and toddler in a shared task, it seems likely that joint making activities with older children and their parents or caregivers could also foster important and potentially therapeutic processes in the child and also perhaps in the adult.

DAP has the potential to offer the parent and child opportunities for joint engagement tasks and encourages discussions of the task as well as an appreciation of the other person's perspectives. It can also focus on moments of attunement when warmth and playfulness emerge. Like other dyadic approaches, it can develop the caregiver's capacity for reflective functioning, address how the caregiver's own Internal Working Models are enacted in the relationship with the child, and facilitate reflective conversations between caregiver and child.

RYAN: STRENGTHENING CONNECTIONS

Ryan (aged 8) has lived with his maternal aunt Dot (aged 45) for nearly a year. His early life was spent with his mother and her different partners. However, his mother's deteriorating mental health following years of domestic violence led to Dot stepping in and becoming Ryan's long-term caregiver. Dot had never wanted children herself (she has described herself to the therapist as feeling more at home with animals) but she has been good at providing routines and boundaries for Ryan. Emotionally she does not feel very connected to him. The art therapist is offering dyadic parent–child work to help build the relationship between them, to enhance Dot's understanding of Ryan's behaviour, to facilitate communication and to encourage some playfulness in the relationship. They have met weekly for eight weeks, with the therapist meeting with Dot between each session. What follows is a description of a typical session at this stage in the therapy using a joint engagement approach.

Starting the session: Checking-in

The therapist has designed a regular routine for Ryan's sessions to help him with the transition at the beginning and end of each session. She uses her large collection of postcard-size photos from magazines. Sessions start with Dot and Ryan viewing the postcards spread out on the table and each choosing one image. The images vary and may be people, landscapes, animals and the insides and outsides of buildings. They are then invited to say why they have picked the particular image. Today Dot has picked a photo of an old dog lazing in the sun.

'Our dog Bess has been poorly', she says.

The therapist knows that Ryan is very attached to Bess, and so she asks him how he feels about Bess. However, Ryan ignores her and sits hunched up with his arms folded, staring at the photo he has chosen of a snarling tiger. He then turns towards Dot.

'You shouted at me for losing my school jumper', he says crossly.

The therapist notes there has been a rupture in the relationship, which has not been repaired. It needs some immediate attention. She has seen Ryan angry before and also noticed that Dot can sound harsh towards Ryan without necessarily meaning to be.

'Are you feeling as angry inside as that tiger looks?' the therapist asks.

Ryan nods.

'You are upset with Dot for shouting at you and probably anxious about Bess too', she says.

Ryan nods again. The therapist also wonders if he felt misunderstood by Dot because she knows he struggles at school and finds it difficult to look after his belongings.

Dot seems to realize she has let her own feelings of anxiety about Bess get in the way of her ability to think about Ryan's feelings. She tells him that she is sorry she shouted. They seem to have got some way to reparation. The therapist wonders whether getting on with the art making might be the best way to complete the repair and help them to move on.

Art making

The therapist collects up the photos, leaving the image of the sleeping dog and the tiger available, and then places some models Ryan and Dot made last week on the table. She had suggested they build a model together using cardboard boxes, packaging material and other items she had in a large basket. Ryan and Dot had worked alongside each other but built separate models. Dot had glued together six toilet roll holders and, laying them on the table, had said it was an obstacle course for dogs. They had to run through each roll, turn and run through the next and so on. Ryan had started to build what he said was a space rocket.

'Mine's rubbish', Ryan says, seeing that his carefully glued rocket from the previous session is falling apart.

'I think you need more than two hands to glue it,' the therapist comments, 'perhaps Dot could help.'

Dot suggests he hold the rocket while she uses a brush and plenty of glue to stick parts of it back together. While they do this, Dot suggests her obstacle course could be used to make a solid base for Ryan's rocket.

'Yes,' Ryan says, looking up with a smile, 'and it can be a space rocket for dogs!'

The therapist, Ryan and Dot all laugh and it seems that the atmosphere between the two has been broken.

Ryan's body visibly relaxes. Dot and Ryan work together happily and creatively on joining Dot's model as a base for the 'dog' space rocket.

The ending

As with the routine at the beginning, the therapist has put a structured ending phase in place. The routine they have established is that they all help with clearing up the art materials and then Ryan and Dot sit together on the small sofa for some quiet reflection. During this reflecting time the therapist usually encourages Dot to share something positive that she has taken from the session and something she has appreciated about Ryan.

Today Dot says that it was a brilliant idea to make it a spacecraft for dogs. Ryan smiles and Dot puts her arm round his shoulder, which he accepts without moving away.

'Are you still feeling like that snarling tiger?' she asks with a chuckle.

Ryan shakes his head.

'Can we go home now and see how Bess is?' he asks.

'Of course,' Dot continues, 'let's see if Bess is well enough for a little walk with us both before you go back to school.'

Narrative coherence

The narrative coherence approach is a way of working that aims to facilitate the co-creation of meaning around a specific event or co-construction of a shared narrative of the child's life events. The focus is on trauma processing, perspective sharing and narrative coherence. For caregivers, children and young people with complex backgrounds, making and showing can be an easier and less daunting way of communicating. The timing of dyadic work with a focus on co-constructing a coherent narrative needs to be carefully judged and the caregivers need to be well prepared. The co-construction of a child's story will usually have more than one phase, with the first phase being careful planning between therapist and caregiver. Together, the therapist and caregiver begin by going through the events in the child's life that need exploration. For adoptive parents, as in the vignette below, this may well be the part of the child's history they did not have direct experience of. Going through adoption records to get the facts as they were recorded can be a complex task for parents on their own, and the therapist may be able to help or offer support with this. Following this, the caregivers and therapists will need to discuss and decide together what information is developmentally appropriate to share with the child before the dyadic work itself begins. In the vignette that follows, although narrative coherence is the focus of the work, it involves the young person and parent jointly engaging in the art making, showing how one session can include more than one approach.

MILLY: ACKNOWLEDGING SADNESS AND PAIN IN AN ADOPTION

Milly (aged 13) was referred to the art psychotherapist for dyadic work to give her a more coherent story about herself. She has cerebral palsy, which affects her walking, speech and learning. Tess and Rosemary, her adoptive parents, have told her she is adopted but have not explained anything more because they thought she would not understand. Now they have accessed help from the Child and Adolescent Mental Health Service (CAMHS) because Milly is self-harming (her arms are covered in scratches and bites). The assessment indicated that Tess and Rosemary needed help to understand Milly's developmental needs, the impact of her neonatal and pre-adoption placement experience and how to share the difficult parts of their adoption story.

The therapist has spent time with Tess and Rosemary, going over Milly's early life. Milly's birth mother was a drug addict and Milly was removed at birth because of the abuse and neglect of two older siblings. They know that Milly remained in hospital for three weeks because of her low birth weight and difficulties feeding, and to monitor her withdrawal symptoms from her mother's cocaine addiction. She then had two different fostering placements before her adoption placement at the age of 13 months.

Rosemary will bring Milly to the dyadic sessions because of Tess's work commitments, but both will meet with the therapist between dyadic sessions. Milly has already had two DAP sessions, which were spent getting to know each other and thinking about Milly's favourite things, one of which is the *Lion King* film.

Session 3

Milly jumps up and down and claps her hands with excitement when the therapist reminds her that today it is not the *Lion King* they will be thinking about: it will be Milly's own story. They settle round the art therapy table and Milly moves her chair close enough to put her arm round her adoptive mother.

The therapist picks up a tub of modelling material and breaks off three chunks. She hands a piece each to Milly and Rosemary and starts manipulating the third piece herself.

'As it gets warm it becomes easy to mould', she says.

Milly quickly starts pressing and poking the white modelling material. Rosemary is surprised how light and dry it is. They spend some time getting used to the feel of it. Then the therapist asks if between them they could mould a small baby. She knows that Milly has a collection of dolls at home and loves playing with them so it is no surprise when she says that she wants it to be like her 'Susie baby doll'.

'How shall we do this Milly? Would you like to make the baby's head while I do the body?' Rosemary asks.

Milly nods and they set to work. Milly watches and copies her mum pushing, pulling and pressing the modelling material.

'You'll need a sort of round shape for the head, so why not try rolling your piece with your hand like this', Rosemary says.

She demonstrates rolling the modelling material on the table with her flattened hand. Milly copies and enjoys the achievement of making her piece of model magic into a ball shape.

'That's great,' Rosemary says. 'Can you make the shapes for the eyes, ears, mouth and nose now?'

'You do that', Milly replies.

'Let's do it together then', says Rosemary.

They move their chairs closer together.

'I think we can just tweak the side bits here to make the ears', Rosemary says.

After the ears, Rosemary takes the lead in making the other features of the baby's face. Next they decide to join the head to the body shape Rosemary has already made.

'That's a funny baby without arms and legs', Milly comments when the head is securely attached.

So they start making arms and legs. At first this involves rolling sausage shapes. Milly enjoys doing this and continues making these while Rosemary attaches legs and arms onto the body of the baby.

'That's a very beautiful-looking baby,' the therapist says, 'I think she needs to be wrapped up.'

The therapist passes a box of oddments over and Milly chooses some pink fluffy material for the baby to be wrapped in. The care with which the baby has been made is exactly what the therapist hoped for.

'We are going to pretend that this baby doll is you, Milly, when you were a baby', the therapist says, watching for Milly's reaction.

Milly claps her hands and looks at her mum.

'Me when I was a baby', she says.

The next part of the session had been rehearsed with Rosemary in the preparation sessions. The therapist knows how anxious Rosemary will be feeling because she is worried about telling Milly the story of her life before living with them. She thinks it will spoil something in their relationship. However, the therapist was struck in the introductory sessions with Milly and Rosemary how unprompted and clearly Milly could tell the narrative of the *Lion King* in her sand play with animal figures. She feels certain that Milly is ready for some developmentally appropriate explanation of the story of her adoption.

Rosemary gently cradles the baby, and looks directly into Milly's eyes.

'I've always been very sad that you did not grow in my tummy and that I wasn't there when you were born', she says.

'Why didn't I come out of your tummy?' Milly asks.

'I couldn't have babies growing in my tummy so Tess and I decided to adopt a baby that couldn't live with its own parents', Rosemary says in a faltering voice.

'I love you, Mummy,' Milly says spontaneously, putting her arms around Rosemary.

The atmosphere in the room is quietly intense and all three of them gaze at the baby.

'Did you know that you came out of another mummy's tummy, Milly?' the therapist asks.

Milly screws up her face and nods.

'Freya told me that my other mummy didn't want me', she says.

Rosemary looks horrified and is at a loss as to how to respond in the moment.

'But Freya moved away five years ago and you haven't seen her since then', she says.

'She told me on the beach at the seaside', Milly responds defiantly.

Milly gets up and moves over to the large round sand tray. Sitting on one of the small chairs, she starts repeatedly covering one hand with the soft moist sand and then exposing it. She quickly becomes engrossed in this activity. The therapist beckons to Rosemary and they both move over to the sand tray.

'It sounds as if you've known for a long time that you came out of another mummy's tummy, but you and your mummy have never spoken together about it before', says the therapist.

'I didn't know you knew, my love', Rosemary says gently, putting her arm round Milly's shoulder. Milly gets up and flings her arms around her mum and starts sobbing. They both cry.

'I wish I'd come out of your tummy', Milly says.

'I do too', Rosemary replies.

The session is near its end and the therapist feels this is enough narrative work for this session. She suggests they put the baby carefully into a box for next time and end the session as they have done previously, with Milly choosing a story from the bookshelf for Rosemary to read her.

Conclusion

In this chapter we have drawn on the history of art therapy with children and adolescents to indicate how and why using art materials can help children and adolescents who have experienced early relational trauma. We have presented a model of DAP based on our clinical experience and empirical research, which we believe can be widely used by art therapists working with this client group and their parents or caregivers.

The three approaches described fit well with published accounts of dyadic art therapy such as those given by Proulx (2003) and Regev and

Snir (2015). We would concur with these authors on the importance of providing the parents and caregivers with adequate support and information to facilitate their full participation.

Qualified art therapists often have considerable experience of delivering non-directive, reflective and mentalizing interventions, and this makes them well placed to offer a creative dyadic intervention aimed at enhancing caregiver sensitivity, and reflective functioning in both caregiver and child. The vignettes illustrate the dyadic approaches described. All therapeutic work with these families presents challenges, and the timing, context and support systems for the therapist, the child and the caregivers need careful consideration before embarking on this work.

References

Acquarone, S. (2004) *Infant–Parent Psychotherapy: A Handbook*. London: Karnac Books.

Adamson, L. B., Bakerman, R. and Deckner, D. F. (2004) 'The development of symbol-infused joint engagement.' *Child Development 75*, 4, 1171–1187.

Ainsworth, M. D. S., Bell, S. M. and Stayton, D. J. (1978) 'Infant–Mother Attachment and Social Development: Socialisation as a Product of Reciprocal Responsiveness Signals.' In M. Richards (ed.) *The Integration of a Child into a Social World*. Cambridge: Cambridge University Press.

Ambridge, M. (2001) 'Using the Reflective Image within the Mother–Child Relationship.' In J. Murphy (ed.) *Art Therapy with Young Survivors of Sexual Abuse: Lost for Words*. Hove: Brunner-Routledge.

Bakermans-Kranenburg, M. J., van Ijzendoorn, M. H. and Juffer, F. (2003) 'Less is more: Meta-analyses of sensitivity and attachment interventions in early childhood.' *Psychological Bulletin 129*, 2, 195–215.

Baradon, T. (2005) *The Practice of Psychoanalytic Parent–Infant Psychotherapy: Claiming the Baby*. Hove: Routledge.

Bowlby, J. (1969) *Attachment*. Volume 1 of *Attachment and Loss*. London: Hogarth Press.

Brenninkmeyer, F. (2007) *Family Work at PAC: Overview of the Theoretical Frameworks and Practice Principles*. London: Post Adoption Centre.

Burnell, A. and Vaughan, J. (2003) 'A model of post-placement therapy and support for adoptive families.' In H. Argent (ed.) *Models of Adoption Support: What Works and What Doesn't*. London: BAAF.

Case, C. (1990) 'Reflections and Shadows: An Exploration of the World of the Rejected Girl.' In C. Case and T. Dalley (eds) *Working with Children in Art Therapy*. London: Routledge.

Case, C. (1995) 'Silence in progress: On being dumb, empty or silent in therapy.' *Journal of the British Association of Art Therapists: Inscape 1*, 26–31.

Case, C. and Dalley, T. (eds) (1990) *Working with Children in Art Therapy*. London: Routledge.

Dalley, T. (1984) 'Introduction.' In T. Dalley (ed.) *Art Therapy: An Introduction to the Use of Art as a Therapeutic Technique*. London: Routledge.

Dalley, T. (2008) 'The use of clay as a medium for working through loss and separation in the case of two latency boys.' In C. Case and T. Dalley (eds) *Art Therapy with Children from Infancy to Adolescence.* London: Routledge.

Drucker, K. L. (2001) 'Why Can't She Control Herself? A Case Study.' In J. Murphy (ed.) *Art Therapy with Young Survivors of Sexual Abuse. Lost for Words.* Hove: Brunner-Routledge.

Gillespie, A. (2001) 'Into the Body: Sand and Water in the Art Therapy with Sexually Abused Children.' In J. Murphy (ed.) *Art Therapy with Young Survivors of Sexual Abuse. Lost for Words.* Hove: Brunner-Routledge.

Hall, P. (2008) 'Painting Together in Art Therapy: Approach to Mother–Infant Relationships.' In C. Case and T. Dalley (eds) *Art Therapy with Children.* London: Routledge.

Hanney, L. and Kozlowska, K. (2002) 'Healing traumatised children: Creating illustrated storybooks in family therapy.' *Family Process 41,* 1, 37–65.

Hendry, A. (2005) 'After the Break: An Investigation into Art Psychotherapists' Work with Adopted Children and Their Parents'. Unpublished MA thesis. Final Report. London: Goldsmiths College.

Hendry, A. (2016) 'The Imprint of Another Life: Assessment and Dyadic Parent–Child Art Psychotherapy with an Adoptive Family.' In J. Meyerowitz-Katz and D. Reddick (eds) *Art Therapy in the Early Years: Art Making as a Therapeutic Intervention with Infants, Toddlers and Their Families.* London: Routledge.

Henley, D. (2005) 'Attachment disorders in post-institutionalized adopted children: Art therapy approaches to reactivity and detachment.' *Arts in Psychotherapy 32,* 1, 29–46.

Henley, D. (2007) 'Supervisory responses to Child Art Therapy.' In J. Schaverien and C. Case (eds) *Supervision of Art Psychotherapy: A Theoretical and Practical Handbook.* New York, NY: Routledge.

Hosea, D. (2006) '"The brush's footmarks": Parents and infants paint together in a small community art therapy group.' *International Journal of Art Therapy 11,* 2, 69–78.

Hughes, D. (2004) 'An attachment-based treatment of maltreated children and young people.' *Attachment and Human Development 6,* 3, 263–278.

Jefferies, B. and Gillespie, A. (1981) 'Art Therapy with the emotionally frozen.' *Journal of the British Association for Adoption and Fostering 106,* 4, 9–15.

Kozlowska, K. and Hanney, L. (2001) 'An art therapy group for children traumatized by parental violence and separation.' *Clinical Child Psychology and Psychiatry 6,* 1, 49–78.

Lachman, M., Stuntz, C. and Jones, N. (1975) 'Art therapy in the psychotherapy of a mother and her son.' *American Journal of Art Therapy 14,* 4, 105–116.

Landgarten, H. (1975) 'Group art therapy for mothers and daughters.' *American Journal of Art Therapy 14,* 2, 31–35.

Lobban, J. (2012) 'The invisible wound: Veterans' art therapy.' *International Journal of Art Therapy 19,* 1, 3–18.

Lusebrink, V. B. (2004) 'Art therapy and the brain: An attempt to understand the underlying processes of art expression in therapy.' *Art Therapy: Journal of the American Art Therapy Association 21,* 3, 125–135.

Malchiodi, C. A. (2014) 'Art Therapy, Attachment and Parent–Child Dyads.' In C. A. Malchiodi and D. A. Crenshaw (eds) *Creative Arts and Play Therapy for Attachment Problems.* New York, NY: Guilford Press.

Meyerowitz-Katz, J. (2003) 'Art materials and processes – A place of meeting: Art psychotherapy with a four-year-old boy.' *Inscape: The Journal of the British Association of Art Therapists 8,* 2, 60–69.

Nelson, P. B., Adamson, L. B. and Bakerman, R. (2008) 'Toddlers' joint engagement experience facilitates preschoolers' acquisition of theory of mind.' *Developmental Science 11*, 6, 847–852.

Nowell-Hall, P. (1987) 'Art Therapy: A Way of Healing the Split.' In T. Dalley, C. Case, J. Schaverien, F. Weir *et al.* (eds) *Images of Art Therapy: New Developments in Theory and Practice.* London: Tavistock/Routledge.

O'Brien, F. (2004) 'The making of mess in art therapy: Attachment, trauma and the brain.' *Inscape: The Journal of the British Association of Art Therapists 9*, 1, 2–13.

Proulx, L. (2003) *Strengthening Emotional Ties through Parent-Child-Dyad Art Therapy.* London: Jessica Kingsley Publishers.

Regev, D. and Snir, S. (2015) 'Objectives, interventions and challenges in parent–child art psychotherapy.' *The Arts in Psychotherapy 42*, 50–56.

Rubin, J. A. (2005) *Child Art Therapy.* Hoboken, NJ: John Wiley & Sons.

Sagar, C. (1990) 'Working with Cases of Child Sexual Abuse.' In C. Case and T. Dalley (eds) *Working with Children in Art Therapy.* London: Routledge.

Schur, J. (2001) 'Parent–Child–Therapist Communication in Dyadic Art Therapy. Some Thoughts about Family Art Therapy.' In L. Kossolapow, S. Scoble and D. Waller (eds) *Arts – Therapies – Communication: On the Way to a Communicative European Arts Therapy* (Vol. 1). Munster/Hamburg/Berlin/London: Lit Verlag.

Taylor Buck, E., Dent-Brown, K. and Parry, G. (2012) 'Exploring a dyadic approach to art psychotherapy with children and young people: A survey of British art psychotherapists.' *International Journal of Art Therapy 18*, 1, 20–28.

Taylor Buck, E., Dent-Brown, K., Parry, G. and Boote, J. (2014) 'Dyadic art psychotherapy: Key principles, practices and competences.' *Arts in Psychotherapy 41*, 2, 163–173.

Waller, D. (2006) 'Art therapy for children: How it leads to change.' *Clinical Child Psychology and Psychiatry 11*, 2, 271–282.

Woolgar, M. (2013) 'The practical implications of the emerging findings in the neurobiology of maltreatment for looked after and adopted children: Recognizing the diversity of outcomes.' *Adoption and Fostering 37*, 237–253.

Chapter 7

HEALING RHYTHMS

Music Therapy for Attachment and Trauma

———————————— JOY HASLER ————————————

Rhythms of life

Internal and external rhythms keep us alive and connected to other people. As Maya Angelou says, 'Everything in the universe has a rhythm. Everything dances' (Angelou and Buckley 2014). Nature has rhythms, all life has rhythms, we are surrounded by sound frequencies that are rhythmic and we organize our lives in rhythmic patterns. We develop skills through rhythmic repetition, and our brains develop neural pathways through rhythms. We use rhythmic actions for greetings and goodbyes. Rhythms rouse, relax and regulate us. Rhythms activate all parts of the brain, from lower-brain movements to mid-brain patterned emotional responses, to higher-brain rhythmic responses and cognitive processes. Rhythms can be automatic (e.g. laughing, walking or chewing) or they can be deliberate actions to achieve a goal that requires rhythmic resonance and synchrony (e.g. using carpentry tools, playing ball games or dancing with a partner). Internal and external rhythms keep us alive and connected to other people.

Our brain develops pathways by recognizing repeated patterns and rhythms that become clusters, and are then translated into behaviours. Patterns can be static, but rhythms are dynamic and have an energy of their own. The process of developing life-engaging rhythms starts before birth and then develops through rhythmic engaging activity between the infant and the key attachment figure.

The rhythms of parent and child engagement resonate and change together as they become attuned in a flow through the rise and fall of energizing and soothing.

> In play episodes, the pair are in affective resonance, and in such, an amplification of vitality affects and a positive state occur, especially when the mother's psychologically attuned external sensory stimulation frequency coincides with the infant's genetically encoded endogenous rhythms. (Schore 2003, p.116)

It is hardly surprising, then, that making music, which is sequencing sound and silence using rhythmic tempo, tone and timbre, has been used for healing for centuries. The profession of 'Music Therapy' emerged in the mid-20th century as research found evidence to back this healing power, and now it is used within nearly every area of improving health and well-being with individuals and with groups.

In the field of 'attachment' and infant development, many authors and researchers, including Dan Stern, Allan Schore, Dan Siegel and Colwyn Trevarthen, use musical terms to describe what happens between a parent and child. They compare the development of attachment to a dance. Even the word 'attunement' is a musical term used to express parent–infant resonance.

In this chapter I intend to explore how music can be used to engage parents and traumatized children in activities that can help stabilize the family, build positive attachment patterns, develop positive self-worth and increase resilience. I will give examples of activities that can be used for dyadic exploration or for a whole family as a group.

The healing power of music

Music is multi-sensory and engages the whole brain. It is therefore a powerful tool that can be used to help repair damage caused by developmental trauma. Music is processed by the whole brain. NeuroRhythm, a music therapy service in the USA, say that 'research shows that music enhances the brain providing more efficient therapy' (NeuroRhythm 2016). The different aspects of music that are processed by different parts of the brain include:

- rhythm – mainly left brain

- tone and melody – mainly right brain

- connection between left and right brain, therefore between rhythm and melody – corpus callosum (which is particularly damaged by early trauma)

- sight, sound and movement senses – visual, auditory and sensory cortex

- processing emotions – amygdala

- memories and context – hippocampus

- decision making – pre-frontal cortex.

Dr Mark J. Tramo (2001), Director of UCLA's Institute for Music and Brain Science, says: 'When individuals are preparing to tap out a rhythm of regular intervals, the left frontal cortex, left parietal cortex, and right cerebellum are all activated. With more difficult rhythms… more areas in the cerebral cortex and cerebellum are involved.' In addition to this, music impacts on the child socially, intellectually and emotionally.[1]

Music presents the child with imaginative opportunities and challenges, and with a sense of achievement and enjoyment. Music helps children to develop the ability to order and sequence, which are key processes in the development of secure attachment patterns and understanding the environment. Music also helps to regulate stress and is used by people in all cultures to co-regulate with a distressed child. Rocking, patting the child's back and making whooshing sounds are all rhythmic representations of inter-utero sounds, which then create the safe feelings needed for regulation. Perry (2006) says that patterned, repetitive rhythmic activity is essential to the early development of the brain. One of the most powerful sets of associations created in utero is between the patterned, repetitive rhythmic activity of the maternal heartbeat and the feelings of being safe and comfortable.

Daniel Stern says that vitality dynamics are critical for anything alive to fit into its environment, and he puts musicality at the centre of what happens in the 'vitality dynamics' of interaction between people.

Communicative musicality is largely based on the coupling of vitality dynamics between people. 'Musicality' is composed

---

1 For further information, I recommend Beth Powell's article 'Feel the beat: The impact of rhythm on the brain' in the US journal *Adoption Today* (June 2012, pp.16–17).

of pulses formed by timing, in the rhythmic sense, and its temporal contouring, and the development of force in time. This is the backbone of vitality dynamics where 'being with another' is accomplished by sharing the vitality dynamic flow. (Stern 2010, p.53)

Furthermore, Malloch and Trevarthen (2010, p.6) say: 'Our shared musicality can be harnessed to our intention to reach out to others, and in this we see the potential healing nature of our desire for companioning others through time.'

Music and trauma

Developmental trauma causes significant damage to the brain at a critical time in the child's development. Neglect over a period of time has its own rhythms, which is why it has such a powerful effect on the brain. But brains are amazing and develop new pathways designed to protect the child if overwhelming anxiety or fear is triggered. The trauma-triggered stress causes blocks to accessing the cognitive higher-brain functions, which include cognitive problem solving, and the child becomes stuck in the lower-brain fight/flight/freeze mode. So the child develops patterns of control, hypervigilance and dissociation with the resulting fragmentation, to create the feeling of safety needed to be able to pursue everyday tasks. But these patterns, which are so protective in the toxic environment, cause the child many difficulties in the environments where most people feel safe and have assumptions that everyone should feel safe. This causes problems for the child in exploring, learning, socializing and developing general well-being. It also causes difficulties for those who work or live with the child because usual parenting strategies do not change the child's patterns of protective behaviours.

Music has a strong element of play, which is an important contribution to early brain development and building relationships, but Jaak Panksepp says: 'In all species that have been studied, playfulness is inhibited by motivations such as hunger and negative emotions, including loneliness, anger, and fear' (Panksepp 1998, p.18).

Trauma and trauma-triggered memories have exactly this effect – they inhibit play, which then affects learning and socializing, and causes the disorders that go with feeling unsafe. Music offers parents and children opportunities to co-regulate so that they can play – play with sounds, rhythms and dynamics. Music also connects to the memory part of the brain, and a child can hold in his mind the fun he had with his parent, so hearing or singing a song on his own can enable him to revisit the closeness he and his parent shared in that memory. Parents of traumatized children, through music, can build up moments of playfulness connected to memory that will lead to co-regulation of an anxious and fearful child.

Musical activities that involve others take the healing power of the rhythmic moments into the field of relationships and can be used to build secure and stable attachments, develop trust and help self-regulation. These activities develop new pathways in the brain that can circumvent the blockages caused by the trauma. Music helps to regulate the anxiety and reconnect with higher-brain cognitive thinking, which is designed to solve problems at the same time as stimulating the 'have fun' play button. Musical moments include mindfulness, mirroring and mirth. Cathy Malchiodi describes mirroring as 'a form of nonverbal, right hemisphere communication that naturally occurs in secure attachment relationships through gesture, postures and facial expressions that transpire between caregiver and child' (Malchiodi 2015). These processes are all part of an infant's development of attachment and social engagement. They help the child develop trust that he is worth being cared for, has people available who care about him and is able to ask for his needs to be met. This is the development of resilience.

One part of the brain particularly damaged by early trauma is the corpus callosum, which is responsible for communication between the different sides of the brain. This causes the child difficulties in learning from experience, learning from wise words of helpful adults and understanding what is happening when in fight/flight mode. This damage can also be seen musically in the inability of some children to play regular beats using a left/right action with beaters. If we ask a child to follow us in a simple walking rhythm that gradually gets faster, many children affected by trauma cannot keep this up and one hand stops working. Using alternate hands involves using alternate sides of the brain, and if the connection is damaged, then this becomes a problem. Drumming using both hands alternating in a regular rhythmic action can help to redevelop the left/right communication.

However, these activities need to be relational – not just sending a child to bang drums on his own.

The brain develops socially and rhythmically, therefore relational and rhythmic engagements are necessary elements in the healing of injured brains. Kathy Brous cites Bruce Perry in her article on how rhythm regulates the brain. She quotes Bruce Perry's list of requirements in activities for healing trauma as 'relational, relevant, repetitive, rhythmic, rewarding and respectful' (Brous 2014).

Introduction to music therapy

Musical instruments offer multi-sensory experiences that can be therapeutic tools. These tools include:

- building a therapeutic relationship

- engaging curiosity, which encourages exploration through visible interest

- engaging curiosity about how to make the sound and how to vary the sound

- enjoyment when an interesting sound is achieved

- interest/attention/acceptance from the therapist

- representation of emotions through the way the sound is formed

- triggering memories

- building sequences to tell a story or narrative

- appreciating that someone else is holding you in mind.

Music therapy is about providing therapeutic space and opportunities to express and share feelings and experiences that are hard to put into words for whatever reason.

Music therapy uses these qualities and the musical components of rhythm, melody and tonality to provide a means of relating within a therapeutic relationship. In music therapy, people work with a wide range of accessible instruments and their voices to create a musical language which reflects their emotional and physical condition; this enables them to build connections with their inner selves and with others around them. (BAMT 2016)

Music therapy with attachment and trauma

Music therapy in the field of attachment means offering opportunities for families to share the power of creating and imitating patterned and rhythmic activities through playing music together. Through rhythmic fun activities, interwoven with other creative arts and play therapies, music can be used to transform effects of trauma, enhance the attachment relationship, develop trust and increase resilience for children and parents. Mercedes Pavlicevic, a music therapist in South Africa working with traumatized children, says: 'Transformation does not deny, ignore or render meaningless the rage, frustration and fragmentation – but allows the "duality" of musical energy to emerge. In this way, the musical act can also be one of creativity, relationship and ultimately self-healing' (Pavlicevic 2002, p.115).

Music becomes a catalyst for engagement, which can be an alternative to the negative forms of engagement that the child and family feel stuck with. To develop secure attachment patterns, the child needs to engage in activities that are shared with a key attachment figure and that require the whole brain to be working, so that connections between the different parts of the brain are rewired and repaired. Music provides these opportunities and so, through music therapy, the process of positive non-threatening engagement can be initiated and developed.

By communicating with music, the child does not need to have face-to-face contact, which many children who have experienced trauma find difficult. According to Stephen Porges, whose research has made the link between Polyvagal Theory[2] and the Social Engagement System,[3] 'music therapy provides a special portal to reengage the social engagement system that does not require an initial face-to-face

---

2   The term 'polyvagal' combines 'poly', meaning 'many', and 'vagal', which refers to the important nerve called the 'vagus'. Polyvagal Theory is based on the functions of a part of our nervous system that automatically regulates several major organs such as the heart, lungs and gut.

3   The Social Engagement System involves pathways that travel through several cranial nerves. These pathways regulate the expression, detection and subjective experiences of affect and emotion.

interaction' (Porges 2016). This can open the door to parents and carers of traumatized children who struggle to find ways to reach their stressed child. The Life Change Health Institute in Dublin have documented the connection of the Polyvagal Theory to the Social Engagement System with the scientific impact of listening to and playing music, and have shown impressive possibilities for therapy.

> Based on the Polyvagal Theory we have been able to deconstruct Music Therapy into biobehavioural processes that stimulate the Social Engagement System. When the Social Engagement System is stimulated, the client responds both behaviourally and physiologically. First, the observable features of Social Engagement become more spontaneous and contingent. The face and voice become more expressive. Second, there is a change in physiological state regulation that it is expressed in more regulated and calmer behaviour. The improved state regulation is mediated by the myelinated vagus which directly promotes health, growth and restoration. However for some clients, especially those who have been traumatized, face-to-face interactions are threatening and do not elicit a neuroception of safety. If this is the case, then the Social Engagement System can potentially be triggered through vocal prosody or music, while minimizing the direct face-to-face interactions. (Life Change Health Institute 2015)

In therapy sessions we do not expect to see for some time the concerning behaviours children display at home. Usually this is hidden until the child feels that his control (his protective strategy) is being challenged, or he feels the need to test his limits and his developing trust in the therapists. 'Trust' is scary because it increases the likelihood of being let down, which must be avoided. What we observe in the child's less challenging behaviours lets us know that the family is having to cope with difficult and possibly dangerous behaviours such as the need for the child to be in control through aggressive and destructive behaviours at home. To stabilize the family and help the child feel safe, we need to work from base-brain up. That means simple playful rhythmic non-verbal interactions in which we explore a new musical communication that enhances feelings of safety, and moves the child into the mid-brain functions of emotional processing. Verbal reasoning is blocked when the child is anxious, so we need another language to connect with him in his fight/flight state. As musical communication is effective for regulating babies, so music can be used to help parents connect with their dysregulated child. Eminent researchers in the field of developmental trauma, such as Bessel van der Kolk, Bruce Perry, Pat Ogden and others, are recommending rhythmic activities to regulate trauma-triggered anxieties.

In the therapy sessions we try to create a pattern of raising and reducing anxiety for the child. This is similar to the rhythm of an infant interacting with his parent in a game of 'peek-a-boo' – 'Where is she?', 'There she is' – or speaking to a child and leaving gaps for him to respond. In the session, through turn taking, we can create a similar rhythm of raised slight anxiety with 'Will I get a turn?', and then reducing anxiety with 'Yes, it's my turn'. This is repeated in a rhythmic pattern that builds the ability to predict and ultimately to trust.

To address the difficulties parents and carers experience at home, including managing the behaviours the traumatized child uses to protect himself, the therapist needs to meet with the parents and the community around the family, to create a common understanding of the child's needs, and appropriate responses to the child's protective behaviours. Bruce Perry recommends that 'the therapeutic approach must address the process of helping to create a "therapeutic web"' (Perry 2006, p.46). This is about helping to create a new context for the therapy sessions through helping parents, carers, wider family and friends and school staff to develop new patterns and rhythms of engaging with the child. It is in this context that music therapy with families can be most effective.

We hope parents will be willing to share in the music making, but this can sometimes be quite a challenge if they did not consider themselves to be 'musical' at school. They may perceive music as about performance rather than enjoyment. We need to overcome the parents' anxieties about joining in, so we start by playing with sounds, and then 'music' becomes something we discover together.

Musical activities as part of a trauma-healing programme need to include factors that match the criteria as set out by Bruce Perry in his Neurosequential Model of Therapeutics (NMT). He stresses the importance of the relational aspect of activities for healing the brain; says they need to be 'patterned, repetitive and rewarding experiences'; and recommends music and drumming (Perry and Dobson 2013, p.257).

We recommend that the following elements are included in the music making of therapy with traumatized children and their families:

- Music making to be shared with one or more people, preferably including the key attachment figure.

- Participants should to be able to explore (play with) the instruments manually, visually, audibly and socially.

- Participants to have a choice of instruments – these can be restricted to different drums, or small percussion instruments.

- There should be minimal verbal instructions, sometimes using sign language or conducting.

- Music making should have a purpose, such as:

  » to enjoy and share exploring patterns of sounds

  » to build a story line

  » to create a representation of something – action, feeling or character

  » to take turns, as in conversation

  » to work out a sound effect

  » to create a piece of music together.

- There should be a sense of being heard, received and accepted.

- There should be a balance of direction and non-direction.

- Play to be for varying lengths of time to account for the child's focusing limits.

Within an attachment therapy programme, musical activities can have various aims, which can include (but are not restricted to) the following:

- To help the child feel safe.

- To find out what is going on between family members.

- To develop the ability to create and repeat a sequence.

- To explore non-verbally different emotional expressions.

- To explore different characters and how they might behave.

- To reduce and regulate stress.

- To integrate dissociative parts.

- To have shared fun and be playful.

- To build a story, which can encompass some aspects of the trauma narrative.

- To have everyone's contributions accepted, welcomed and appreciated.

- To develop safe boundaries and positive means of keeping the boundaries.

- To develop rhythms of reciprocity – turn taking.

- To develop a means of communicating things that are challenging.

Music therapy activities with families living with the effects of trauma
FOLLOW THE LEADER

This is a game to let different people take the lead and enjoy being heard and followed. To start the game we ask parents to choose instruments for the children, and children to choose instruments for the parents or therapists. This can be quite a challenge for children with attachment difficulties because they want to be in control. After a couple of changes of leader, we invite anyone to change his instrument to one of his own choice to reduce any build-up of anxiety. Different people take the lead as chosen by the previous leader. This opens up an anxiety for the child about whether he will be chosen. It also presents difficulties about who to choose next and how to make these choices. Some traumatized children find it very difficult to make choices.

When following someone else's lead, the child may try to take control by playing when the leader stops or by playing something very different to the leader. This should be expected and a response worked out before the start of the game. The child can be assumed to be testing the boundaries, and testing to see if he will get a negative response. There can be a choice of prepared responses, none of which can be negative:

- Ask the leader how he felt when he was not followed – therefore giving attention to the leader rather than the child who is fighting being a follower.

- Suggest to the child that he might like to play a solo, and then offer him one minute. At the end of this time, return to the game. This may need to be repeated until the child appreciates that he will not get a negative response.

- Ignore the interruptions and then indicate: 'Yes, that was difficult to follow, wasn't it? Well done.' It is likely that the child moved in and out of following the beat, so give affirmation for the times the beats were together.

- (With younger children) suggest that the particular beater does not want to play the game. Would the child like to try a different beater?

- Invite the child to use a puppet to play the game.

KEVIN

The Norris family arrived with Mum and Dad and their two children, Katie (aged 10) and Kevin (aged 8). After introductions (starting routines), we played a game of 'Follow the Leader'. Very quickly it became clear that Kevin was determined to disrupt Mum's turn. I experimented by inviting Dad to be the leader. Kevin followed exactly what Dad played. I turned to Mum and invited her to be the leader again. Kevin played against her rhythms and played loudly when she played quietly.

I used our 'pause' signal and asked whether they had had an argument. Mum said that yes, Kevin had accused her of taking the special pen he got for getting his spellings right.

'But I don't know what he is talking about', she said.

We explored what had happened and the resulting story was this: Kevin had made a cake at school, which he wanted to give to Mum. On the way home he dropped it. We all empathized with this disappointment. I asked him what he did with that disappointment.

'When I got home I tried to pick a fight with Dad but he wouldn't have one, so I picked an argument with Mum', he replied.

We continued to used free improvisation to draw Kevin and his mum together and they started chatting (now feeling safe enough to use higher-brain processes) about how they were going to make a cake and what they would need. Then, while they had a cuddle, Dad and Katie and the therapist played music for them. The family went out happily.

IMPROVISING ABOUT FAMILY EVENTS

This activity enables the child to explore how other people feel and behave, and to have some fun portraying different members of the family, including pets.

Choose a family event, which could be a daily routine or a specific event such as a birthday. Together, decide on instruments to represent different members of the family. Then think about what happens at home in that event. Invite people to be someone different than themselves – therapists could take on people who are not there. Which person starts? Which person tells everyone what to do? Who are the noisy ones, and who is quiet? What happens next? Build the event musically and thoughtfully and then play it through. If the child's concentration cannot be sustained, have a break and come back to it. Focus on a conversation that he is not part of to give him time to watch for a while, or invite him to change his character.

LOTTIE AND LISA

The Jones family arrived with their two adopted daughters, Lottie (aged 11) and Lisa (aged 8). The girls were half-siblings who had experienced severe neglect. Lottie had stolen food to keep herself and her baby sister alive. But, now in their adoptive family, Lottie was seen as the difficult child. Her behaviours were typical of a child with an avoidant attachment pattern. The parents were very worried because Lottie was aggressive with other children and had been excluded from her new secondary school. She was telling other people that she did not want to be adopted.

In the therapy sessions we explored the sounds, took turns conducting and played music for people who were important to Lottie and Lisa. Lottie could stay focused for short times but then turned away or tried to distract her mum from the music. But as we continued, Lottie's focus increased. She began to listen to what other people were playing and played quite moving music when it was her turn to lead.

One day Lottie asked if she could play something for her Auntie. We agreed without asking why. Lottie moved closer to her mum to play. She chose a xylophone to play on with soft beaters. Her music had a journey from being quietly melodic to being fast, angry, loud, chaotic and then back to quiet melodic music. Lottie knew that everyone was listening to her. We had a quiet moment after she finished and then asked her about her Auntie. Lottie told us about her Auntie (her mum's sister), who had been expecting a baby and lost it. Lottie was able to relate this experience to her own losses and how she felt when she had been moved from the foster carers she had grown to love. We all chose instruments for the different people in her life and played her story in music, with the feelings expressed non-verbally. Mum told her she was brave and offered her a hug. Lottie accepted the hug and became quite relaxed. Lisa quietly sat with Dad without trying to attract attention to herself, which was hard for her. They were enjoying a special moment that they had shared in Lottie's story.

GUESS THE ANIMAL

This is an activity to introduce music as the means of communication for expressing feelings and character traits. This game can be played offering a range of instruments, or one instrument, such as a large 'Gathering Drum' or large 'Ocean Drum', with the family sitting round it.

Think of an animal and what it does. Find an instrument to tell us something about that animal – whether it is fierce or friendly, shy or cheeky, fast or slow, and whether it crawls, flies, slides or jumps. Then everyone else can guess what it is and what it is doing. It is often easier to play feelings in animals than to play our own feelings. This can then be developed into a game of having two animals interacting: Are they friends or enemies? Are they listening to each other? Are they doing something together? The aim is to portray through music the feelings of animals and to explore how this can be communicated to others through the sounds of the instruments.

JUSTINE

Justine (aged 9) had been born to a teenage mother who was involved in the drug culture although she said she was not using drugs herself. Justine was born early and had spent several weeks in a Special Care Baby Unit. She then lived with her mother who did not make eye contact with her except when angry and who left her on her own while she went out. After nine months, during which time the mother was offered a lot of support, Justine was taken into care; and at 2 years old she was placed for adoption. By now, communication between Justine and Diane, her single adoptive mother, had broken down so that it was either non-existent or angry and aggressive. Diane did not like to be in the same room as Justine. She hated the fact that loving her was so difficult.

In our music therapy sessions it became clear that they both found it difficult to make eye contact. Diane found it difficult to look at the face of her daughter, who would return the look with a blank expression. So they were stuck, each feeling the rejection of the other and not able to enjoy being together.

At first, playing music was difficult, and Justine did everything she could to irritate her mother. We stayed on safe topics about animals, which they both loved. Gradually, through playing music they discovered that they could have fun and safely share emotional expressions including sadness or anger. From thinking about animals in frightening or safe situations, they moved to thinking about things that happen in their family and what feelings are expressed there. They became more affectionate with each other. They learned to listen to each other safely. The music did not take away totally the discomfort with eye contact, but it did give them a chance to develop a positive relationship.

HOLDING

The adults choose instruments that play a rhythm – these can also be tuned rhythmic instruments – and the child is offered a range of instruments that make a variety of sounds. The adults play and sustain a regular beat at the speed of the most relaxed heart beat.

The child is given freedom to play what he likes and to whatever tempo he chooses. There is no expectation that he should follow the adult's beat.

What happens almost invariably is that the child moves in and out of meeting the beat. This is comparable to a toddler in a play centre who moves in and out of contact with his parent. If the parent stops talking, the child turns towards the parent to see what is happening. In the same way, if the adults change the beat or pause, the child checks what is happening, showing that he is listening all the time.

ROBERT

Robert came to therapy with his maternal grandparents, who were his Special Guardians. He had lived with his birth parents until he was 5 years old, where there was a lot of domestic violence. He moved out to a refuge with his mother, but was then abandoned by her when she returned to live with his father. Robert went to live with his grandparents, whom he had hardly known because his mother had broken all contact with them. Robert was aggressive about a lot of minor things and particularly targeted Nan when Grandad was not there. Nan reported these behaviours to Grandad, but he never saw them.

Through the music in the therapy sessions Robert would try to annoy them, playing loudly, playing instruments that he thought they would not like and interrupting them if we tried to take turns. He seemed to particularly target Nan, which was how it was for them at home. Grandad was surprised. Robert was fine with him at home and he believed the problems between Robert and Nan were because Nan was too soft with him. Now he saw how deliberately Robert was targeting Nan. At first he wanted to be angry with Robert, but in the therapy we helped him see that this was Robert giving them a message that he was fearful and that we needed to find out what was triggering the fear. It appeared that he did not trust Nan in a mothering role. His mother had rejected him so he was letting Nan know what that felt like. Nan and Grandad started to support each other and through the music have fun with Robert.

We played holding music, where the grandparents and the therapists (two because of the risk of aggressive behaviours) played music to a regular beat. There was still variation within that beat, but we continued playing, like footsteps walking along. We invited Robert to choose what instrument he wanted and play what he wanted. At first he increased his loud aggressive music with occasional pauses to see what effect this was having, but the beat kept going. He began to join in with the beat for a few beats, then move away and then back again. The next session, he said he did not want to play anymore. He may have been finding the closer relationship with his grandparents quite threatening. They were present, holding him in mind, being patient and positive. He could not irritate them so he tried a new strategy to disrupt their plan. This was expected and we were ready for it. We chose other activities, such as making up musical stories and exploring different feelings within the stories. These activities involved taking turns, which Robert had found very difficult but was now enjoying. This led to them playing all sorts of music together and laughing a lot.

Conclusion

Rhythms are part of the world around us and part of our musicality. Music is processed in the whole brain and then links to the other organs of the body, which means it is a total experience that also links to memory. As such, it is a powerful tool for healing trauma. Through offering opportunities for parents and children to explore sounds and rhythms, and improvise together, they can:

- stabilize attachment relationships

- integrate the fragmented parts of the brain

- play out personal narratives safely without needing words or direct eye contact

- recognize that they can be listened to and held in mind

- develop the ability to take turns and wait for their turn – reciprocity

- enhance their personal sense of self as someone worth being cared for

- reduce anxiety and regulate stress

- increase resilience

- increase enjoyment and fun in the family

- increase opportunities for positive peer social engagement.

Through musical rhythmic activities the child can develop the relationships he needs to support him and encourage him through into adulthood – to help make aspirations come true.

References

Angelou, M. and Buckley, R. (2014) *101 Quotes and Sayings from Maya Angelou* (Kindle edn).

BAMT (British Association for Music Therapy) (2016) *What is Music Therapy?* Available at www.bamt.org/music-therapy.html, accessed on 11 November 2016.

Brous, K. (2014) *Perry: Rhythm Regulates the Brain.* Available at www.mentalhealthexcellence. org/perry-rhythm-regulates-brain, accessed on 11 November 2016.

Life Change Health Institute (2015) *Music Therapy and Trauma: Insights from the Polyvagal Theory.* Available at www.lifechangehealthinstitute.ie/music-and-polyvagal-theory, accessed on 11 November 2016.

Malchiodi, C. (2015) 'Neurobiology, Creative Interventions and Childhood Trauma.' In C. Malchiodi (ed.) *Creative Interventions with Traumatised Children.* New York, NY: Guilford Press.

Malloch, S. and Trevarthen, C. (eds) (2010) *Communicative Musicality: Exploring the Basis of Human Companionship.* Oxford: Oxford University Press.

NeuroRhythm (2016) *Music Therapy and the Brain.* Available at www.neurorhythm.com/ files/9714/2524/6924/Music_Therapy_Science.pdf, accessed on 11 November 2016.

Panksepp, J. (1998) *Affective Neuroscience: The Foundations of Human and Animal Emotions.* New York, NY: Oxford University Press. p.18

Pavlicevic, M. (2002) 'Fragile Rhythms and Uncertain Listenings: Perspectives from Music Therapy with South African Children.' In J. P. Sutton (ed.) *Music, Music Therapy and Trauma.* London: Jessica Kingsley Publishers. p.115.

Perry, B. (2006) 'Applying Principles of Neurodevelopment to Clinical Work with Maltreated and Traumatized Children.' In N. Boyd-Webb (ed.) *Working with Traumatized Youth in Child Welfare.* New York, NY: Guilford Press.

Perry, B. and Dobson, C. (2013) 'Neurosequential Model of Therapeutics.' In J. Ford and C. Courtois (eds) *Treating Complex and Traumatic Stress Disorders in Children and Adolescents.* New York, NY: Guilford Press. p.257.

Porges, S. (2016) *The Polyvagal Theory.* Available at www.lifechangehealthinstitute.ie/music-and-polyvagal-theory, accessed on 12 October 2016.

Schore, A. (2003) 'Early Relational Trauma.' In M. F. Solomon and D. J. Siegel (eds) *Healing Trauma.* New York, NY: W. W. Norton. p.116.

Stern, D. (2010) *Forms of Vitality.* Oxford: Oxford University Press.

Tramo, M. J. (2001) 'Biology and music: Music of the hemispheres.' *Science 291,* 5501, 54.

Chapter 8

MAKING A DRAMA

Interview with a Dramatherapist Who
Works with Adoptive Families

———— MOLLY HOLLAND AND JOY HASLER ————

Introduction

The word 'drama' originates from ancient Greece and literally translates as 'things done' (Harrison 2015). Dramatherapy uses action techniques associated with drama, such as role play, drama games, improvisation, puppetry, masks, theatrical performance, storytelling and myths. It combines theatre and psychotherapy to enable clients to explore difficult and painful life experiences through an indirect approach (BADth 2011).

According to Emunah (1998), the aim of the therapy work is the intentional and systematic use of drama to achieve psychological growth and change. The therapeutic element comes from engaging in the process of dramatic art, not the final enactment, so the emphasis is on the client's experience and not the standard of performance (Langley and Langley 1983).

The dramatherapy method has its roots firmly in psychodrama, developmental play, ritual and roles. It can be argued that role theory (Landy 1993) is at the core of the dramatherapy method and is the significant feature that distinguishes dramatherapy from other forms of creative therapies and healings. At the heart of the dramatic experience, whether in ritual, spontaneous play, creative drama, improvisation or theatrical activity of any kind, is the principle of impersonation – the ability of the person to take on a persona or role (Landy 1991).

Interview

Joy: How did you get to be a dramatherapist?

Molly: My journey towards Dramatherapy started from a very young age when I started to play and realized: 'Gosh, isn't it fun being something other than me. Isn't it fun to be the witch, or the dragon, or the Mum.' I can be so many things. And I think I suddenly started to realize also that it was fun to be things that scared you and how powerful that was. As a child I read Maurice Sendak's (2000) *Where the Wild Things Are* and that really affected me. I played out being a wild thing and suddenly I wasn't so scared any more. Through being one of them I understood that they're actually a bit sad when Max goes. Bizarre! These big things that scared me had feelings.

And so I started to realize that drama is this real collaborative cementing activity. If you stop worrying about being the best, or the most polished performance, you can just begin to enjoy playing. I studied drama for a degree, which was very practical. I learned skills such as being able to talk to people, to hold eye contact and becoming aware that if I'm feeling a little bit down today I won't sit like this: I'll sit like this and I will feel better. I learned that my posture can change how I feel. Wow, my body's really connected to this world.

People would talk to me about drama and go, 'Oh, are you an actress?' No, I just love drama and would love everyone to love it.

When I finished my degree I worked as a teaching assistant in a special school, and it's here that the drama training was helpful. People asked me, 'How are you interacting with the children in such a confident, playful, but not patronizing way?' And I just thought this is so natural, I'm performing, we're performing together. It goes back to the importance of mirroring, being spontaneous and working with what someone gives you. So that was how I related with non-verbal autistic older boys who had a lot of energy. I was inspired by the Son-Rise [Embrace Autism][1] programme, which is an intensive therapy from the States built on the importance of mirroring. It's about working with non-verbal autistic children

---

1   For more information about the Son-Rise Program, visit www.embrace-autism.org.uk/son.ht

through mirroring, and gradually introducing short turn-taking games which in turn introduces things like social skills. It is very much working at the pace of the child with what is important to them.

From there I started to do after-school drama clubs. I was amazed at the effect it had on the children and their parents. They would come to the sessions and watch their children perform. The child that's performing is being witnessed within a safe structure.

Joy: Tell me about working with families.

Molly: I realized that the work I was doing could be valuable with parents and children together, so when I joined the Catchpoint team we worked in the here and now using stories, developing characters, making connections and working with the imagination. I learned how children's brains could become overwhelmed and unable to make connections to the thinking brain. Through the drama in the sessions we found we were taken into the overwhelming state where we seemed to have lost connection with parts of the child. We were in a dance to keep the child aware and engaged. I would create a 'pause' like a director's pause, then be curious – 'I wonder what is happening here?' – and bring the drama back to a safe place for them.

Joy: How did you find working with parents as participants?

Molly: The challenge in working with parents and carers has been recognizing their expectations. There is something special about working with 'love' and the conditions that create love. The parents we work with have an idea of how they want it to turn out. They come with an issue they want us to deal with in the session, and our role can be about meeting them half-way but keeping them on board, which can be difficult. So I realized that working with parents and children together is not about pleasing them, but about working with the glue – that bit between them. As the therapist you are there to sustain their relationship and keep the communication open. So it's about communicating, observing and then feeding back. Through being an observer, the therapist has an overview of the session with the ability not to lose the interaction, but to keep the drama going and seeing the whole story.

There are difficulties when, as the therapist, you are engaged in the drama and there are disappointments. What does this mean for the parents and children? Just feeling the disappointment with them without feeling shame, and recognizing the line between the two. I have felt shame in sessions because we are challenging someone to take a risk and to do something new. Sometimes there is shame because there can be disappointment, which is powerful. It is one thing to be working with a family and another to be actually experiencing the feelings in the drama.

Joy: Have you got some specific tools you use in dramatherapy?

Molly: One drama activity I have found helpful has been working on 'family journeys'. We start with a map, saying where we want to go today, and they choose something like clay or play-doh, which might be used to create an island. Then they might use the hammock and imagine trees and then monkeys in the trees. Each person has the choice about where they want to go, which could include swimming across the river, climbing a mountain or walking through jungle, and then we put it together and the journey becomes a shared experience. This creates a sequence and a structure that is mapped out. Difficulties and dangers arise, like someone falling in the water or wanting to jump over the crocodiles.

Not long ago, with a family, we started off with 'How are we going to get there?' The child, Terri, picked a magic carpet, but this magic carpet could not fit anyone else. Terri kept flying off on her own. Mum chose a hot air balloon and she took off in this balloon. The magic carpet got closer, and then got too close to the hot air balloon, which was now on fire. Terri said, 'Oh no, you're going to crash', and Mum said, 'I'm still going, I'm still going.' So gradually we got to the island where there was a big lake. Terri said, 'I'm going to swim across on my own', and Mum said, 'I'm going to put some stones down to jump across.' Then they needed to encourage each other when there were bigger gaps between the stones, saying, 'You can do it, you can do it.' And so by helping each other they reached the end. You cannot do it on your own. We are all in it together, so much together, but at the end we can retell the story, which is another way of processing and reflecting on what happened.

Sometimes I put some fabric down that can be a picnic blanket to sit on and we have an imaginary dinner while we talk about what we've been doing. Or I get out a cooking bowl and we make a 'recipe' of the session. This happened and then this happened, and then it all gets put into the bowl. Now let's taste it. Or we might take a camera on a journey to take photos so that we can show people when we get home: 'Look where we went; we did this and we did that.'

We might reflect on the positives of a shared experience, because some of the children we work with have 'misshapen glasses' and they can't see the positive elements. If 10 per cent is negative, that is what they will talk about. So together we can look back and find the gem of the session – a little jewel, however small it is – and we can do this through imagery.

With other families we create an imaginary bag that the family can use to hold all the difficult feelings that hurt each other. Then when the child is feeling relaxed, they can get them out and look at what's in the bag and decide what they want to do with them.

I worked with Tina, a 15-year-old, on her own rather than with her parents, although we had worked with Tina and her parents together previously. I saw Tina for a couple of sessions before she went away on a trip. We created her own story book using the six-part story method. This is a method devised by Alida Gersie (Dent-Brown 2011), inspired by Vladimir Propp and Algirdas Greimas. The six parts are:

1. Main character in their setting.

2. Task facing the main character.

3. Things that hinder the task.

4. Things or characters that can help.

5. Main action – turning point of the story.

6. Aftermath – what follows main action.

This six-part story method is a way of assessing the child's response to adversity, because there is an obstacle in the story and the child needs to find a way of overcoming it. So Tina told a story about a girl who had no happiness. It was very much her own story. She found it very difficult to end the story. The wonderful thing about the six-part story is that even at the end it is not the end. Whatever the child ends with you can say, 'And then what happened?' Tina's story was negative but she acknowledged that this wasn't the end. I think for her this was quite powerful: the recognition that the story can go on and there will be something else that will happen. She retold the story through figures. We did it in freeze frame so that we could imagine how they would respond to each other and what they said to each other. There were lots of colours and lots of figures picking on her, which is how she perceives reality. We were able to look at what was happening, and then we took pictures and printed them off so we could look again. This enabled her to see the situation in the story from the perspective of the other figures. This had an impact on her relationship with her father, who featured in the story. Tina recognized his sense of humour and playfulness, and how loving and mischievous he is. She acknowledged that he makes her feel good.

Joy: How does dramatherapy heal the effects of developmental trauma?

Molly: There is a projection in dramatherapy described as EPR – Embodiment, Projection and Role. Dr Sue Jennings (2002) relates this to the mother–infant relationship: 'EPR charts the "dramatic development" of children, which is the basis of the child being able to enter the world of imagination and symbol, the world of dramatic play and drama. The early attachment between mother and infant has a strong dramatic component through playfulness and "role-reversal". Even in pregnancy the mother is forming a dramatic relationship with her unborn child.'

This is explained as a baby experiencing the world through their body and through their senses. Then you start to discover other things and connect with other people, so you start projecting characteristics onto toys, and then you take on roles, and the child can identify with these roles. Some are bad and some are good, so you can play out which is which and put qualities into characters. EPR moves in the direction from base-brain up rather than top-brain down, which is how recovery from trauma works. With Tina we had to move back to embodiment because she had moved to a place in her story that she wasn't ready to be in. Then we could move on to projection and then the role which was freeing for her. She started to take on roles when talking about her different characters, her different personalities, the personalities of the characters, and the power that went with their roles. It is very powerful for people who don't have very good emotional boundaries to create a story where they can determine which roles and boundaries can be played out.

The ability to tell a story is an amazing sign of having an overview from which to encapsulate and experience within a story the sequence of beginning, middle and end, and be able to re-tell experiences through the story without having to worry about whether it is the 'truth'. Through the child's stories we can see the roles they are taking on – positive or negative, hero or victim, adventurer or destroyer. And the child can change roles and play with what each role represents. This enables them to have an overview of a role and to regulate themselves in the process.

At Catchpoint we work in therapy pairs. At first I found this difficult, but I soon realized that this way of working enhances our training and that we are stronger together. It is about feeling more empowered and learning together. I found recently, when working with the art therapist, that you come to realize the power of art and drama together. It made me realize how important it is to mix and change, and create a combination to match what each family needs. We developed non-verbal cues about what each of us was doing and who was taking the lead. Either of us might notice something that needed to be followed up, and then a trust develops that helps us work together in supporting the family. After the session we debrief and this can be profoundly helpful in being able to share how we felt and what we noticed, and then to plan future sessions.

Joy: Can you tell me about some of the specific work you have done with families?

Molly: Recently we worked with Mum and Callum (aged 7). As they arrived I could hear Callum coming down the corridor in a whirlwind of excitement. As they came in Mum gave me an aside comment (asides can be so useful, like in a theatre where the audience are told what is going on). She said, 'He has been like this since he was with Dad.' She and Callum had had the morning together and Callum was quite calm, and then as soon as Dad arrived, he took off. When we started the session Callum was using a baby voice and showing his need for Mum, alongside a sense of shame which wasn't explained. He became increasingly agitated. We did some 'arm-art' (face painting on each other's arms), which is quite sensory and is seen as a gift to each other. Callum said he didn't want it on his arm, which is a form of rejection, at the same time as holding his arm out for more. When Mum did some art on his arm he then got cross and said, 'I don't want it there.' Mum decided she was going to leave the room (parents can opt to talk to a therapist while watching the session on a video). As she got up, Callum wrapped himself round her legs and she slipped and fell. Callum hid his face in the cushions and was clearly distressed. They were both experiencing a lot of emotions. I called in another therapist, Jo, to help because I could see that Mum needed to talk to someone. So Mum had someone to support her and Callum had a new face (that he knew well), which brought in new energy. Earlier Callum had been playing with the wolf puppet, 'Wolfie', so Jo gave this to him. He kept his head under the cushions but put his hand in the puppet and started to respond by nodding and shaking his head in answer to Jo's questions. Mum, watching on the video, was excited because she usually gets total shut-down.

I think Callum was stuck in his internal conflict and chaos, with one part wanting to shut down and another part wanting to connect. Wolfie was acting as a bridge between his two parts. Mum then sent him a written message and pushed it under the door. Jo read it out to Wolfie. This is a sort of script which lets you write something when you are out of the situation that lets you look back and think. Mum wrote, 'I love you always but I did not want to stay in because I did not want to give you some of my upset feelings.' Eventually Callum came out of his hole and asked Mum to come back in, which she did. He threw his arms round her as she came into the room. He was able to say that he was feeling really tired, and Mum and the therapists were able to confirm this and thank him. Mum and child were re-attuned.

The process in this session moved from embodiment to projection and ended with getting into roles that allowed empathy. This is also the process of moving from base-brain regulation, to mid-brain reflection, to top-brain thinking and sharing how you feel, which fits with Dr Bruce Perry's recommendations: Regulate > Relate > Reason (Perry 2014).

In drama you have three elements: props, characters and story. A script can be used to write down the ideas, put them in order and play around with them. The child and parent together can make choices, listen to each other and change their minds. They have the freedom to make things happen in the story, decide what they need and which characters they want, but it needs to be collaborative, which is therapeutic. It's about attunement.

Joy: Are there families that find dramatherapy difficult as a therapeutic medium?

Molly: For the families we work with, dramatherapy is about the opportunity to rewrite experiences, to share new experiences and create fantasy together This might be making a den, creating an island or exploring a jungle. It is new and also shared in the here and now. We have had families who are worried about being involved in drama and say, 'You're not going to make me put on that hat', or who are worried about being made to look stupid. This may be where the role of the clown is important. To be able to look silly or do silly things and finding out that it is safe and non-judgmental. I don't judge. I am just curious. There is no right or wrong. We are just going to see what happens and then explore what happens next. Most families come to enjoy the creative space and the shared fun.

Joy: Thanks, Molly.

References

BADth (2011) (The British Association of Dramatherapists) *Dramatherapy*. Available at http://badth.org.uk/dtherapy, accessed on 11 November 2016.

Dent-Brown, K. (2011) 'Six-Part Storymaking" a tool for CAT practitioners.' *Reformulation* 36, 34–36.

Emunah, R. (1998) *Acting for Real: Drama Therapy Process, Technique, and Performance*. New York, NY: Brunner-Routledge.

Harrison, J. (2015) *Ancient Art and Ritual*. CreateSpace (Independent Publishing Platform).

Jennings, S. (2002) *Healthy Attachments and Neuro-Dramatic-Play*. London: Jessica Kingsley Publishers.

Landy, R. (1991) 'The dramatic basis of role theory.' *The Arts in Psychotherapy 18*, 1, 29–41. Available at www.sciencedirect.com/science/article/pii/019745569190005U/part/first-page-pdf, accessed on 12 October 2016.

Landy, R. (1993) *Persona and Performance: The Meaning of Role in Drama, Therapy, and Everyday Life.* New York, NY: Guilford Press.

Langley, D. and Langley, G. (1983) *Dramatherapy and Psychiatry.* London: CroomHelm.

Perry, B. (2014) 'The Welcome Address.' Symposium of the Child Trauma Academy, Banff, Alberta.

Sendak, M. (2000) *Where the Wild Things Are.* London: Random House.

Chapter 9

WHEN PLAY THERAPY IS NOT ENOUGH

Using Eye Movement Desensitization and Reprocessing/Bilateral Stimulation in Combination with Play Therapy for the Child with Complex Trauma

—————— RENÉE POTGIETER MARKS ——————

Johnny plays out the same game every week. The dinosaur has been locked away. He is scared, but no matter what he does he just cannot escape the dragon. Again this week, as in so many weeks before, no one can help. He plays this game with a robot compulsion and the anxiety in the room is palpable.

Introduction

I was working with children who had experienced complex trauma, when I began to question whether the play therapy methods I was using were helping. It was the very repetitive play of children that provoked my frustration and concern and led to many questions. My curiosity was about their need to repeat play that appeared to be linked to the traumatic experience – I wondered if they were 'stuck' in traumatic experiences and whether the repetitive play was having any effect. Yet, I remained passionate about play therapy as the most effective entrance into the internal world of the child. Oaklander (1988, p.160) says that 'play also serves as a language for the child – a symbolism that substitutes for words'.

My supervisor referred to the 'processing' and provided a blanket answer to my questions – that it is all 'part of the process of the child'.

I questioned whether I should allow the children to continue to replay their traumatic experiences week after week – and for how long? This process felt indeed like a maze with 'twists and turns, false starts and dead ends' (Cattanach 1992, p.68).

Play therapy

There are many definitions of play therapy as well as different views in terms of directive and non-directive play therapy. Boyd-Webb states that 'Play Therapy ingeniously undertakes the hard work of child psychotherapy in the appealing guise of play' (2007, p.45). Oaklander says: 'For the child, play is serious, purposeful business through which he develops mentally, physically and socially. Play is the child's form of self-therapy, through which confusions, anxieties and conflicts are often worked through' (1988, p.160). Meanwhile, the British Association of Play Therapists (BAPT) describes play therapy as:

> the dynamic process between child and Play Therapist in which the child explores at his or her own pace and with his or her own agenda those issues, past and current, conscious and unconscious, that are affecting the child's life in the present. The child's inner resources are enabled by the therapeutic alliance to bring about growth and change. Play Therapy is child-centred, in which play is the primary medium and speech is the secondary medium. (BAPT 2013)

Landreth (2012) differentiates between the play of adjusted and maladjusted children. He finds maladjusted children either quieter or talking more rapidly during the first sessions. He has noticed they are also more cautious and deliberate, use few toys, play in a small area and can be more aggressive and destructive in their play.

Eye Movement Desensitization and Reprocessing

Francine Shapiro originally discovered Eye Movement Desensitization and Reprocessing (EMDR) in 1987, and the core of EMDR is Adaptive Information Processing (AIP) (Shapiro 2001). EMDR was first used in an adult population and later extended and adapted for use with children. Morris-Smith and Silvestre (2014, p.2) state that 'traumatic memory is encoded in a state-specific way and does not get processed, it becomes "frozen". It is stored as it was perceived at the time, in pictures, emotions and sensations and gives rise to dysfunctional reactions.' Different trauma-related symptoms could develop, as it appears that the trauma processing is 'blocked'. The AIP is facilitated by the EMDR or Alternating Bilateral Stimulation (ABLS/BLS), which 'enables information processing of the blocked, frozen information and thus enables traumatic memories to be metabolised or digested by the information system to healthy resolutions' (Morris-Smith and Silvestre 2014, p.2).

The speed and effectiveness of trauma processing with the use of EMDR astounded me during training. Enthusiastically I envisaged using it with children who I was seeing in therapy. I was perplexed when at that time I was told that I 'could not' use it with children who suffered complex trauma. It was unthinkable to me that such a potent therapeutic process could not be used with these children. More questions arose: Could EMDR be combined with play therapy in order to help children who suffered complex trauma? Would EMDR be able to help children who are repeating their traumatic experiences to process them quicker? Van der Kolk, McFarlane and Weisaeth (1996, p.8) state: 'Thus, in dealing with traumatised people it is critical to examine where they have become "stuck" and around which specific traumatic event(s) they have built their secondary psychic elaboration.'

SAM: LEARNING FROM EXPERIENCE

My concerns were growing with 10-year-old Sam's repetitive war games in the sand tray, with no change in his behaviour. For eight weeks, we were playing war in the sand tray. Both sides nearly became extinct, until he finally won with a marginal victory. I decided at the end of the following session to do EMDR with Sam, but I found that he could not make sense of the protocol and was still unable to name his main emotion about the abuse. Later this made sense to me as I understood more about the significant changes in the brain of the traumatized child. Although I tried the eye-movements as I had been taught, Sam was unable to follow my hand. Much later I discovered, during Neurosequential Model of Therapeutics training with Dr Bruce Perry in 2011, that many children who suffered early complex trauma are unable to fluently track an object with their eyes. During my Institute for Neuro Physiological Psychology (INPP) training,

I tested 50 children with complex trauma and found that 76 per cent of this population were unable to fluently track an object with their eyes. I agreed with Sam that I would use alternative tapping of his hands. This is often referred to as bilateral stimulation during trauma processing and can be used instead of eye movements. Other examples of bilateral stimulation are tapping hands alternately, drumming with alternate hands, marching and walking.

Sam was thinking about the abuse from his stepfather while tapping continued. He suddenly crawled under the table and moved into a foetal position. I continued the tapping and after a couple of minutes Sam crawled out on the other side and announced that he was going to 'punch' his stepfather. He drew the face of his stepfather on paper, stuck it to a big cushion, and punched relentlessly until he fell to the ground, exhausted. Sam never played the war game again. We continued with direct work targeting his abusive experiences combined with play, tapping and allowing his body to do what it needed to do, and three months later Sam was doing so well in all areas of his life with significant behavioural changes and therapy ended. I managed to receive annual feedback from Sam's family. He never displayed emotional and behavioural difficulties again and is a successful young man. This process inspired me to continue to explore a different way of using play therapy in children who have suffered complex trauma.

Rationale for exploring different ways of working

Most children are referred for therapy due to behavioural difficulties. It is questionable whether behavioural modification is effective in the long term with children who have suffered complex trauma. Adults around the child who endeavour to modify the child's behaviour, including sanctions and rewards, can leave the traumatized child feeling increasingly incompetent owing to his inability to modify his behaviour, and more often reinforce the 'rubbish' feelings that the child already carries.

Harrison-Breedt (2015, p.14) states, regarding the child who has suffered from complex trauma:

The fears and subsequent behaviours will be more rigid or fixed if the child has needed these ways of being to survive...

Attempting to modify the behaviour without understanding the roots of it will at best be ineffective but more likely create significant internal conflict and miss the true needs of the child.

The behaviours that children who have suffered complex trauma display might look similar to those of non-traumatized children, but the process of treating them needs to be different. Unless the root of these behaviours, namely the traumatic experiences, is directly addressed during therapy, the behaviours are likely to persist and even increase in intensity. Malchiodi and Crenshaw (2015) refer to Terr (1990, p.293) who states that 'trauma does not ordinarily get better by itself. It burrows down further and further under the child's defenses and coping strategies.' Malchiodi and Crenshaw (2015, p.3) further state that 'in order to reach these children effectively, therapists must use both developmentally appropriate methods and interventions that address traumatic memories and provide emotional relief'.

The main difficulty for play therapists working with the child who suffers complex trauma is that the child often tries to 'move away' from the metaphor or exploration that is connected to the trauma or behaviours. This is with either a flight response or avoidance. In her Affect Avoidance Theory Silberg (2013, p.22) defines dissociation as 'the automatic activation of a pattern of actions, thought, perception, identity, or relating (or affect script), which are overlearned and serve as conditioned avoidance responses to affective arousal associated with traumatic cues'.

Avoidance causes the child to move away from the trauma in such a way that it can totally disempower the therapist. Silberg (2013, p.84) also states: 'In some cases, the child appears to be so wrapped up in her fantasy world that it may feel counter-therapeutic to engage in symbolic fantasy play during therapy. In these cases, carefully tying what is discussed in the symbolic play to real behavior and events is important.' This concept introduces a novel concept in play therapy; but if play therapy is adapted to connecting the symbolic play to the past experiences as well as the present behaviours, it brings significant insight and relief for the child and can lead to significant behavioural changes.

Trauma changes the brain of the child (Perry 2006; Siegel 1999; Stien and Kendall 2004; Struik 2014). Traumatic memories are stored in the implicit memory system in the right hemisphere of the brain, and in trauma the brain mainly processes the information visually. The most common recall of traumatic memories is in visual form (Chapman 2014). Play therapy is in essence a visual and sensory process. Traumatized children have an elevated baseline in terms of emotional regulation and reactive stress hormones (Siegel 1999). This implies that the child with complex trauma might experience rapid elevation of internal stress when confronted with a toy or exploration regarding a metaphor relating to the trauma. Avoidance or dissociation is often the only choice, but at the same time avoids the moment of potential trauma processing.

Alternatively, the child might be attracted to the toy, which reminds the child of the trauma. It might be used in a way in which the child will replay the trauma in an effort to master the overwhelming feelings and sensations relating to it. Both avoidance and compulsion might be a response to stress hormones or an effort to regulate emotions. If these behaviours become repetitive, the question remains: Is the child processing trauma or might the child be stuck in the very trauma that he is trying to move away from? Adler-Tapia and Settle (2008, p.241) refer to 'looping' as a 'form of blocked processing'. Looping occurs when the child is providing the same information at least 2–3 times and there is a sense that he is not progressing with the trauma processing towards finding the resolution. Van der Kolk *et al.* (1996, p.8) refer to trauma memories and state that iterative learning might take place and 'repetitive exposure etches them more and more powerfully in the brain'. It appears possible that through repetitive play of trauma events, or looping, the child might actually be reinforcing the trauma-related neuron connections in the brain and during this process entrenching the trauma-based behaviours. If this is possible, how ethical is it from a neurobiological perspective to allow or encourage children to keep repeating the trauma through play without any other intervention? Play remains a very important modality in child therapy and it became vitally important to me to find an alternative way to process traumatic experiences of children with complex trauma, while still using the modality of play.

In my experience, it is the case for both adults and children that having a flashback usually leads to becoming highly distressed and dysregulated. Children who are looping are not necessarily distressed, and appear to use the looping as a way of avoidance, albeit subconscious, or emotional 'stuckness'. In this process, the child does not 'relive' the trauma but rather uses the metaphor to explain his 'stuckness' in the trauma. Bilateral stimulation appears to move the child through the trauma to an effective resolution.

EMMA: UNSPEAKABLE
TRAUMA CAN BE PROCESSED

Emma was a 13-year-old girl whose adopted placement was on the verge of disruption. Extreme violence on a daily basis towards the mother brought her to the verge of a nervous breakdown. Initially it felt impossible to gain the trust of Emma. She accused me of being 'just another stupid therapist'. I was the last therapist in a long line of therapists who saw Emma over many years. Referring to her previous experiences of therapy, Emma stated: 'They all just played with me; nobody helped me – you are just the same.' It took six months to gain her trust.

After eight months the violence stopped. Emma's regressive behaviour became her main concern. Emma arrived one day at the session asking me why she was behaving at times as if 'I am little'. I asked Emma whether she had any idea, but she shrugged her shoulders. I asked her if she had any memories about when she was little. Emma shook her head. We moved to the sand tray, which became the place where Emma was able to express herself the best. The concept of EMDR/BLS had already been introduced to Emma by using a book for children explaining EMDR. Emma also had a choice about whether she would prefer to hold the 'buzzers'[1] in her hands or put them in her shoes or socks. Emma placed the buzzers in her socks and I switched them on.

'Emma, can you show me about being "little"?' I asked.

'How do I do that?' she replied, frowning.

'Try not to think with your brain; focus on how you feel inside, feel it here', I said, pointing to my tummy area.

Emma pulled the toy box closer and started to rummage through it. A baby girl figurine emerged. Emma placed her on an adult bed in the sand tray. Next to her, Emma placed

---

1   'Buzzers' is an electronic device (from NeuroTek) that provides bilateral stimulation and is used during EMDR (Adler-Tapia and Settle 2008).

a mother figurine. The room was silent apart from the buzz-buzz sound. Emma stared at the scene.

'What happened next?' I asked.

Slowly, as if life threatening, Emma lifted up a toy dinosaur and moved it towards the bed where it pushed the baby off the bed and took baby's place next to the mother. Emma started pushing the baby into the sand, head first, deeper and deeper until only a white speck of the nappy was visible.

'What is happening, Emma?' I asked.

Staring, Emma opened her mouth. No sound emerged. It is not unusual for children processing trauma to struggle with verbal expression: 'Broca's area – the part of the left hemisphere that is responsible for translating personal experience into communicable language – showed a significant decrease in oxygen utilization during exposure to traumatic reminders' (van der Kolk et al. 1996, p.233). This is the unspeakable trauma, which is often present in children who suffered complex trauma. In my experience, trauma processing continues effectively with continuous bilateral stimulation, despite the silence.

Emma continued to show how the dinosaur and mother were fighting: mother throwing baby aside, just to sink into the sand once again. Finally, Emma found a tepee and placed it at the other end of the sand tray. She lifted the baby from the sand and placed her inside the tepee. There was some sense of relief and finally the tepee was replaced with figurines of the adopted parents holding the baby. Both parents, who were present throughout, were visibly touched. Emma looked up and said, 'I know!' Relief flooded her as she described what happened from the start. For the first time, Emma was finally able to talk about what happened as well as express her feelings and how she thought about herself at the time. The session ended with Emma sitting with her adopted parents telling her how proud they were of her.

Morris-Smith and Silvestre (2014, p.3) refer to the groundbreaking research of Pagani et al. (2012): 'Their findings point to a highly significant activation shift following EMDR therapy from limbic regions with high emotional valence to cortical regions with higher cognitive and associative valance.' With EMDR a better cognitive understanding of the impact of the trauma develops, which enhances control over behaviour in the present. Emma never needed to repeat this activity again, and became more able to manage infantile behaviours, especially in public areas.

Impact of trauma

With increasing evidence from neuroscience that trauma affects the brain of the child, especially when the child has suffered early complex trauma, we need a different therapeutic approach when working with these children. Perry (2006, p.29) states: 'Chaos, threat, traumatic stress, abuse and neglect are bad for children. These adverse experiences alter a developing child's brain in ways that result in enduring emotional, behavioural, cognitive, social and physical problems.' The child also has to adjust to the traumatizing environment (van der Kolk 2005). This leads to trauma-based behaviours that are much more complex to change and can also cause 'simplified repetitive play' (Yehuda 2016, p.143).

Trauma-based behaviours as well as repetitive play serve as a desperate way to find a solution out of the pain, terror and 'stuckness' of the trauma experience. Trauma-based behaviours also appear in anticipation of more traumatic experiences. They can also lead to transferring the trauma replay, feelings and behaviours onto innocent people around the child, where the child instantly views them as either a perpetrator or victim. This mostly leads to attachment difficulties, problems in peer relationships, social isolation and victimization. These behaviours are often dissociative and are a means to protect the child against the environment or people who might be perceived as hostile. Trauma-based behaviours cause the child to vehemently avoid trauma stimuli during therapy or lead to repetitive looping in trauma play. It can also lead to a child being in control of the therapist, demanding action. Even worse, the therapist might be invited to become the victim of the child or the perpetrator in the play. In these moments the therapeutic alliance might be dangerously at risk and even leave the therapist impotent to help the traumatized child.

Trauma feelings, sensations and internal experiences are powerful and frightening for children. They need a brave therapist who is 'strong' enough to 'hold' these experiences for them, while they explore and process their trauma in a safe way. Children often told me that their anger or 'big feelings' would 'kill' me, 'destroy' the building or become so big that we will all 'explode'. The child needs to know that the therapist is present, calm, grounded, brave and strong enough to hold whatever happens in the room without becoming part of the process as a victim or a perpetrator. They are the safe pillar the child can lean on, while being in the process with the child to find the solution to overwhelming trauma.

Trauma memories also appear to be processed in the brain differently from neutral memories (Teicher *et al.* 2003). Van der Kolk *et al.* (1996) state that traumatic memories do not fit in a contextual memory. Further, van der Kolk, Burbridge and Suzuki (1997, p.99) say: 'Dissociation causes memories of the trauma to be organized, at least initially, as sensory fragments and intense emotional states that may have no linguistic components.' As trauma is best remembered through images and sensations, play is an ideal way for the child to externalize these fragmented experiences. The therapist has to connect these fragments with the past traumatic experiences as well as the present behaviours in order to enable the child to gain a full understanding of his internal landscape. If this is done with continuous bilateral stimulation, the child appears to move out of the looping and will either suddenly progress the play where previously unknown information starts to unfold, or display significant body movements, depicting some traumatic experience. In other cases, children start to draw or write information, or try to express what is happening inside them in some way. It appears from these behaviours that children move from looping into another process where the original trauma information is being accessed. With the continuation of the BLS, the children are able to process the traumatic memory underlying the initial looping: 'BLS appears to activate both sides of the brain, which facilitates more complete processing of distressing events' (Waters 2016, p.354).

Adapting play therapy for work with complex trauma

Play therapy can be effectively adapted to be used with traumatized children. Once the traumatized child is emotionally regulated at home and in the therapy room, the child is ready to access trauma memories very effectively using metaphors and symbols.

First the play therapist might need to integrate some directive approaches: 'My integrated approach is documented elsewhere, but suffice it to say that therapy can include the purposeful integration of directive and non-directive strategies' (Gil 2006). Struik (2014) also encourages the therapist to work directly with the trauma of the child who suffered complex trauma.

The therapist has to be constantly aware of the possible avoidance or potential affect dysregulation that might take place during therapy. Herman (1997, p.155) describes the recovery of trauma in three stages: the first is establishing 'safety', the second is 'remembering and mourning' and the third is 'reconnection with ordinary life'. These guidelines have been widely accepted by trauma therapists. Struik (2014) wrote extensively about enabling the child with complex trauma to find sufficient safety and stabilization in order to start with trauma processing.

Once the child's attachment figure can provide safety and effective emotional regulation to the child, trauma processing can start. In practice it appears that many children who suffered complex trauma are not able to establish a 'safe place', which is commonly used in EMDR. Some of these children find a safe place, but once found, threatening objects or people might intrude. In reality this defies the object of a safe place. In practice it appears to be the best policy to ensure a safe parent, foster carer or attachment figure who can be present in the therapy room during the trauma processing. This excludes any person who was responsible for the trauma.

The attachment figure attends therapy sessions armed with a safe smell that is used at home – for example, lavender (Gomez 2013). Chewy foods (e.g. carrots, apples, crunchy foods or chewing gum), as well as a water bottle or lollies that the child can suck, are very beneficial to ground the child. These can be used effectively at the first signs of emotional dysregulation to promote a calm state where trauma processing can continue. Movement or sensory activity can be used to improve the emotional regulation of the child (Ogden, Minton and Pain 2006). It is imperative for the child to experience the parent and therapist as powerful enough to hold the child emotionally and not to move away from the trauma or the metaphor.

JAMES: FINDING A WAY OUT OF BEING STUCK IN TRAUMA MEMORIES

James was a 5-year-old adopted boy who displayed aggressive behaviour at school. His peers became victims and school started to receive complaints from other parents. Different strategies were put in place, but to no avail. The adoptive parents were pressurized to address this behaviour, but none of the discussion, threats, promises and pleading had any effect. The problem escalated to the point where school started to contemplate excluding James. A visit to the school indicated compassionate teachers, out of their depth and in despair, caught between wanting to help James and protecting the other children. They reported that during times of aggressive behaviour they noticed his pupils were dilated. The headmistress described it by saying his 'eyes became black'. Dilated pupils in children can be a sign of trauma recall and high internal anxiety or a 'flashback'.

During the assessment James seemed a pleasant, talkative boy with brown hair and big brown eyes. He did not like the teachers at his school and stated that his friends were hurting him. James had been living with his adoptive parents for three years, but it was evident that he had significant attachment difficulties.

The therapy process started with attachment-based therapy. Both parents engaged during therapy in attachment-based activities with James using Theraplay techniques. They repeated these activities at home on a daily basis. Four months later, James appeared more securely attached to his parents. His eye contact with them had improved; he was able to spontaneously seek and receive physical nurturing from them; aggressive attacks on his peers had reduced radically; and trauma processing was introduced.

James was exposed to severe domestic violence, drugs, abuse and neglect as an infant. The presence of his adoptive mother during therapy remained his biggest source of comfort and safety. The smell of lavender, which she used during the sessions, permeated the room. James started to process the domestic violent incidents.

As EMDR is used as an integrative part of the psychotherapeutic process, the use of the 'buzzers', which is used for BLS, is discussed with the child during the early phases of therapy. In the next session, I watched in amazement how James never complained, walked into the room, accepted the buzzers and started to do the work, as if he somehow instinctively knew this was his exit ticket out of the traumatic life he experienced.

During one session where the dollhouse was used, James placed the birth parent figurines near the front door. Once again, James showed with the figurines how the birth parents were shouting, screaming, punching and hitting each other. The baby figurine was sitting on the floor nearby, watching. Another punch and Mother figurine fell over, followed by relentless punching from the father figurine. James froze, pupils dilated.

'I wonder what is happening for you now James?' I asked.

James looked up at me with his big eyes and then stared back at the scene in front of him. Helplessness and hopelessness saturated the atmosphere. No words, and no body movement. Just the silence, and the buzz-buzz sound.

'What does the baby need to feel better?' I asked, introducing a cognitive interweave, which is an EMDR technique to enable the person to move from trauma looping or 'stuckness' to further processing.

A fleeting, speechless look with more staring followed.

'James, who can help the baby? You can choose anybody', I said in another attempt.

There was still no response. Silence.

'I wonder if we could bring the social worker in and see if she could help the baby?' I suggested.

James gave a slight nod. I found a female figurine and handed it to him. He placed her next to the scene with the parent figurines.

'What is happening now James?' I asked.

Staring, buzz, buzz, buzz and buzz. My cognitive interweave was not working.

What if the social worker could not save him from this trauma or left him too long? She appeared frozen, just like the child in front of me. I found a police figurine. There was a faint smile when James took it out of my hand. He placed the police figurine next to the front door and stared.

'What is happening now James?'

Staring, buzz, buzz, buzz, buzz and buzz. I quickly assessed the situation. There was a sense that James was back in the house, parents fighting and being in a life and death situation, which was overwhelming and left him in a frozen state. I recalled the information of Schaer (2005), who states that trauma in the body cannot be processed unless the body is enabled to do what it was unable to do at the time of the trauma. In front of me I had the epitome of helplessness and a frozen state.

I mentally scanned the content of my toys through the closed cupboard doors. James was staring, frozen. I got up, took out the police outfit, hat, badge, handcuffs and the baton. James looked up when I stood in front of him.

'James, that policeman cannot do anything, so we need a real, powerful police officer who can do something to help baby', I said.

A smile, and James got up. I switched the buzzers off. The mother helped dress James. He eagerly co-operated. The buzzers resumed as James looked down at the scene in front of him. He smiled. He moved towards the mirror, looked at himself and re-adjusted the hat. He had a broad smile and changed stature. James sat with his mother again and looked at the scene in front of him. A thoughtful stare followed. He pushed the social worker figurine over and placed both her and the police figurines back in the toy box.

'What is happening now, James?' I asked.

He looked at me.

'I am the police', he stated emphatically.

He took the handcuffs out of his pocket, took the small figurine and started to handcuff him. Although the figurine was hopelessly too small for these handcuffs, James pretended to handcuff him, got up, went to the toy cupboard and got the toy jail out. He used the small key to open the door and pushed the father figurine inside and locked the door. He pushed the jail to the back of the cupboard. A big sigh followed, then a smile, and I noticed that his pupils were less dilated.

'He's gone!' James exclaimed.

'Wow, what a brave police officer you are – just like that', I exclaimed.

James smiled and the tension in the room started to dissolve as James swung the baton around in bravado.

'He can never do that again – he is now locked up!' he said.

(Steele and Malchiodi (2012, p.3) state that 'before traumatic memory can be encoded, expressed through language, and successfully integrated, it must be retrieved and implicitly externalised, in its symbolic (iconic) sensory forms'.)

'That is amazing, James. You ended it all. All by yourself. How brave are you!' I said.

James smiled while returning the mother figurine to the toy box. He draped himself over his mother and she embraced him, while telling him how much she loved him. She read the book about the 'big Mummy love', and James moulded into his mother's embrace.

James finally processed the traumatic memories, which he experienced before the age of 14 months. Perry (2013, chapter 12) states that 'trauma during infancy has a profound impact on the developing child; and sadly most traumatised infants end up "remembering" the trauma in one way or another for the rest of their lives'. James was finally free from this burden.

One question remains. Did I actually re-traumatize James through this process or did the re-traumatization happen each time James attacked his friends at school, replaying the violence that slowly became part of his social repertoire? In either case – James hurting his friends or during trauma processing – his pupils were dilated and he experienced trauma recall. Did the therapy that is described above 'stop' the trauma re-enactment or reinforce it?

James never needed to return to the same trauma scene. It was completed. The trauma was fully processed. There were no further incidents of aggression. According to Gomez (2013, p.7) 'during the reprocessing phase of EMDR therapy, the memories containing traumatic material are assimilated and integrated'. James progressed well at school, and many years later he is a kind and helpful young person with positive peer relationships.

Conclusion

There has been an increase in research in neuroscience and trauma processing over the past 10–15 years. There also appears to be an increased number of children with complex trauma who are inevitably referred to therapists with a generic training in counselling, some form of psychotherapy or play therapy. Due to the complexity of the plethora of problems of these children, it appears that their long-term recovery might be compromised in certain cases by the use of generic techniques.

There is also a growing awareness amongst clinicians treating children with complex trauma that 'there might be more' that they need to know about this population of children, in order to deliver effective treatment and improve their long-term mental health and secure more positive relationships across the board for them. These children often struggle with attachments and socialization and experience rejection from adults and peers alike owing to their behavioural problems. Behavioural strategies often do not provide the solution as at the core of these problems there are often significant attachment difficulties as well as unprocessed trauma due to abuse, neglect, exposure to interpersonal violence or early painful medical interventions.

Delivering a more effective treatment plan to children with complex trauma can be both a trial of extremes as well as an exhilarating journey. Another aspect that can be a battle on its own is the capriciousness of the effects of different treatment techniques on individual children, which often leads to further challenges for the therapist.

As the child is living internally with the trauma, he will continue to live with the discomfort of the trauma unless it is processed. The therapist has the challenge of 'waking up the sleeping dog', enabling the child to see that it no longer has power over him, and enabling the child to 'tame the sleeping dog' (Struik 2014). May we, as therapists, give hope to the children and continue to do effective trauma processing with the words of Levine (1997, p.41) in mind: 'Trauma is not a life sentence.'

References

Adler-Tapia, R. and Settle, C. (2008) *EMDR and the Art of Psychotherapy with Children.* New York, NY: Springer.

BAPT (British Association of Play Therapists) (2013) *History of Play Therapy.* Available at www.bapt.info/play-therapy/history-play-therapy, accessed on 13 October 2016.

Boyd-Webb, N. (2007) *Play Therapy with Children in Crisis. Individual, Group and Family Treatment.* New York, NY: Guilford Press.

Cattanach, A. (1992) *Play Therapy with Abused Children.* London: Jessica Kingsley Publishers.

Chapman, L. (2014) *Neurobiological Informed Trauma Therapy with Children and Adolescents: Understanding Mechanisms of Change.* New York, NY: W. W. Norton.

Gil, E. (2006) *Helping Abused and Traumatized Children: Integrating Directive and Nondirective Approaches.* New York, NY: Guilford Press.

Gomez, A. M. (2013) *EMDR Therapy and Adjunct Approaches with Children: Complex Trauma, Attachment and Dissociation.* New York, NY: Springer.

Harrison-Breedt, C. (2015) 'Trauma: A Gestalt Play Therapy Perspective.' *BACP Children & Young People.* September, 13–16.

Herman, J. L. (1997) *Trauma and Recovery*. New York, NY: Basic Books.

Landreth, G. L. (2012) *Play Therapy: The Art of the Relationship*. New York, NY: Routledge.

Levine, P. (1997) *Waking the Tiger: Healing Trauma*. Berkeley, CA: North Atlantic Books.

Malchiodi, C. A. and Crenshaw, D. A. (2015) *Creative Interventions with Traumatized Children*. London: Guilford Press.

Morris-Smith, J. and Silvestre, M. (2014) *EMDR for the Next Generation: Healing Children and Families*. Reading: Academic Publishing International.

Oaklander, V. (1988) *Windows to Our Children*. Highland, NY: Gestalt Journal Press.

Ogden, P., Minton, K. and Pain, C. (2006) *Trauma and the Body: A Sensorimotor Approach to Psychotherapy*. New York, NY: W. W. Norton.

Pagani, M., Di Lorenzo, G., Verado, A. R., Nicolais, G. *et al.* (2012) 'Neurobiological correlates of EMDR monitoring – An EEG study.' *PLoS ONE 7*, 9, e45753.

Perry, B. D. (2006) 'Applying Principles of Neurodevelopment to Clinical Work with Maltreated and Traumatized Children. The Neurosequential Model of Therapeutics.' In N. Boyd-Webb (ed.) *Working with Traumatized Youth in Child Welfare*. New York, NY: Guilford Press.

Perry, B. D. (2013) *Brief: Reflections on Childhood, Trauma and Society*. Houston, TX: Child Trauma Academy Press.

Schaer, R. (2005) *The Trauma Spectrum: Hidden Wounds and Human Resilience*. New York, NY: W. W. Norton.

Shapiro, F. (2001) *Eye Movement Desensitization and Reprocessing: Basic Principles, Protocols and Procedures* (2nd edn). New York, NY: Guilford Press.

Siegel, D. J. (1999) *The Developing Mind: Toward a Neurobiology of Interpersonal Experience*. New York, NY: Guilford Press.

Silberg, J. (2013) *The Child Survivor: Healing Developmental Trauma and Dissociation*. New York, NY: Routledge.

Steele, W. and Malchiodi, C. A. (2012) *Trauma-Informed Practices with Children and Adolescents*. New York, NY: Routledge.

Stien, P. T. and Kendall, J. (2004) *Psychological Trauma and the Developing Brain: Neurological Based Interventions for Troubled Children*. London: Haworth Press.

Struik, A. (2014) *Treating Chronically Traumatised Children: Don't Let Sleeping Dogs Lie!* New York, NY: Routledge.

Teicher, M. H., Andersen, S. L., Polcari, A., Anderson, C. M., Navalta, C. P. and Kim, D. M. (2003) 'The neurobiological consequences of early stress and childhood maltreatment.' *Neuroscience and Biobehavioural Reviews 27*, 33–44.

Terr, L. (1990) *Too Scared to Cry*. New York, NY: HarperCollins.

van der Kolk, B. A. (2005) 'Developmental trauma disorder. Towards a rational diagnosis for children with complex trauma histories.' *Psychiatric Annals 35*, 5, 401.

van der Kolk, B. A., Burbridge, J. A. and Suzuki, J. (1997) 'The psychobiology of traumatic memory. Clinical implications of neuroimaging studies.' *Annals of the New York Academy of Sciences 21*, 821, 99–113.

van der Kolk, B. A., McFarlane, A. C. and Weisaeth, L. (1996) *Traumatic Stress – The Effects of Overwhelming Experience of Mind, Body and Society*. New York, NY: Guilford Press

Waters, F. S. (2016) *Healing the Fractured Child: Diagnoses and Treatment of Youth with Dissociation*. New York, NY: Springer.

Yehuda, N. (2016) *Communicating Trauma: Clinical Presentations and Interventions with Traumatized Children*. New York, NY: Routledge.

Chapter 10

DANCE MOVEMENT THERAPY IN ATTACHMENT WORK

'Repetitive, Rhythmic, Relevant, Relational,
Respectful and Rewarding'[1]

———— Hannah Guy and Sue Topalian ————

*Tell me, and I will forget. Show me, and I may remember. Involve me,
and I will understand.*

Chinese proverb, attributed to Confucius, c.450 BC

Introduction

In this chapter we will illustrate how Dance Movement Psychotherapy
(DMP) can be used to promote attachment between adoptive parents,
long-term foster or kinship carers and children who have attachment
difficulties and have been exposed to complex trauma following early
abuse or neglect. We will do this by describing our underpinning
theoretical basis and interventions used in our therapeutic practice.

DMP is one of the creative therapies. It is defined as 'a relational
process in which client(s) and therapist engage in an empathetic
creative process using body movement and dance to assist integration
of emotional, cognitive, physical, social and spiritual aspects of self'.[2]
While dance has had a significant role over millennia in healing rituals

---

1   Perry (2015, p.xi).
2   For details, see the home page of the Association of Dance Movement Psychotherapists'
    website at www.admp.org.uk, accessed on 11 November 2016.

across the world, modern psychotherapeutic use of dance emerged in the USA in the 1940s, in the work of Marian Chace (1896–1970). Chace's work with shell-shocked soldiers, victims of sexual abuse and psychiatric in-patients validated dance as a therapeutic profession, using movement to support clients in identifying and communicating their feelings (Sandel, Chaiklin and Lohn 1993).

DMP has been developed in the UK from the 1970s onwards, and is now used with many different client groups, in both individual and group settings. Like art, music and drama therapists, dance movement psychotherapists train to Master's degree level, and undertake their own psychotherapy for three years. Dance movement psychotherapists are registered with the Association of Dance Movement Psychotherapists (an organizational member of the UK Council for Psychotherapy).

Theoretical background

Our therapeutic approach draws on two main strands of research and practice. Our agency's approach is based on decades of study of attachment, and neuroscientific research into the effects of complex trauma on brain development. It is principally informed by:

- The Neurosequential Model of Therapeutics (NMT) (Perry and Dobson 2013).

- Dyadic Developmental Psychology, including relating to children with playfulness, acceptance, curiosity and empathy (Hughes 2007).

- Theraplay, which encourages building of relationships through attachment-based play. Interactions focus on structure, engagement, nurture and challenge (Booth and Jernberg 2010).

- Trauma-Focused Cognitive Behavioural Therapy (TF-CBT) applying arts therapies to work with families. TF-CBT brings together various components, including psycho-education about the effects of trauma, teaching relaxation techniques and promoting affective expression and regulation. It enhances cognitive coping and processing through understanding of the connections between thought, feelings and behaviours.

It works with trauma narrative and processing, and desensitizes through gradual exposure to trauma reminders. It encourages safety and relationship skills development (Cohen, Mannarino and Deblinger 2006).

The second strand is DMP theory and practice. There are various psychotherapeutic approaches to DMP. The current authors are trained in a person-centred approach, based on the work of Carl Rogers (1902–1987) and his successors. Key to this approach is the understanding that each person has within himself an 'actualizing tendency' and that the therapist's role is to provide an environment of unconditional acceptance, empathy and personal congruence in which this can function to lead the person into healing, growth and development (Rogers 1951).

DMP is based on the understanding that body, mind, emotions and spirit interact (Association of Dance Movement Psychotherapists 2015). Emotions are experienced physically, associated with, for example, changes in body temperature, heart rate and muscle tension, in synch with brain activity. Neuroscience describes how trauma impacts on the body and brain through the autonomic nervous system, and how hyper-arousal can persist when flight or fight has not been possible in early trauma (Perry 2001). The brain stores memory. Body memory is the storing and recall of sensations that make up emotions and physical states such as pain, through the interconnection between the brain and the body's nervous system (van der Kolk 2014). Sometimes the corresponding facts are also stored and recalled; sometimes they are not (Rothschild 2003). A person's posture and movement may reflect his 'stance' towards life and others, based on body memory of repeated emotional or sensory experience. In paying attention to bodily sensations, posture and movement, unconscious material, forgotten memories and associations can be accessed (Stanton-Jones 1992). A change in physical movement can prepare a person for a change in his emotional state and unblock suppressed feelings from the past (Levy 1988). Group DMP with chaotic and disorganized children in an in-patient psychiatric unit found that it encouraged the development of body image, self-awareness, awareness of others, improved impulse control, frustration tolerance, gratification delay and ability to get along with others (Erfer and Ziv 2006).

Dance movement psychotherapists are also trained in Rudolf Laban's (1879–1958) Movement Analysis, a system devised to record and map movement scores to prolong the lifespan of dance works (Laban and Ullman 1985). In order to maintain the authenticity of a dance, the system was applied to all the main characteristics of the work, including individual movements and the 'effort factors' of 'time', 'weight', 'space' and 'flow'. This provides dance movement psychotherapists with an objective tool to observe and record the qualities of an individual's somatic (physical), mental and emotional development over a course of therapy.

DMP uses a number of key approaches:

- *Kinaesthetic empathy* involves 'tuning into' and reflecting the qualities of the client's mode of movement in a way that enables the client to feel accepted, seen and understood (Fischmann 2009). This could be seen as applying through movement Carl Rogers' (1961) core conditions: congruence (being aware of and acting on one's true internal responses), unconditional positive regard, and empathy. In the group/ family therapy situation, the therapist creates an environment where kinaesthetic empathy can happen between group/ family members. This helps to build attachment, echoing the way that good enough parents do this in the baby's pre-verbal period (Gerhardt 2004, p.37). In addition, the client can see himself reflected in others, enhancing self-awareness.

- *Mindfulness enhanced by movement* encourages a sense of grounding, of being present in one's body, of one's breath, and awareness of self in relation to others and the space around (Russell and Arcuri 2015).

- *Playful experimentation with new ways of being and relating* is a non-threatening, accepting, creative environment for caregivers and children that supports the potential for change (Golding and Hughes 2012).

- *Improvisation* involves creativity, which is often a vehicle for the emergence of metaphorical or symbolic material (Meekums 2002) that may be verbally acknowledged and explored, or remain unspoken but influential.

- *Shared rhythm* is used to build attachment and a sense of strength in the group/family. Again, this echoes the way attachment builds in early relationships: 'A group moving together seem to have one rhythm and one pulse… As feelings are expressed in shared rhythm, each member draws from the common pool of energy and experiences a heightened sense of strength and security' (Chaiklin and Schmais 1994, p.21).

- *Music* may be used to support this sense of connection, drawing people into a shared atmospheric field.

- *The circle formation* is significant and often used. This 'permits equal sharing, visual contact among group members, and a sense of security in a clearly defined space' (Chaiklin and Schmais 1994, p.27).

- *Props* such as balls, pieces of material, balloons, elastic and hoops are frequently used and can become symbolic, or provide a means of creating boundaries or enabling connections between participants (Meekums 2002).

DMP is particularly appropriate for work with attachment and early trauma. Babies do not use words, and are right-brain dominant. Perry (2013) observes that traumatized children have poor function in their brainstem and diencephalon, and need patterned, repetitive activity to help remedy this. He writes that healing practices work because they are 'repetitive, rhythmic, relevant, relational, respectful and rewarding' (Perry 2015, p.xi). Perry also notes that traditional healing rituals include story, relationship, dance and music: 'While these therapeutic practices may not at first seem 'biological'…they…will assuredly provide the patterned, repetitive stimuli required to specifically influence and modify the impact of trauma, neglect, and maltreatment on key neural systems' (2015, p.xii). Dance is by its nature rhythmic, repetitive, relational and rewarding.

Literature review

For those who would like to read further, the impact of trauma on the body and addressing this in individual therapy are explored by Babette Rothschild (2000, 2003). Kim Etherington's research (2003) brings together accounts of the impact of trauma on emotional and physical health. Bonnie Meekums (2002) provides a general introduction to the practice of DMP in the UK.

There is published case material about DMP with parents and children with attachment and trauma difficulties. Meekums (1992) records extended group work with four mothers and toddlers designated at risk of abuse. Harvey (1995) gives a detailed account of work with a 3-year-old sexually abused adopted child and her mother. Blau and Reicher (1995) write of building attachment through movement between parents and young children in a variety of situations. Treefoot (2008) describes a course of DMP with a 2-year-old with attachment difficulties and her mother. Tortora (2009) and Dulicai (2009) each describe their applications of DMP to therapeutic work with families.

Mount St Vincent Creative Arts Therapy Department is a group of creative therapists working in a long-established US treatment centre for children with severe emotional and behavioural challenges due to trauma, abuse or neglect. Their book (see Perry 2013) provides a brief introduction to the application of arts therapies to NMT, including DMP. This includes examples of dance movement activities for enhancing sensory integration, self-regulation, relationship and cognition.

The setting

The setting for the work we describe is a therapy centre in the South-West of England that works with families where children have been placed for adoption or long-term fostering following abuse or neglect. The agency provides guidance, support and attachment-focused therapy for individual families, and some one-to-one therapy with young people with the agreement of the parents. The agency employs drama, art, play and music therapists as well as dance movement psychotherapists. Therapeutic work is undertaken in therapy rooms equipped for all of these creative modes. Therapists generally work in pairs alongside families. This enables modelling of the dyadic parental working relationship, ensures safety in unforeseen circumstances, makes a variety of arts therapies available, and allows for a greater depth of observation and reflection on sessions.

Illustrative vignettes

DMP interventions may be planned to work on specific areas of development, or may be freer flowing, with general aims leading to unplanned creative parent–child interactions. The vignettes below reflect both planned and free-flowing work, and give a feel for how practice reflects theory in specific interventions.

The examples are composite, based on therapeutic sessions with a number of families, rather than on a single identifiable family. While every child and family are unique, similar patterns of thought, feelings and behaviours are often seen in different children who have experienced early trauma, and so variations on similar interventions may be helpful for different families.

Sessions are structured with a clear beginning and end, and creative activities are appropriate to the needs of the child. Activities depend on previous assessment of the child's needs, what the child presents on arrival to the session, and what is observed by the therapists as the session unfolds.

BOBBY AND HER ADOPTIVE PARENTS

Opening the session

Bobby (aged 5) attends weekly sessions with her adoptive mother and father. Bobby has been with her adoptive family for one year. This session took place nine months after the commencement of therapy. Bobby exhibits anxiety, short attention span, difficulties with trust and a low sense of self-worth. Bobby frequently presents a need to remain in control of the therapeutic environment and often disengages. She can struggle with emotional regulation and displays high levels of anxiety through her behaviour:

- running from one side of the room to the other
- disengagement from Mum
- exploration of the room without seeking reassurance from Mum
- hiding underneath the table
- not waiting her turn.

General therapeutic aims for Bobby are to: develop a more secure attachment to her parents; achieve better regulation of her anxiety; improve her ability to take turns; improve her attention span; and increase her resilience and a positive sense of self.

Sessions start with a verbal check-in, giving Bobby and her parents a chance to share something that she has enjoyed, and something that has evoked a feeling of disappointment. Mum and Dad shared Bobby's recent display of sadness on leaving her godmother's home following a weekend away. This then enabled Bobby to share her own thoughts on the experience: happiness at receiving a cuddle from Mum and Dad to soothe her upset, yet a continuing feeling of sadness.

The therapist observed Bobby's energy levels during the check-in, seeing her sudden and dynamic shifts on the couch as an indication of raised anxiety, and decided to initiate 'Shake Awake' to introduce the next part of the session.

The family members were asked to each share a different body part to shake awake – for example, shaking of the head from side to side, enthusiastic flicks of the toes and a sudden back-and-forth movement with the shoulders. These gestures enable the family to channel any held energies, as well as give the therapist an idea of what might be an appropriate intervention to follow. Bobby presented high levels of energy and interaction during this time. Sharing movements in a fun activity provided Bobby with the opportunity to move rhythmically with her parents and to initiate frequent eye contact and smiles, demonstrating an enjoyment of the shared experience.

Feedback in the verbal check-in enables Bobby to feel heard as well as seen. Children in trauma recovery often use behaviours rather than words as a tool to let parents know what they are thinking. Voicing feelings for these children may evoke painful memories that may be difficult to manage. The caregiver is often encouraged to give an example of how he sees others express their emotions, enabling the child to develop an understanding of how feelings can be expressed. It also demonstrates how an emotion can give a non-verbal message, which may communicate a very different message from the verbal one.

The introduction of physical activity following a check-in can provide an opportunity for free self-expression and externalization of feelings without the restriction of language, leading to gaining a greater level of control over the present moment. Any feelings that may have been evoked during the check-in can be safely channelled and explored through body, voice and improvisation.

Middle of the session: 'I am the Music Maker, I am the Dancing Daisy' – turn taking, waiting, accepting parental control

Bobby voiced a preference for playing the role of the Music Maker, creating sound through a variety of available instruments. However, when papers were drawn from a container, both Bobby and her father picked out 'Dancing daisies', a role which involves moving and vocalising to the Music Maker's sounds. This initiated a decline to participate on Bobby's part, and she sat out. Continuation of the game without Bobby encouraged her to re-join the group and move with Dad in time with the music. Roles were swapped after a brief time, enabling Bobby and Dad to choose an instrument to accompany Mum's dance with the therapists.

Turn taking is a key component of activities to encourage children to experience deferred gratification. Waiting is often highly challenging for a child recovering from trauma (Wesselmann, Schweitzer and Armstrong 2014).

When the intervention continued without Bobby's presence, it highlighted to Bobby that she had a choice and that she *can* determine the outcome: to sit out and watch, or join in with the fun. It also models to the parent who is in 'control' and how this can be integrated into the home environment, encouraging the child to experience trust with the parental figure. The child can express himself freely as he wishes without feeling a need to control the self and others, and without the need to detach from the family unit, maintaining a level of autonomy within the family dance.

End of the session:'The Goodbye Groove' – sequencing

The ending ritual for Bobby's sessions is a 'Goodbye Groove' devised by the group with movement to accompany the words. A standing circle enables a sequence to unfold by going around the circle and inviting each participant to contribute a gesture to correlate with a word – for example, 'Au revoir' or 'Until next time'. The group follows the movement and word/s of each participant before sequencing them all together: a high reach, then touching the toes, into an explosive star jump, enabling a cohesive activity to bring the session to a close.

An ending ritual through movement is helpful with younger children, as it is a clear signal of the end of the session approaching, and allows a 'wind down' time.

Following the lead of the individual provides a mirror for the child to gain insight into the way the world sees him. Mirroring enhances a sense of connection. Bobby and her family revisit the Goodbye Groove at the end of each session, enabling them to be creative and make it their own. In a therapy setting this can be a tool that enables parent and child to devise something between them, enabling a shared experience to form.

Sequencing is a key component of therapeutic activities, as it can support change in the neural system. Dysfunction in the brain is caused by poor regulation. However, as neurons have the capacity to shift in response to 'moderate, predictable and patterned' experiences (Perry and Szalavitz 2006, p.41), sequencing allows for healing and the establishment of positive neural patterns.

Somatic (bodily) attunement between parents and child in varying movement qualities is threaded throughout this session – for example, in the vibrancy of the 'Shake Awake' and the rhythmic beat of the drumming and dancing.

GABE AND HIS ADOPTIVE MOTHER

The dice – practising unpredictability and not being in control

Gabe (aged 9) was adopted six years ago with a younger brother. Gabe came to therapy owing to low levels of self-esteem and concentration, challenging and aggressive behaviour and poor peer relationships at school. Gabe has been coming to therapy with his adoptive mother for seven months.

Gabe and his mother take a turn at rolling a large foam dice, the outcome requiring a number of unspecified gestures, providing them with an opportunity to freely express themselves in, for example, a bottom wiggle four times, a loud screech two times, running around the room six times, etc.

Using the dice as a warm-up tool gave Gabe experience of determination of events as an external force and something that we cannot always control – a life situation that is often a struggle for Gabe. It illustrates experientially how although we may not always like an unpredictable outcome (e.g. a number one on the dice), we have a choice in how we decide to respond, and this choice, like our behaviours, can then impact on others.

The dice exercise explores the concept of unpredictability, which is particularly frightening for those who have experienced situations where unpredictable events can cause harm or neglect. Remaining in control of a situation can reassure an individual that the outcome is a safe and secure one. Individuals who have experienced trauma may have invested their trust in an adult and been betrayed. Learning to trust is paramount to the therapeutic process.

Improvisational creative interaction elicits joy. It takes participants into a place that is positive, present and playful. Developmental neuroscientist Allan Schore (2011) states that, in the first year of life, shared joy is the key to attachment. The playfulness of this activity enabled Gabe to remain engaged while the difficult issue of unpredictability was being explored, with the element of shared fun providing an element of containing safety.

We often tell clients how their role within the session can make us smile, laugh or feel excited. This lets the child know that he is responsible for the therapist feeling this way and therefore drip feeds the message 'I am OK, I'm not rubbish, I made Mummy/the therapist smile!!', and reinforces how choices can impact on the way others feel.

'Balls and Bumble Bees' – story and improvisation

An unstructured activity often follows a more set exercise to provide a greater level of creative freedom and to enable a therapist to observe what a looser boundary evokes relationally and in behaviours.

Mum and Gabe were invited to move in the space and access any external prop in response to a piece of poetry introducing imagination and creative play. Mum chose to use a malleable sensory ball as a passing bumble bee, enabling a kiss to be placed on her son's cheek. The pair were asked to take note of any movement or gesture they would like to use again in order to create a performance-like ending.

The use of the ball demonstrates how a prop can bridge a gap between parent and child and provide an opportunity for indirect connection.

Imagination and creativity with a parent can reinforce the parent as the key relational figure, and encourages verbal and non-verbal communicative tools to aid mutual understanding in a non-threatening way. Strengthening the relationship between parent and child through the creative process increases an awareness of each other, and provides scope for the fruition of understanding and trust, 're-choreographing family dynamics' (Devereaux 2008, p.59). Mutual appreciation of their creative input becomes possible as well as emphasizing the reciprocal roles of the parent–child relationship. DMP can create a setting that enables a child to experience his own way of relating while simultaneously enabling him to explore new ways of interacting with his environment. Several of Bruce Perry's core components for healing trauma and attachment disorders (Perry 2015) are evident in this exercise, particularly relationship, respect, relevance and reward.

ANNIE AND HER FOSTER CARERS

The storm in the forest – sensory integration, somatic attunement and symbolism

Annie (aged 6) lives with her long-term foster carers. She has difficulty focusing and regulating her emotions, and this is reflected in her bodily movement. She is generally fast-moving, darting about in different directions, always noticing what is happening around her, and often distracted by surrounding details. Her emotions can flare up into tantrum-like behaviour when she does not feel safe. This creates difficulties for her at school, resulting in frequent exclusions. Annie will try to distract from conversation about feelings by diversionary activity. She shows some affection to her carers but at home can be overwhelmed by feelings she does not understand, and behave in a rejecting and destructive way for lengthy periods.

The primary aims of the intervention described below are to improve Annie's emotional regulation and to facilitate development of a shared language for her to begin to verbalize the intensity of her feelings, in a non-threatening, fun way.

This intervention follows on from talking about disappointing things, during which Annie began to become uncomfortable and fidgety.

The therapist announced that we were all going to be trees, standing together in a wood, rooted to the spot. The trees are standing very still, basking in the sunshine, feeling the warmth. Gradually a small breeze begins to rustle the leaves, and rises through a 1–10 scale up to gale force. The group moves accordingly, still rooted to the spot, but with arms and bodies moving about fiercely in all directions, battered by the wind and rain, thunder and lightning. Activity moves down again through the scale, until once again the trees are standing still enjoying the sunshine. (The 1–10 wind scale concept was used later in the session to help Annie talk about levels of anger.)

As her foster carers described her anger, Annie was moving into hyper-arousal triggered by shame. The introduction of an imaginative movement activity engaged her, lowered her level of arousal and brought her back to the group. The circle formation created a secure, equal space where she could see everything that was happening. The latter is particularly important for children who are anxious.

Traumatized children often have underdeveloped skills in the areas of sensory integration, self-regulation, relationship building and cognition (Perry 2015). Children with underdeveloped basic sensory integration skills find it difficult to bring together messages from the seven senses – sight, hearing, smell, taste, touch, proprioceptive (sense of relationship between different parts of their body) and vestibular (sense of relationship of the body to the earth and surrounding space). According to Perry, reparative work on this area is required before more advanced development can occur (Perry 2013). The forest intervention encourages co-ordination between sight, hearing and sense of where the body is in relation to itself, others, and the ground. It took Annie into an unfamiliar mode of movement – rooted to the ground, controlling the escalation and de-escalation of her upper body movement. Such movement exercises help children to experience that they have control over their own body, to decrease muscle tension and to change posture. Relaxation of physical tension is associated with relaxation of emotional tension.

The raising and reduction of arousal levels within each session reinforces pathways that allow the child to use relationship with his adoptive parents/carers to help him to regain equilibrium, in the same way that babies learn to regulate their overpowering emotions through good enough parents matching and lowering their level of affect.

Annie had missed out on this attunement in babyhood. In this exercise, carers and child unconsciously mirror each other's movements as the 'storm' builds, experiencing shared joy in the story and the creativity it engenders together.

The 1–10 measurement of wind speeds was later used as an analogy to provide a language for talking about levels of emotional agitation. The physicality of the movement experience brought the scale to life.

On another level, the intervention has an unspoken – felt rather than articulated – symbolic significance. The subliminal imagery is of the foster family as a glade of trees, different but together, weathering storms but returning to times of peace and enjoyment.

KIYANA AND HER ADOPTIVE MOTHER

Rainbow cloth and balloons – somatic attunement and emotional connection using music and props

Kiyana (aged 13) is of mixed Jamaican and white UK heritage, and was adopted when she was 3 years old. Always challenging, she was placed in residential care a year ago, her single adoptive mother having become increasingly afraid of and stressed by her threatening behaviour. Kiyana and her mother attend therapy sessions fortnightly, with the aim of repairing their relationship, and assessing the possibility of Kiyana returning home. A residential care key worker is also present to enable shared understanding and continuity between therapeutic work in sessions and in the residential setting. The dynamic in therapy reflects the complexity of the situation, allowing this to be observed and worked with.

The therapist introduced a large sheet of translucent rainbow voile and four large balloons, and explained that we would bounce the balloons on the material to atmospheric music. Kiyana briefly joined in and then ran underneath the sheet, hitting the balloons off. After a while Kiyana made connection with Mum, and the therapist invited both to go under the sheet to hit the balloons off. They then lay down under the sheet, hands and feet punching upwards, as the therapists and care worker tried to keep the balloons on. After some time the therapists laid the rainbow sheet over Mum and Kiyana. They lay in a relaxed state as the music continued and moved into a cuddle, with Kiyana (who does not usually reveal her vulnerability) crying softly.

The colourful material and balloons (props chosen for their inability to cause harm) created a playful atmosphere, with play's positive and experimental associations. The music created a shared rhythm. Kiyana and her mother formed an alliance as they joined in a similar kicking and punching movement. The activity allowed Kiyana and her mother to turn movements that had previously been negatively associated with violence into play in which both of them were 'on the same side'. This could perhaps be seen as symbolizing them working towards the common purpose of reunification. As the session continued, the atmospheric music and the movement qualities of the balloons and the voile generated a calm and soothing atmosphere, enhancing a peaceful closeness between Kiyana and her mother, and a release of emotion through tears (very rare for Kiyana).

In the kicking and punching side by side there was complementary rhythm in movement, breath and voice; in the stillness that followed there was physical contact and moulding, as the two bodies nestled into each other. Both phases showed a match of movement qualities and interactive synchrony (changes in gestures or postures that begin and end at the same time), following the focus of the child. Attunement between babies and parents is largely mediated through touch, cradling, movement, shared facial expressions, mutual gaze and embryonic sounds, rather than words. Unconscious mirroring between parent and child builds attachment (Fonagy and Target 1997). The spontaneous moving-together witnessed here replicates the pre-verbal, attachment-building, physical interaction that adopted and looked after children have often missed out on in babyhood.[3]

Schmais (1985, p.23) writes: 'Some rhythmic activities seem conducive to casting a spell-like atmosphere that unites the group.' This session was one of those moments.

There is safety in creative work, which allows release through playing out emotions, allowing emotional distancing while deepening the experience (Grainger 1990).

Conclusion

All of us are physical beings. Western society has tended to focus on the importance of the mind, neglecting the body connection. DMP works on the principle that mind, body and emotions are interconnected, and that a change in one can precipitate a change in the whole system.

Our earliest personality formation took place in our pre-verbal period, through bodily interaction with our prime caregivers. Parental love, or abuse and neglect, were experienced somatically. Children in general more openly experience their emotions in physical terms. For children who have experienced abuse and neglect in their earliest years, interaction in a loving relationship is fundamental to healing. Current research suggests that activities that make for effective progress are rhythmic, repetitive, relational, respectful, relevant and rewarding (Perry 2015). These are all fundamental to DMP, when used with family groups. This chapter has provided descriptions of DMP in practice and the role of the moving body in a therapeutic process, in light of current research and theory. DMP can help address the roots of trauma and problematic attachment behaviours, creatively supporting the child through positive integration into the family unit.

References

Association of Dance Movement Psychotherapists (2015) Accessed at www.admp.org/uk/dance-movement-psychotherapy/what-is-dance-movement-psychotherapy on 14 January 2017.

Blau, B. and Reicher, D. (1995) 'Early Intervention in Children at Risk for Attachment Disorders.' In F. Levy (ed.) *Dance and Other Expressive Arts Therapies*. London: Routledge.

Booth, P. and Jernberg, A. (2010) *Theraplay: Helping Parents and Children Build Relationships through Attachment-Based Play* (3rd edn). San Francisco, CA: Jossey-Bass.

---

3   For further discussion of this in relation to DMP, see Harvey (1995, pp.169–170).

Chaiklin, S. and Schmais, C. (1994) 'The Chase Approach to Dance Therapy.' In P. Lewis (ed.) *Theoretical Approaches in Dance Movement Therapy 1*. Dubuque, IA: Kendall Hunt.

Cohen, J., Mannarino, A. and Deblinger, E. (2006) *Treating Trauma and Traumatic Grief in Children and Adolescents*. New York, NY: Guilford Press.

Devereaux, C. (2008) 'Untying the knots: Dance/movement therapy with a family exposed to domestic violence.' *American Journal of Dance Therapy 30*, 58–70.

Dulicai, D. (2009) 'Family Dance Movement Therapy: A Systems Model.' In S. Chaiklin and H. Wengrower (eds) *The Art and Science of Dance Movement Therapy – Life is Dance*. London: Routledge.

Erfer, T. and Ziv, A. (2006) 'Moving toward cohesion: Group dance movement therapy with children in psychiatry.' *The Arts in Psychotherapy 33*, 3, 234–246.

Etherington, K. (ed.) (2003) *Trauma, the Body and Transformation: A Narrative Inquiry*. London: Jessica Kingsley Publishers.

Fischmann, D. (2009) 'Therapeutic Relationships and Kinesthetic Empathy.' In S. Chaiklin and H. Wengrower (eds) *The Art and Science of Dance Movement Therapy – Life is Dance*. London: Routledge.

Fonagy, P. and Target, M. (1997) 'Attachment and reflective function: Their role in self-organisation.' *Development and Psychopathology 9*, 679–700.

Gerhardt, S. (2004) *Why Love Matters*. Hove: Routledge.

Golding, K. and Hughes, D. (2012) *Creating Loving Attachments*. London: Jessica Kingsley Publishers.

Grainger, R. (1990) *Drama and Healing: The Roots of Dramatherapy*. London: Jessica Kingsley Publishers.

Harvey, S. (1995) 'Sandra: The Case of an Adopted Sexually Abused Child.' In F. Levy (ed.) *Dance and Other Expressive Arts Therapies*. London: Routledge.

Hughes, D. (2007) *Attachment Focused Family Therapy*. New York, NY: W. W. Norton.

Laban, R. and Ullman, L. (1985) *Mastery of Movement* (4th edn). Plymouth: Northcote House.

Levy, F. J. (1988) *Dance Movement Therapy – A Healing Art*. Reston, VA: American Alliance for Health, Physical Education, Recreation and Dance.

Meekums, B. (1992) 'The Love Bugs: Dance Movement Therapy in a Family Service Unit.' In H. Payne (ed.) *Dance Movement Therapy: Theory and Practice*. London: Routledge.

Meekums, B. (2002) *Dance Movement Therapy*. London: Sage.

Perry, B. D. (2001) 'The Neurodevelopmental Impact of Violence in Childhood.' In D. Schetzy and E. P. Benedek (eds) *Textbook of Child and Adolescent Forensic Psychiatry*. Washington, DC: American Psychiatric Press.

Perry, B. D. (2013) 'Foreword.' In M. Heibert, J. Platt, K. Schpok and J. Whitesel (Mount St Vincent Creative Arts Therapy team) *Doodles, Dances and Ditties: A Trauma-Informed Somatosensory Handbook*. Denver, CO: Mount St Vincent Home.

Perry, B. D. (2015) 'Foreword.' In C. Malchiodi (ed.) *Creative Interventions with Traumatised Children*. New York, NY: Guilford Press.

Perry, B. D. and Dobson, C. (2013) 'The Neurosequential Model (NMT) in Maltreated Children.' In J. Ford and C. Curtois (eds) *Treating Complex Traumatic Stress Disorders in Children and Adolescents*. New York, NY: Guildford Press.

Perry, B. D. and Szalavitz, M. (2006) *The Boy Who Was Raised as a Dog*. New York, NY: Basic Books.

Rogers, C. (1951) *Client-Centred Therapy*. London: Constable & Company.

Rogers, C. (1961) *On Becoming a Person*. New York, NY: Houghton Mifflin.

Rothschild, B. (2000) *The Body Remembers: The Psychophysiology of Trauma and Trauma Treatment*. New York, NY: W. W. Norton.

Rothschild, B. (2003) *The Body Remembers Casebook*. New York, NY: W. W. Norton.

Russell, T. A. and Arcuri, S. M. (2015) 'A neurophysiological and neuropsychological consideration of mindful movement: Clinical and research implications.' *Frontiers in Human Neuroscience 9*, 282.

Sandel, S., Chaiklin, S. and Lohn, A. (eds) (1993) *The Foundations of Dance Movement Psychotherapy: The Life and Work of Marian Chace*. Columbia, MD: American Dance Therapy Association.

Schmais, C. (1985) 'Healing processes in group dance therapy.' *American Journal of Dance Therapy 8*, 1, 17–36.

Schore, A. (2011) 'Joy and Fun. Gene. Neurobiology. Child Brain Development.' Speaking on www.youtube.com on 11 July 2011, accessed on 1 September 2015.

Stanton-Jones, K. (1992) *An Introduction to Dance Movement Therapy in Psychiatry*. London: Routledge.

Tortora, S. (2009) 'Dance/Movement Psychotherapy in Early Childhood Treatment.' in S. Chaiklin and H. Wengrower (eds) *The Art and Science of Dance Movement Therapy – Life is Dance*. London: Routledge.

Treefoot, A. (2008) *Moving Together: Enhancing Early Attachment Using Dance Movement Therapy*. Auckland, New Zealand: Whitecliffe College of Arts and Design.

van der Kolk, B. (2014) *The Body Keeps the Score: Mind, Brain and Body in the Transformation of Trauma*. New York, NY: Viking Penguin.

Wesselmann, D., Schweitzer, C. and Armstrong, S. (2014) *Integrative Team Treatment for Attachment Trauma in Children: Family Therapy and EMDR*. New York, NY: W. W. Norton.

PART 3

COMPLEX TRAUMA AND CREATIVE PRACTICE IN EDUCATION

Chapter 11

ADAPTING TO WORKING IN SCHOOLS WITH THE FAMILY FUTURES' NEURO PHYSIOLOGICAL APPROACH

—————————— Marion Allen ——————————

Introduction

This chapter outlines common difficulties experienced in school by children with a history of complex trauma, and offers a supportive approach to manage these with tried and tested strategies. Family Futures' Neuro Physiological approach is described in Chapter 5. The rationale for the strategies described here are based on this understanding. The research by Bessel van der Kolk (2005), Perry and Pollard (1997) and their associates is fundamental to this understanding. They show how in-utero and early trauma can lead to behaviours and learning difficulties that are very specific to this cohort of children. UK writers (Bomber 2007; Bomber and Hughes 2013; Cairns and Stanway 2004; Fursland, Cairns and Stanway 2013; Geddes 2006) have explored how attachment difficulties and early adverse care need to be understood in order to help children in education. The impact of trauma on the development of executive functioning skills has been examined by Lansdown, Burnell and Allen (2007), Cooper-Kahn and Dietzel (2008), Allen (2008) and Meltzer (2010).

Throughout the chapter, vignettes are used to highlight difficulties and suggest possible strategies to help the child.

'Learn the child'

Within the book *Supporting Education* by Fursland and colleagues (2013), the first tip, 'Learn the child', focuses on the child's narrative, his strengths and difficulties, and the impact of childhood neglect and trauma. The importance of learning about a child's strengths and difficulties and his origin in childhood trauma is central to a school's ability to understand behaviour and introduce a more supportive educational environment. It may be that the child is unable to access his cognitive brain because his primitive and mid-brain states are constantly activated; he may experience a high level of fear and anxiety at school and may demonstrate the primitive responses of fight, flight and freeze.

MICHAEL

Michael (aged 10) lives in kinship care with his maternal grandparents following horrendous abuse from his birth father. He was quickly triggered into the fight and flight response within the school setting, especially when daily routines were upset. Just before the Christmas break, a time that produced particularly harrowing memories as well as a time in school when normal lessons are frequently disrupted, Michael was reprimanded for talking in assembly. He immediately dysregulated, running through school, dismantling displays and decorations, and eventually ran out of the school grounds.

A small trigger for Michael leads to a major outburst at school, which needs an understanding response. This can only be given if staff have background knowledge that puts his behaviour into a context. This background information may be gathered from many sources: caregivers, educational psychologist, paediatric occupational therapist, Child and Adolescent Mental Health Services (CAMHS), an Education, Health and Care Plan, and school behavioural logs.

Observing a child at school in different lessons and at play is another important way of gathering information. This will give information about a child's peer relations, emotional regulation and his ability to manage transitions, start tasks independently and plan, organize and execute them.

KELLY

Kelly (aged 7), a child in foster care, spent much of an observation fidgeting and getting out of her chair but never at the teacher's request. When given work, Kelly moved to sharpen an already sharp pencil, distracting others en-route. When the teacher asked the class questions Kelly shouted out answers despite being asked to allow others an opportunity to respond. During the lesson she wrote only four words. As the teacher started to collect the books, Kelly smuggled hers into her desk and went to the toilet without asking permission. At play, she was clearly angry and became involved in peer arguments, and then stormed off on her own.

From this observation we learn that Kelly is sensory-seeking and needs sensory strategies and resources. She clearly has difficulties with the executive functioning skills of 'initiate', 'plan and organize', 'inhibit' and 'emotional control'. She was visibly shamed about her inability to complete work and was unable to move from feelings the shame triggered.

Working with school staff

Acknowledging the everyday challenges and expectations placed on schools and teaching staff must be part of the work in schools. Teachers feel supported if they are provided with information helping to explain the rationale of the child's behaviour, and are offered strategies to help the pupil. Often these can be used to benefit other pupils.

NICHOLAS

Nicholas (aged 8) has lived in kinship with an aunt since he was 5 years old. He frequently became extremely agitated about minor incidents in the classroom when he had to be reprimanded. In his early years with his birth family he had always been blamed for any difficulties with his siblings. It seemed important that now his feelings of unfairness were validated and a strategy implemented to enable him to move his mind-set on from these classroom incidents. The teacher placed a small plastic dustbin on her desk, and invited him to write his feelings about these incidents down and throw them in the bin. This helped Nicholas move on, and two weeks later the teacher expressed surprise at how many other children were using the bin.

Ongoing support for teachers, mentors or assistants supports staff in their understanding that one day a certain strategy may work and on another it has no impact. Sometimes it is possible to pre-empt a difficulty by addressing a particular subject in the context of therapy.

ELLEN

Ellen (aged 11) was adopted after suffering sexual abuse by her birth father. Family Futures borrowed the school's sex education resources before her class was given these lessons as it was acknowledged that she was likely to find this extremely difficult. By addressing the issue in the therapy programme, she was able to manage the school lessons without dysregulating.

Without knowledge of the possible holistic impact of early developmental trauma, it can be extremely hard for teaching staff to understand behaviour. With this knowledge, an understanding emerges that can lead to a more empathic approach. The child feels understood and thus is able to start to develop an internalized sense of safety, which improves emotion regulation.

Supporting the caregiver in relation to the school

Some traumatized children may be overcome by the need for compliance, exerting all their efforts into being accepted by behaving in a manner perceived as socially and emotionally acceptable. This behaviour at school can lead to heightened externalized behaviour at home, rather like a bottle of fizzy liquid exploding when the lid is removed after being agitated.

JENNY

Jenny (aged 6) was newly placed for adoption. She had suffered extreme abuse in her birth family and little attention in a foster placement. In her new primary school she worked hard to fit in. She took on a compliant persona so that she was not noticed, and appeared to be behaving and managing well. In fact she was in a permanent state of anxiety and struggled with peer relations and reaching her educational potential. This took its toll so that at home she became dysregulated and demonstrated her frustrations and fear in verbal aggression and overt physical violence towards her adoptive mother. Anxious that Jenny might be taken away from them, her prospective adoptive parents did not share their difficulties for a long time. When at last they did so, the school staff sympathized but said they did not see any of these difficulties in the school setting. They needed help to think holistically and understand that behind Jenny's compliance at school was a high degree of anxiety that was contributing to her behaviour at home.

Some permanent new caregivers or adoptive parents are great advocates for their child and fight for the additional help they need; others struggle to do this within the educational and professional network and need an advocate themselves. The behaviour of a child with complex trauma is often bewildering and exhausting and can be isolating for both the child and the family. Support networks can diminish over time as relations, friends, the child's peers and their parents fail to understand the child's behaviour. Being labelled as 'the naughty child's parents' is extremely upsetting and isolating.

Many of these children do not reach their academic potential. For those who are obviously struggling academically, this is usually addressed; but for children who are achieving to the required level, despite their academic potential being somewhat higher, this may not be registered. This is another situation in which parents and caregivers of children with complex difficulties need support. This may be on an informal footing; sometimes knowing that somebody understands and cares is enough. For others much more active involvement with school staff and specialist educational services is needed.

Time at home

When a comprehensive multi-disciplinary assessment has been completed by Family Futures, it may indicate the need for the child to spend some time at home with his carer on a one-to-one basis. This may be especially so when siblings have been placed together or where the child immediately starts an educational placement on arriving at the new carer's home. An afternoon a week at home can provide the child and caregiver with 'bonding' time, which is essential for developing a more secure attachment. For new placements Family Futures recommends a period of time at home allowing the 'new' family to get to know each other and to give the child time to start feeling safe and secure in this new family before facing the anxiety of a new school. Children often benefit from a gradual introduction to school with a phased entry alongside some home learning. Family Futures uses the four elements of Theraplay – the appropriate level of structure, nurture, engagement and developmental challenge to facilitate the bonding process at these times (Booth and Jernberg 2009).

During the school year there may be occasions when attendance at school is too difficult for the child. For example, Michael, in the example earlier, may have benefited from spending time at home instead of having to manage the disruption of the last week of the Christmas term, especially as it was known that this time of the year was particularly hard for him.

Of course attendance at school (or structured home education) is crucial to a child's learning, and the decision for the child to spend time out of school should not be taken lightly, but there may be occasions when being at home rather than school is more beneficial for the child's development, mental health and education.

Delays in executive functioning

Even if the child is functioning in his cognitive brain, it may be that the development of executive functioning is delayed, which can effect learning, emotional stability, self-organization, working memory, self-monitoring and the ability to manage transitions.

JANE

Jane (aged 8) was an academically able adopted child who seemed to manage well in school although she struggled at times with peer relations. She was supported in mathematics, which she found more difficult, but otherwise teachers did not identify any difficulties. However, as Jane progressed through the education system with increased expectations for independent learning, she struggled to manage the everyday organization of her work, particularly starting and completing tasks. Jane worked incredibly hard to hide these difficulties as she desperately wanted to be like her peers, but during observations it was clear she was unable to follow instructions and needed more structure and scaffolding. It was observed that she would watch others and copy them. Her work started to deteriorate. Once school understood the problems and extra support was provided, alongside Jane meeting a mentor at the beginning and end of the school day to help with the transition, her work started to improve. Although Jane did not need an adult by her side constantly, she did need an adult who could monitor her and move in at the beginning of tasks to support her in her understanding, processing and planning.

Sensory regulation

Children's sensory needs must be met to enable academic learning. For many pupils this involves regular movement and the need for adults to be leading the movement, perhaps giving the child tasks such as distributing books and taking messages but also incorporating more structured movement by using a trampoline, pull-up bar, spinning, hanging upside down on wall bars, etc.

FREDDY

Freddy (aged 7), a child in foster care, was extremely sensory-seeking. Teaching staff implemented a 'sensory diet' suggested by Family Futures' occupational therapist, and this improved Freddy's ability to focus. Sensory breaks were built into the day, with the programme incorporating walks around the school wearing a weighted rucksack (as deep pressure across his shoulders soothed him), time in the gym on pull-up bars and time on the trampette.[1] Freddy enjoyed the fun challenges built into these sensory breaks, and school found his concentration improved. The programme involved several breaks during the day, and as teaching staff became more attuned to his bodily reactions, they were better able to time the breaks according to his need.

Fellow pupils were supported in understanding that Freddy needed the extra break to help him concentrate, just as other children needed support with their reading or mathematics.

It is important to recognize sensory needs, as these are part of the foundation for self-regulation. The sensory-seeking child needs movement whereas the sensory-defensive child needs a 'quieter' environment.

SALLY

Sally (aged 14) was in foster care. She was particularly sensory-sensitive. She found managing her affect in noisy, busy settings extremely difficult, and avoided such environments if possible. Within the class setting, she managed very formal, quiet lessons but struggled to complete tasks within practical lessons as she was constantly impacted by low-level noise surrounding her. Permitting headphones playing her choice of calming music allowed her to complete her work in record time.

ADRIAN

Adrian (aged 7) was adopted and he struggled to stand in queues where others could accidentally brush against him. To support him, he was accompanied by an adult to stand at the front of the lunch queue. This enabled him to know he was safe from accidental touch of others and also addressed his internalized fear that the food might run out, following early experiences of severe hunger and deprivation. This

---

1   Trampettes/mini-trampolines are reasonably priced. Once schools recognize the benefit of sensory breaks for one child, they often identify others who benefit from similar strategies.

avoided the daily 'meltdown', and over time, a carefully structured plan and continued sensory work supported him in managing to stand within the line.

An understanding of how 'light touch' can be dysregulating for some children can allow procedures to be implemented to minimize risk.

Emotion regulation – somatic work, mentalization and external regulators

Somatic work is important too. This involves supporting the child in understanding his bodily reactions and emotions – for example, through emotion resources or verbalized observations. Allowing opportunities for mentalization and mindfulness can also support him in managing emotions and the daily stress patterns that have been established (Midgley and Vrouva 2012).

Key adult support is vital to support the child from dysregulating. In 'good enough' parenting the parent is the child's external regulator as he moves from dependence to independence. In those early days, as the baby starts to move away very gradually into the outside world, the parent or substitute figure guides and protects him. A child who did not have consistent and supportive parenting, or whose caregivers were neglectful or abusive, is unlikely to have mastered self-regulation. The provision of a key adult, as an external regulator and with whom the child can develop a trusting relationship, is crucial.

Validation of the child's feelings, difficulties and needs, and understanding the child's perception, are essential. What may seem a very small issue to an adult can be extremely challenging for a traumatized child. The phraseology used, warnings of changes or activities that may be challenging, and offers of support to manage can transform how a traumatized child manages in school.

Separation loss and attachment security

In the Neuro Physiological Psychotherapeutic approach, separation, loss and attachment security are linked to the mid-brain or limbic brain. The key strategy to help these children is to have an adult within the school setting to act as an attachment figure. This helps facilitate their developing Internal Working Models of adults being safe and caring, and supports self-regulation. This in turn allows better access to learning.

JOHNNY

Johnny (aged 6) was a prospective adopted boy who struggled to concentrate on his work within the classroom. He was acutely hypervigilant, a survival strategy learned when in his abusive birth home, and as soon as somebody spoke or entered the room, he focused on them. When supported individually, he was able gradually to develop an internalized sense of safety; sometimes he and his learning assistant would work together in a quiet space and slowly he was able to feel safe enough in the classroom to work when his learning assistant was close.

SUZIE

Suzie (aged 5) was adopted. She had seemed to settle well into school, enjoying the school day in Reception in informal play, listening to stories, etc. At home time, however, Suzie would meet her adoptive mother with screams and tantrums, indicating her internalized fears and demonstrating that she was not feeling as secure as she seemed. School agreed that Suzie's mother could spend time in class to help the transition and to help Suzie identify school as a 'safe' place and know her mother was still going to be there at the end of the day.

Transitional objects from home, photos, permission to make phone calls and the ability to hear messages are useful strategies to help children.

LISA, FREDDIE AND SAMEERA

Lisa (aged 6) was adopted and had experienced 12 placements in her short life. She had a pencil case with slots for photos of her adoptive family, a 'beating heart' cushion she was allowed to use when feeling stressed, and a 'talking tin' with a recorded message from her mother. All these helped her to know she was being 'kept in mind' by her family when she was at school.

Freddie (aged 16) was in foster care and was given a small pebble to keep in his pocket every day, as did all members of the family to provide the link when they were apart.

Sameera (aged 7) was supported by a learning assistant but found it difficult when her supporting adult had breaks during the day. The adult provided her with an object to look after for her when she went on her break and used a timer so Sameera knew when to expect her back.

Challenge

Regarding the level of challenges, tasks need to be differentiated according to the child's capabilities academically, emotionally, socially, physically and neurologically. This leads to raised self-esteem through positivity and success. By providing success criteria, the child knows and understands what he needs to do to get things 'right'. Self-esteem is a step towards reflective capacity, an important factor in self-monitoring.

LEANNE

Leanne (aged 14), an adopted girl, was inspired by a lesson and spent three hours completing homework. She was devastated when it was marked low as she had not covered the points the teacher had wanted.

By providing success criteria, pupils (and parents when supervising homework) can see whether they have covered the necessary points, avoiding this scenario.

TRACEY

Tracey (aged 8) was in foster care. She did not have the fine-motor skills required for writing although she had good ideas. School introduced a computer dictate program and taught Tracey to use this. Alongside this the school and parents helped Tracey develop her manipulative skills with non-shaming activities.

Sometimes it can be a sensory or physical difficulty that impinges on a child's academic progress. Early neglect can lead to underdeveloped muscle tone, gross-motor and fine-motor skills.

GEORGE

George (aged 13) lived in foster care following early abuse. He was an extremely articulate boy who often gave correct and intuitive answers, and contributed well to discussion. However, his written work and homework tasks never reflected his verbal ability. His executive dysfunctioning hampered progress. George struggled to plan and organize his work and because of this he did not try. When this was recognized and he received adult support, chunking tasks into manageable steps and helping structure his ideas, George gained confidence.

Teachers may recognize a child as being academically able and, understandably, give him a more demanding challenge. It is easy to expect an academically able student to manage but there are many factors that impinge on the child's ability to achieve his academic potential.

SUKI

Suki (aged 15) became overwhelmed by the project and coursework expected in Year 10. Although she was academically able, her underdeveloped executive functioning skills of 'initiate', 'plan and organize' and 'organizing resources' meant she was falling behind and missing important deadlines. Her special educational needs co-ordinator (SENCO) recognized this and arranged teachers to support Suki in timetabling the completion of tasks. Without this unified approach of staff, Suki would have been unable to submit her work for evaluation.

Structure and routines

A major factor in helping the child feel 'safe' is to ensure predictability and routine. Traumatized children often need to know exactly what is planned. These children may need plenty of structure, timetables, visual plans and strategies for managing the shift between activities within lessons and between different lessons.

All children need boundaries. A child who has experienced early neglect and/or abuse needs to know he will be safe if adults are in charge. Boundaries need to be clear, consistent and manageable. If the child cannot manage a rule or social expectation, this needs to be recognized and staff need to adjust expectations and adapt the setting or provide the level of support necessary.

ALEX

For Alex (aged 7), a child in long-term foster care, school assembly was too demanding on his neurological and sensory systems. He shifted around the hall on his bottom, distracted other children and made noises. Allowing him to be excused temporarily and using the time in sensory work followed by a gradual introduction to assembly with strategies in place (i.e. being close to a trusted adult and allowing a sensory resource for fiddling) were enough to enable him over time to manage.

It may be that a child manages within the structure of lessons but struggles in unstructured activities. The provision of a trusted adult to act as an external regulator in the playground can provide the boundaried protection that the child so desperately needs.

KEVIN

Kevin (aged 7), an adopted child, had experienced profound trauma in his early life. He needed to know that the adult in the playground was keeping him safe. She would wear a bright red tabard so that wherever Kevin was he could see her. This was all he required to manage in the playground.

Some schools implement clubs for vulnerable pupils, which include physical activities. For many of these children physical movement helps self-regulation so it is vital they have opportunities like this.

Homework

For many traumatized children the completion of homework at home proves too challenging, causing unnecessary family stress. Schools have implemented different approaches – setting a minimum amount, allowing completion of homework at school and/or providing specific adult support within school. It is vital that completion of homework at school is not perceived as punishment for the child and is not scheduled into his break times.

Within lessons it is important to make learning manageable for the child who struggles to plan and organize, initiate tasks or use his working memory. Chunking, structure, prompting, 'errorless learning',[2] simple instructions, idea-generating methods, memory methods and self-monitoring techniques all help.

Sexualized behaviour

The impact of sexual abuse – both being abused oneself and witnessing sexualized activity – can lead to the child acting out sexually within the home and/or school settings. This can include (and this list is not exhaustive) being sexually provocative, using inappropriate or sexualized language, enticing others into sexual activity, inappropriate touch, sexual violence or sexual allegations.

Of course, of primary importance here is to keep the child, other children and adults safe and to monitor the situation.

It is important the child feels safe within the setting and that support is in place to keep the child regulated. This may involve sensory strategies to address the child's nervous system and/or the presence of a trusted adult. Once these aspects are addressed, some cognitive strategies can be implemented.

---

2   Errorless learning is a teaching approach whereby the pupil does not make mistakes as he explores and learns new concepts. It involves adjusting one's expectations, working collaboratively with the pupil, anticipating problems and providing prompts, repetition and consolidation. It is beneficial for highly anxious pupils who lack confidence and have low self-esteem, and particularly appropriate for students who struggle to remember and internalize their learning because of reduced memory skills.

GAVIN

Gavin (aged 8) was newly placed in foster care. He was prone to masturbate in class so he had a photograph on his desk with his hands above the desk as a reminder. Of course a 'script' may need to be given to explain the strategy to other pupils without shaming the child. This idea can be used for other reminders too – for example, a photo with a raised hand for the child who shouts out answers. It may be that the child needs to use a separate toilet, and a 'script' can be provided to ensure confidentiality and self-esteem.

Sometimes adaptations need to be made to the environment or one's expectations.

MARK

Within one school the possibility and practicality of Mark (aged 10), an adopted boy who had suffered early traumatic sexual abuse, being included in a residential adventure week was questioned as he had previously acted out sexually at school. As a result, the school had implemented daily support in order to keep him and others safe. The school was intent on including him and so rented a separate chalet and took two extra members of staff, thus eliminating any worries of him in a dormitory situation and ensuring the safety of the adults against any possible allegations.

Primary and secondary schools and the transition

The structure and demands of secondary school are very different from those of primary school. This transition is massively challenging for all children, but for the traumatized child, fears are intensified. It is vital these children have a well-structured transition programme: visiting the school many times with a trusted adult and being introduced to prospective teaching staff. Focusing on one concern at a time can break down the wall of fear for the child. Once within the school, the initial induction measures in place at the start need to continue. It will almost certainly take longer for a child with this background to develop a sense of safety and familiarity.

Within the secondary setting the cortical brain is in constant demand and it is often at this stage that executive-functioning difficulties become more noticeable. For example, a pupil who struggles with the constant transition between classes may be unable to function well at the beginning and end of lessons. Supporting the pupil in set rituals can help. Teachers can help by ensuring homework is given out and explained during the lesson rather than at the beginning or end.

For children whose working memory is underdeveloped, remembering instructions can be challenging. Staff need to provide the student with simple instructions, checking in a non-shaming manner to see if he has heard, understood and processed them. These children may need extra scaffolding when approaching tasks, with 'chunking' strategies to manage tasks in small steps and help in highlighting the important facts.

The impact of some school behaviour policies

JOSHUA

Joshua (aged 13) was an adopted boy who was constantly in trouble at school for defiance and lack of attention. In fact Joshua experienced heightened anxiety following harrowing early trauma. He was easily shamed and quickly triggered into primitive-brain reactions. He rapidly moved along the sanctions procedures and spent considerable time in isolation, where he was given tasks such as copying out school rules – rules he was emotionally and neurophysiologically unable to manage without constant adult support.

Existing expectations and systems within the education system may provide an impossible scenario for a young person whose early life trauma has left him incapable of self-regulation. Busy, open-plan settings; large institutions; days that involve numerous transitions and shifts of expectations; behaviour policies that include rewards and sanctions; detentions; isolation areas; or charts for escalating behaviour – all are immense challenges for the traumatized child whose neurological, sensory, emotional and adrenal systems may be impacted or underdeveloped. Already harbouring an incredibly low level of self-esteem, the first signs of being unable to manage can quickly escalate into dysregulated behaviour, sanctions and exclusion. For many the self-fulfilling prophesy of failure can quickly become reality.

BENN

Benn (aged 7) was in foster care. When asked by his teacher to move his name down the behaviour chart, he threw his name in the litter bin. Benn had spent his early years in an environment where the adults treated him as unworthy of attention. He had an internalized belief that he was 'rubbish'.

This is a metaphor for all traumatized children in educational settings that do not understand that the child has not reached the holistic developmental milestones expected for his age. The expectations and systems need to be modified throughout the child's education to ensure that he remains engaged in education and is offered the best possible opportunity to become a responsible and caring adult.

A child whose neurological development has been impacted by trauma often wants to manage the school day, desperately wanting to be like his peers and trying hard to manage. It is important to understand that we are not providing an 'excuse' for the child's behaviour, but the rationale. Of course the child needs to conform to meet the expectations of everyday life, the workplace, further education and family life, but the traumatized child often needs a high level of understanding and support to reach these milestones alongside adaptations to expectations and environment.

Conclusion

The strategies suggested are aimed at helping children with a history of complex trauma have a better chance of managing and learning in mainstream school. This approach will challenge some long-standing classroom methods and management. Some behaviour policies, particularly those that evoke shame, will need to be adapted or changed. For the child whose body and brain have not reached the same level of development as expected for his biological age, the school setting, expectations and curriculum can be overwhelming and non-accessible. Many of these children, both primary and secondary, spend time out of the classroom because of the demands placed on them. The school system needs to be tweaked to help them to manage.

Across the country, new legislation (Academies Act 2010; Education Act 2011) has led to the establishment of smaller education settings in which there is greater freedom to provide for the traumatized child. In these schools the focus is on, first, ensuring that children feel safe and secure, and, second, adapting the structure to allow learning within their neurological, emotional, sensory and academic capability. This type of education has benefits for all children.

References

Allen, M. (2008) *Attachment, Developmental Trauma and Executive Functioning Difficulties in the School Setting.* London: Family Futures.

Bomber, L. M. (2007) *Inside I'm Hurting: Practical Strategies for Supporting Children with Attachment Difficulties in Schools.* Duffield: Worth Publishing.

Bomber, L. M. and Hughes, D. A. (2013) *Settling Troubled Pupils to Learn: Why Relationships Matter in School.* Duffield: Worth Publishing.

Booth, P. B. and Jernberg, A. M. (2009) *Theraplay: Helping Parents and Children Build Better Relationships through Attachment-Based Play.* San Francisco, CA: Jossey-Bass.

Cairns, K. and Stanway, C. (2004) *Learn the Child – Helping Looked After Children to Learn.* London: BAAF.

Cooper-Khan, J. and Dietzel, L. (2008) *Late, Lost and Unprepared.* Bethesda, MD: Woodbine House.

Fursland, E., Cairns, K. and Stanway, C. (2013) *10 Top Tips for Supporting Education.* London: BAAF.

Geddes, H. (2006) *Attachment in the Classroom.* Duffield: Worth Publishing.

Lansdown, R. Burnell, A. and Allen, M. (2007) 'Is it that they won't do it, or is it that they can't? Executive functioning and children who have been fostered and adopted.' *Adoption and Fostering Journal* 31, 2, 44–53.

Meltzer, L. (2010) *Executive Function in Education from Theory to Practice.* New York, NY: Guilford Press.

Midgley, N. and Vrouva, I. (2012) *Minding the Child.* London: Routledge.

Perry, B. D. and Pollard, R. (1997) 'Altered Brain Development following Global Neglect in Early Childhood.' The Child Trauma Academy. Society for Neuroscience, Annual Meeting, New Orleans.

van der Kolk, B. (2005) 'Developmental trauma disorder: Toward a rational diagnosis for children with complex trauma histories.' *Psychiatric Annals 35*, 5, 401–408.

UK Acts of Parliament

Academies Act (2010) Ch. 32. Available at www.legislation.gov.uk/ukpga/2010/32/contents, accessed on 12 November 2016.

Education Act (2011) Ch. 21. Available at www.legislation.gov.uk/ukpga/2011/21/contents/enacted, accessed on 12 November 2016.

Further reading

Ayres, A. J. (2005) *Sensory Integration and the Child* (25th Anniversary edn). Los Angleles, CA: Western Psychological Services.

Bomber, L. M. (2010) *What About Me? Inclusive Strategies to Support Pupils with Attachment Difficulties Make It Through the School Day*. Richmond: Worth Publishing.

Bowlby, J. (2005) *A Secure Base*. London: Routledge.

Burdick, D. (2014) *Mindfulness Skills for Kids and Teens: A Workbook for Clinicians & Clients with 154 Tools, Techniques, Activities and Worksheet*. Eau Claire, WI: PESI Publishing & Media.

Dawson, P. and Guare, R. (2004) *Executive Skills in Children and Adolescents*. New York, NY: Guilford Press.

Dawson, P. and Guare, R. (2009) *Smart but Scattered*. New York, NY: Guilford Press.

Forbes, H. T. and Post, B. B. (2006) *Beyond Consequences, Logic, and Control: A Love-Based Approach to Helping Children with Severe Behaviours*. Boulder, CO: Beyond Consequences Institute.

Gioia, G. A., Isquith, P. K., Guy, S. C. and Kenworthy, L. (2000) *Behaviour Rating Inventory of Executive Function – Professional Manual*. Lutz, FL: PAR Psychological Assessment Resources.

McCullough, E., Gordon-Jones, S., Last, A., Vaughan, J. and Burnell, A. (2016) 'An evaluation of Neuro-Physiological Psychotherapy: An integrative therapeutic approach to working with adopted children who have experienced early life trauma.' *Clinical Child Psychology and Psychiatry 21*, 4, 582–602.

Meltzer, L. (2010) *Promoting Executive Function in the Classroom*. New York, NY: Guilford Press.

Post, B. (2009) *The Great Behaviour Breakdown*. Palmyra, VA: Post Institutes and Associates LLC.

Snel, E. (2014) *Sitting Still Like a Frog: Mindfulness Exercises for Kids (and Their Parents)*. Boulder, CO: Shambhala Publications.

Tileston, D. W. (2004) *What Every Teacher Should Know About Learning, Memory, and the Brain*. Thousand Oaks, CA: Corwin Press.

Chapter 12

RULES, RELATIONSHIPS AND RIPPLES

Therapy in a Specialist Residential School

—— SARAH AYACHE AND MARTIN GIBSON ——

Introduction

Ten years ago a trial into the introduction of a psychotherapy service was conceived at our residential school, a specialist provision for boys with social, emotional and behavioural difficulties. At that time, our observation that students were entering the school with increasingly complex presentations at a younger age, a trend supported by evidence from Cole and Knowles (2011), meant that we needed more understanding and support both for the boys and staff alike.

In considering recent research, which highlights that half the people who suffer from long-term mental health problems have the onset of symptoms before the age of 14 (DOH 2011), it is apparent that therapeutic input is needed as early as possible if there is to be any chance of changing the course of many of these boys' lives. In addition, an acknowledgement that schools like ours seem to be facing an enormous challenge in educating pupils, who present with what Carpenter (2010) describes as a tsunami of new conditions, suggests that our rationale to adapt our provision was quite insightful.

From a humble beginning of three part-time, sessional therapists we have developed a dedicated, dynamic, multi-disciplinary therapy team, which is now embedded in the school. This chapter describes some of the learning and challenges we have been privileged to experience since the introduction of therapies into this setting.

The setting

The school is in Northern England and provides specialist education to around 60 boys from the age of 7 to 19, all referred by local authorities within roughly an 80-mile radius. Approximately two-thirds of boys are residential, with the remainder attending daily. All students spend weekends and school holidays at home, which may be with biological parents, in kinship care, with adoptive parents, with foster carers or in Residential Children's Homes. Approximately 25 per cent of boys in the school are in substitute care, the population which our composite vignettes in this chapter focus on. All the boys have Statements of Special Educational Needs (SEN) (or Education, Health and Care Plans) and have usually been permanently excluded from several mainstream schools, leading to experience of pupil referral units, home tuition or long periods of absence from formal education.

The site has a community feel, with three distinct sets of buildings and their associated staff departments: education, care and therapies. Staff and boys sleep on site during the week, living together like enlarged families, with care staff supporting boys through their personal and social development.

The presenting difficulties

The school often becomes the most solid, consistent point in a child's life, when home placements have previously broken down and education has battled to engage him. Despite being primarily commissioned as an educational placement, we increasingly become the detective seeking those places and agencies that are supporting or have previously supported the student. We become the social worker engaging the family and negotiating to understand its dynamics. We become the child's second home and assess his interactions, capacities for friendships and abilities to function in social situations. We become his therapist to look at the world from his viewpoint, thinking about what his behaviour communicates and what he really thinks relationships and the world are all about, and trying to uncover how his experiences have shaped him. We try to provide a foundation to build trust and someone to lean on for support; and yet underneath it all, the expectation is to teach. We are a specialist provision for complex children, with training, experience and expertise at hand.

However, our mainstream counterparts are increasingly expected to adopt these roles and responsibilities too.

These boys have been referred to us because they have been unmanageable in education and carers have received numerous phone calls describing their unacceptable behaviour. The predominant message is that their child cannot be contained. For a family (or supporting team) approaching a new school, feelings of trepidation, fear and anxiety are to be expected. For a pupil to approach our school with a psychological armoury of aggressive behaviour, false confidence, mistrust, propensity to test out and reluctance to engage with adults for fear of being let down, again, is almost the norm.

ALAN: AN OVERVIEW OF A STUDENT

Alan (aged 11) is currently in kinship care and has experienced numerous placement changes since he was removed from his birth family. His relationship with his early caregiver was inconsistent and problematic, furthered by substance misuse and domestic violence, which he witnessed.

In behavioural and emotional terms Alan exhibits obsessive and compulsive traits and high levels of anxiety – he experiences phobias, has an eating disorder and has in the past resorted to self-harming. His self-esteem is low, with little sense of identity and a reluctance to trust others, so he has problems forming successful relationships. The content of his conversations revolves around the 'darker side of life' (e.g. demonic and satanic rituals) and he is seen as being very adept at drawing adults into discussions around these subjects, which fuels his fascination and creates task avoidance. This distraction and interaction causes him to become over-excited, and he then struggles to calm down and refocus. Alan's very caring nature, combined with his anxiety, can also mean that he gets extremely homesick, worrying about his carers during the week.

From an educational perspective, Alan is described as having complex learning difficulties, particularly in relation to mathematical concepts, writing, numeracy skills, processing of information at speed and reasoning with visual and spatial information. Whilst he attends some lessons and can demonstrate engagement, he is easily distracted, particularly by his peers and through interaction with adults. Alan displays a vast level of natural curiosity and an eagerness to learn, but this can lead to investigation and discussion unrelated to the actual class topic.

In Alan's case it seems likely that, as described by O'Neill *et al.* (2010), the consequences of trauma from an abusive environment and disorganized attachment relationship have made the increased likelihood of a risk of multiple academic and behavioural challenges a reality.

A secure base

As one of the first therapists on site, my observation is that a key to the success of the therapy department and its integration into the school community has been the strength of its founder, my co-author, Martin. His calm manner evokes respect, trust and a natural desire from staff to do the best they can. As a well-established senior leader he created the secure base for the therapists to work from with reference to current research and national policies, buffering us from scepticism from all sides and creating a structure in which to work. He trusted our thoughts, opinions and the individual therapeutic processes we were dedicated to and allowed us to influence the development of the service. He has contained us as we have negotiated the journey of engaging and working with these children.

MANAGING ANXIETY

As I negotiated the fine line of trust with one of the more volatile boys I was working with, I found the balance tipped out of my favour as he swiped an expensive piece of equipment from the office and made off out of the building with it tucked neatly under his arm. As I went across campus in pursuit, somewhat flustered and slightly panicked, I was thinking to myself, 'How on earth am I going to resolve this!?' I passed my manager and quickly explained to him what was going on. His response as he carried on walking by was, 'Well, if the boys did what you expected, it wouldn't be such an interesting job.' His calmness gave me containment of my anxiety. The lightness of his response re-grounded me.

The fact that he carried on walking showed that he had faith in me to manage. And so I did.

The therapy team

Our service has developed considerably since its conception, always keeping in mind the client group and aiming to provide the best service for its complexity of need. We recognize that long-term work is essential and it can take up to 12 months to gain trust and find a way to begin the therapeutic work to address the primary reasons for referral. The foundations are possibly the most important part of the work. Our interventions tend to span years, with regular reassessments by the team to make sure the therapist and discipline is still the best match to the boys' developing needs.

We work holistically to consider the needs of the whole child. Our on-site location provides connection with others' observations in a variety of different settings: education, care, off-site trips, home visits. We form part of an internal 'Team Around the Child', regularly thinking with teachers, learning-support assistants and care workers, supporting the development of the child and his relationships with others.

The psychotherapeutic aspect of the team is predominantly creative psychotherapy from the disciplines of art, music and drama. These are complemented by a horticultural therapist, neuro-linguistic programming (NLP) practitioner, social counsellor and family counsellor. Further multi-disciplinary aspects are added to the team by our speech and language therapists and occupational therapists. The theoretical interests of the team span child development, psychodynamics, transactional analysis, Jungian theory, psychoanalysis, attachment theory, systemic family dynamics, sensory integration and affective neuroscience to name but a few. The department is a fertile thinking space.

Over the past five years the creative psychotherapies team has strengthened and found more opportunities for multi-disciplinary working, exploring the crossovers we have with different disciplines on site. Learning about sensory integration from our occupational therapist has provoked a reconsideration of art materials and furthered the importance of activities and movements that revisit early child development. Ideas and tips from our dramatherapist have helped to support the boys who do not have the confidence to make a mark but will still engage their imagination through role play. Listening to the clinical practice of our music therapist has highlighted the role and value of music for boys who struggle to communicate, so that when an art therapist finds himself sitting next to a boy facing the piano, he can explore a musical way to make connections. The benefits of such an integrative, creative approach in psychotherapy are becoming increasingly recognized in affective neuroscience (Schore 2012).

This process of cross-fertilization was enhanced by a challenge to lead a keynote presentation in our annual school conference. By unpicking a case that had involved varied clinical input, we illustrated the theory and practice of our interventions, how they connect and support each other and also their benefits in relation to supporting a boy's development and engagement in education. Months of work and a series of experiential sessions allowed each of us in turn to guide the team members through their own particular discipline. Our methods of learning and exploring influenced our presentation and we endeavoured to engage our audience in similar ways, creating a parallel process of the way our boys learn.

The rationale for our approach: playful, creative and connected intervention

As a school we have a duty to educate; however, as pointed out by Coughlan (2010), mental health difficulties create a significant barrier to learning for students with SEN, which supports the concept of employing multi-modal interventions (Cooper 1999).

The conditions that lead students to attend our school can often involve every system of the body. Van der Kolk's definition of developmental trauma (2005) acknowledges the extent of affect that early experiences have on a child's emotional conduct, educational engagement, attainment, psychological development and social functioning. Supporting research by Melillo (2009) proposes that rather than treating inattention, poor socialization or a reading problem in isolation, a combination of systems (including sensory, digestive, motor, cognitive, emotional and academic) should all be addressed together. It therefore makes sense for a child to be treated with a connected and integrated approach through a curriculum that meets his educational, social, health and emotional needs.

Keeping in mind this global affect of trauma, as a team we also note that the traumatic experiences of the children we work with have a very raw quality to them – different to that if working with older clients or adults. This may be in part due to the chronological closeness to the traumatic events and also be related to the sequenced development of the different key areas of the brain, as noted by Perry (2008). The overwhelming trauma spills out in a jumble of mess and confusion, metaphor, gesture, transference and projection that is highly emotive and challenging to make sense of. Their memories and experiences, implicitly held and communicated, have yet to receive a developed cognitive strategy to successfully manage and change their resonance to clearer, more connected, contained thoughts located within narrative, time and space.

Research into therapeutic work with trauma indicates that it is not the re-telling of the trauma using words that helps the person process and resolve the feelings involved; it is a process of symbolization that actually helps the psychological movement of the experience away from the trauma sensations that linger (Wilkinson 2010). As metaphor connects all the creative therapies, through consideration of gesture, music, sound, imagery (expressed or visualized), stories and language, its foundations can be observed in early child development.

Stern (1985) explored inter-subjectivity and the process of mother–child affective attunement, focusing on the capacity of the infant to find comparable meaning across different sensory modalities, so creating a form of pre-verbal language and dialogue. Modell expanded these observations to suggest that this cross-sensory understanding represents 'a profound connection between affect and metaphor' (1997, p.108).

Klein (1998) spoke about the process of symbolization as a fundamental part of psychological development in children, which again echoes the validity and importance of imagery, in every guise, as a form of communication. Panksepp and Biven (2012) too promote the need to address the emotional ailments arising from early developmental problems by using multi-modal approaches that address underlying emotional dynamics and connect at non-verbal primary process levels.

Teenage boys will rarely openly verbalize the issues that are on their mind. Here the creative psychotherapist steps in to offer a less threatening means of expression that uses imagination and playfulness, the latter often something the boys have missed out on. The importance of play is now underpinned by the recognition of the involved brain system and its importance in the epigenetic development of the neocortex, also suggesting that greater understanding of the processes around play may be key to understanding certain problematic childhood emotional problems (Panksepp and Biven 2012). Considering themes and metaphors in stories and myths, different resolutions and responses, as well as difficult thoughts and feelings, can be explored at a safe distance (Casson 2004; Jones 1996). We have also noted that the kinaesthetic aspects of creative exploration often provide a physical sensation of sorting through and making sense of, which supports a parallel process of organizing jumbled emotions.

At the foundation of the layers of theories we consider, psychodynamic theory underpins all of our creative psychotherapists' training, enabling them to acknowledge and work with the patterns of relating that our clients have learnt. These aspects of functioning frequently hinder their development in mainstream society and create the barriers to learning seen in our classrooms.

As we consider our theoretical influences on our journey and practice, it is interesting to note that the school's shift in ethos also parallels research in affective neuroscience, recognizing the need to move in psychotherapeutic treatment from a cognitive or behavioural approach to one that relies more on relational, affect-regulation (Schore 2012) in order to connect with and meet the needs of our clients.

The therapy space

The often chaotic and heightened presentations of the boys we work with means we have to work harder to provide containment. Some feel physically too threatened to sit alone inside a room with a therapist, so we may use the garden. Frequently, when adult focus becomes too intense – which happens particularly for looked after children – a request for a game of hide and seek allows them to negotiate contact and disengagement, exploring how it feels and allowing them to test out the connection of the therapeutic relationship.

NICK: TO SEEK AND BE FOUND

Nick has lived in a children's home since he was young, separated from all his birth family with whom he witnessed domestic violence and was neglected and subjected to sexual abuse. Nick is keen to explore the whole therapy building, searching in cupboards, toying briefly with what he finds but moving on unsatiated by each discovery. It seems that searching is the drive. Having connected with the rooms and the other therapists, we settle into the play room, finding some figures in the doll's house. After only several sessions, I am pleased to find Nick focused, as his play only tends to last a few minutes. Just as I am considering this development, he stops to suggest a game of hide and seek. It is late in the day and the other therapy rooms are empty, so I agree and the house becomes our boundary. I am to count first and not look, staying in the play room. As I count I listen to his footsteps hurrying away and making their way down a set of stairs. As I reach the final number, I shout to him that I have started seeking and walk around the building, verbalizing my actions, looking and wondering as I go.

He instigated the game to separate from me, to allow him to control our contact. It is a turn-taking game that will help us to get to know each other and let him know that I am willing to play. My seeking is an act of holding him in mind, wanting to make contact again, seeking a reconnection. I'm verbalizing a process of looking for something, someone, of having a need for something I am unable to find or have lost. The game has so many different levels to it, each time allowing me to experience aspects of that particular child's experience. When it is my turn to be found, sometimes I notice that my heart thumps with anxious excitement as I hear the seeker walking past without finding me, indicating his experience of being hidden. With another child, I find myself forgotten – they are not interested in finding me – but instead when I give up my role of hiding, I find that they have engaged themselves in something new to do, leaving me lonely and obsolete. With another, it is the thrill of the chase that is highlighted, with emotive shrieks expelled as the child runs from his hiding place, in flight from the threat of being caught. For some children, even the brief separation that this game provides is too much to bear and therefore by request we introduced walkie-talkies, providing an auditory connection as we play. Every game is different yet allows important aspects to be communicated and worked through.

From the outset, our therapy rooms have been dedicated, valued spaces, offering a safe place to consider and explore often difficult thoughts and feelings. As the provision has grown, so too has the space we have occupied, leading to a dedicated building with its own garden. Therapy is the norm for our boys and they recognize the different stance of our staff and often bring themselves to the door, or loiter in the garden waiting to be noticed and invited in if they find themselves struggling in class and in need of support.

Many therapists in education have to be the container as they battle for temporary therapy spaces. Our provision of containment does extend outside the therapy room, to use the whole building and sometimes beyond (engaging the boys in their houses, on the outdoor gym equipment or coaxing them off the roof) within the school grounds, but we have a more secure and layered level of containment: the security of the team.

Assimilating therapies into the school setting

Significant work has been done with the staff over the years to help assimilate the therapists into the workforce – for example, informal conversations with keyworkers and teachers, and experiential sessions of the different therapy disciplines on training days. Slowly, we've broken down barriers to become more accepted and more supportive of the staff in their work. Our perspectives are listened to and our consistent, thoughtful stance helps slow people down to maintain a proactive thought process rather than finding themselves in a position of reactive 'doing', which is commonplace in many settings. The change of ethos is recognizable throughout the staff community, with all staff thinking about behaviour as a form of communication to be unpicked and understood. Staff recognize the value of all the different disciplines on site, calling people together when students become stuck, or too difficult, or display signs that concern them. Thinking has become more connected.

The site is a close-knit community with a warm, supportive and family feel to it, with even a number of marriages forming within the staff group over the years. Due to this model of functioning, we notice themes ripple through the staff, ignited by the students' actions. Students affect other students, creating patterns of behaviour that inspire others; the behaviour becomes more prolific, leading the pressure on staff to increase and test their patience and resilience to the limits. When greater numbers of students feel out of control it often makes the staff themselves feel that they are out of control. Feelings of helplessness, hopelessness, that nothing will make a difference, that they are useless, transfer from students to staff. Managers, supervision and the therapeutic underpinning help staff to notice and think about the events from a different perspective, assisting them to separate and not be engulfed by the behaviour. In this environment, staff well-being and mindfulness are essential.

It is at these times of feeling under attack that putting in a positive action to break the cycle of negative behaviour can sometimes become unfathomable for the staff. The staff have been subjected to a multitude of feelings, often including physical and verbal aggression, and yet someone involved (usually a manager) stops to suggest that we offer a positive experience for the perpetrating boy, something the boy will really like such as an afternoon out or an activity that breaks away from the daily routine. It can raise exasperation for the staff who have been 'through the mill', the perception being that we are then rewarding the student for doing this. It can even be taken personally.

But we do this with good reason: he is a child with attachment difficulties, whose self-esteem is so low that his default position is 'feeling shit', reinforced by the relationship patterns or emotional neglect in his early years – patterns that he seeks to continue because he knows no other way of being, and that he has just successfully evoked in the staff around him. We do this to break the pattern and show him that we recognize his value and his worth and that we can react with care and compassion for his needs; we want to ease his fears and can see beyond the behaviour he has learnt and adopted to keep him safe.

This is often a place where his therapist steps in, helping to support the staff by listening to their difficult experiences of the child, exploring them, validating them and then helping staff to connect them to the child's experiences of adults and early years. Understanding helps break the cycle. We help support the development of connections on all levels – interpersonal relationships that in turn affect and re-wire patterns of thinking and experience at a personal and so at a neural level. We also offer a different perspective to the child: a child-centred approach that can help him realize how others react to him and why people become upset or exasperated. We help support the containment of the child's difficult feelings and experiences, both as he experiences it and as those around him experience it, negotiating the conflict between.

SEBASTIAN: CONTAGIOUS FEAR

Sebastian is a particularly dysregulated boy, whom staff are fearful of, despite his small size and age. He is unpredictable and there is a wildness when he explodes, lashing out at staff physically, verbally, often spitting. His therapist has a sense that he has been chronically abused from a young age, but nothing has been recorded in his history of this nature. He is a looked after child.

Jane, a member of the education staff, has been involved in an incident with Sebastian in the classroom, where he has turned on her, without perceived warning or reason, physically assaulting her and verbally abusing her. Jane is disgusted by him and by his actions. She wants him to be punished, perceiving his actions as completely unreasonable. She had done nothing to him to warrant it. It is unacceptable. She does not want to go near him again; she does not like him and he doesn't even appear to want to apologize.

Sebastian's therapist has seen him when he is overwhelmed and uncontainable. She has also seen the small child underneath, who is vulnerable, frightened and desperate to stay in control of his overwhelming emotions and physical, non-verbal memories of trauma. He has never been taught how to put things right. Once a situation has gone wrong, it tumbles into a negative spiral that cannot be undone, like falling down a well with no concept of what a ladder is. Despite all of this, his therapist finds that her response to him is not of fear but more maternal in nature.

Sebastian has a level of trust in his therapist, so he manages to stay in the room when she suggests that they sit and talk to Jane together. They do this in a space where

Sebastian feels comfortable, but even then he hides his face and can't find any words to say. His therapist explains to Jane how distressed Sebastian is by his actions towards her. She is surprised, she did not know. His therapist explains how overwhelmed he feels when things go wrong, and his instinct is to run and hide. He does not know how to put things right – he has never been helped to do this.

Jane's distance to him softens as she begins to connect with his experiences. His therapist has also spent some time with her beforehand to explain what she knows of Sebastian and what she suspects his experiences of adults are, and how this has made him fearful and self-loathing. The balance shifts and Jane can see him more clearly – the vulnerable, frightened child underneath. Sebastian can hear that he is understood as the therapist speaks. He can hear that Jane still wants to know him but also wants to understand him better. He can hear that they see through his hatred to the child underneath. He manages to lift his head to make eye contact and mumbles a small 'Sorry'. It is his first and helps pave the way for more reconnections even when he feels he has destroyed everything. He has learnt that people can understand him, and experienced a sense of something being repaired. Jane feels as though a weight is lifted from her and starts to view him differently. She wants to help him too.

The development of a therapeutic ethos has shifted the behavioural management response to something more considered and bespoke, affecting how we perceive and enforce rules and boundaries. One rule does not fit all – successful methods of resolving misdemeanours differ between students and, even then, what works one day may not work the next. Boundaries are a constant consideration and take negotiation to maintain. We imagine them as a flexible, elastic membrane around the school that stretches and strains under different pressures but ultimately always finds a place to hold, stand firm and keep the staff and students safe.

Some particular challenges: assimilate or separate

A further consideration for our modelling of a secure base within school is the continuous battle between the influence of staff and of home life for our boys. Many students return to a home setting daily, others weekly. Every week they negotiate two sets of rules, boundaries, relationship models and, often, significant differences in adult contact. The communities they reside in may also have cultural differences, simply in their dynamics, ways of functioning and place in society.

This realization fuelled the introduction of our family counsellor to 'plug the gap' in our service and try to prevent the unravelling of our work when the boys returned home at weekends. With careful negotiation and sensitivity, and constant liaison with the team, the family counsellor attempts to mould the home environment on behalf of the boys in their absence and prepares the parents and carers to offer a warm welcome on their return with the same unconditional positive regard that the children receive at school.

With time and patience, we begin to help the students integrate a healthy model of an adult caregiver, to support them to re-develop their ideas and patterns of relationships. After years of work with some boys, we reach a point where the balance tips and they negotiate a painful realization that the staff in school, who are paid to care and keep them safe, provide greater well-being, consistency and consideration for them than their own foundations. We are aware that to accept one way of being could potentially create misalignment in the other arena of their life. To exist successfully and 'fit' in one place may mean dismissing the learnt behaviour from the other setting, creating a disjointed place to be. These maladaptive strategies are the aspects that have kept the boys safe, allowing them to find a way to keep moving forwards. To remove these strategies or breach them can be perceived as a physical threat to the boys' being.

It is a complicated position to negotiate, even more so for a child who is trying to grapple with his dysregulated emotions and fathom out a sense of identity: finding a way to be and survive the places he encounters whilst still being true to himself.

We have also had to find a place of separateness in order to function properly as a service, recognizing its importance and, again, how this idea can be applied to staff working on site. At the staff well-being training day, we spoke about compassion fatigue and mindfulness, highlighting the essential position of finding themselves, reconnecting with their bodies to ground themselves momentarily outside of the dynamics they find themselves in, in order to be able to reflectively consider their work. That is no easy task in a workplace as fast-paced and unpredictable as ours, but it is ultimately essential. To be engulfed completely into the dynamics evoked by our students would be unhealthy and unhelpful, making it impossible to maintain the stance of the thinking, consistent adult.

In parallel, the individual members of the therapy team, despite their undeniable unity and integrated working ethos, undertake their own off-site clinical supervision with carefully selected clinicians to ensure they remain separate enough to think and function. This practice is currently extended to senior managers.

Conclusions

The process of implementing therapies has evoked significant learning. These are our thoughts for others embarking on the same journey:

- A solid foundation is vital. An advocate for the service at senior leadership level is key to creating roots and stability within the school community.

- Staff education is a priority during the establishment period of the service. Any mystery surrounding therapy needs to be dissolved so that staff can confidently support the students to attend and also connect in conversation with the therapists themselves.

- A dedicated, neutral space on site is the ideal. Our physical location has supported our acceptance as part of the school community, to the extent that engaging in therapy is the norm. The protection of this space as purely for therapy indicates its value.

- Connection is key. Within the therapist's role, time is allocated for connection and conversation with other staff on site. When we reached a point of employing multiple therapists, their connection with each other created a multi-disciplinary thinking space and so significant developments in practice.

- In our provision the therapists have been encouraged to create a service of best fit for the client group and to put this into practice. For example, we work with students for years, not weeks. We also create individual pathways of treatment for each boy, dependent on need.

- Therapists belong to a profession that requires engagement in regular professional development. The benefit is that the team members, supported by the school, engage with the most interesting and current thinking they can find, attending seminars and conferences across the country and feeding ideas back into the school.

During our exploration and consideration of psychotherapeutic practice, diverse theoretical thinking, the needs of our students and the dynamics of our setting, we have found new paths and created bridges. We have tested out ideas, failed in places, changed track and tried again. Based in a facility whose primary function is learning, in the creation of our team we have also modelled for our students and colleagues a process of education based on experience, connections and confidence to explore. As Szalavitz and Perry (2010) highlight the fundamental importance of empathy and relationships to emotional, psychological and social health, the introduction and inclusion of therapies has promoted this focus within our school community's consciousness.

References

Carpenter, B. (2010) *Think Piece 3 – New Generation Pedagogy: Evolving and Personalising Teaching for Children with Complex Learning Difficulties and Disabilities (CLDD).* London: Specialist Schools and Academies Trust Publication.

Casson, J. (2004) *Drama, Psychotherapy and Psychosis.* Hove: Brunner-Routledge.

Cole, T. and Knowles, B. (2011) *How to Help Children and Young People with Complex Behavioural Difficulties.* London: Routledge.

Cooper, P. (1999) 'Emotional and Behavioural Difficulties and Adolescence.' In P. Cooper (ed.) *Understanding and Supporting Children with Emotional and Behavioural Difficulties.* London: Jessica Kingsley Publishers.

Coughlan, B. J. (2010) *Think Piece 6 – Critical Issues in the Emotional Wellbeing of Students with Special Educational Needs.* London: Specialist Schools and Academies Trust Publication.

DOH (Department of Health) (2011) *No Health without Mental Health: A Cross-Government Mental Health Outcomes Strategy for People of All Ages.* London: HM Government. Available at www.gov.uk/government/uploads/system/uploads/attachment_data/file/213761/dh_124058.pdf, accessed on 12 November 2016.

Jones, P. (1996) *Drama as Therapy: Theatre as Living.* London: Routledge.

Klein, M. (1998) *Love, Guilt and Reparation and Other Works 1921–1945.* New York, NY: Vintage.

Melillo, R. (2009) *Disconnected Kids.* New York, NY: Penguin.

Modell, A. H. (1997) 'Reflections on metaphors and affects.' *Annual of Psychoanalysis 25*, 219–233.

O'Neill, L., Guenette, F. and Kitchenham, A. (2010) 'Am I safe here and do you like me? Understanding complex trauma and attachment disruption in the classroom.' *British Journal of Special Education 37*, 4, 190–197.

Panksepp, J. and Biven, L. (2012) *The Archaeology of Mind. Neuroevolutionary Origins of Human Emotions*. New York, NY: W. W. Norton.

Perry, B. D. (2008) 'Child Maltreatment: A Neurodevelopmental Perspective on the Role of Trauma and Neglect in Psychopathology.' In T. Beauchaine and S. P. Hinshaw (eds) *Child and Adolescent Psychopathology*. Hoboken, NJ: John Wiley & Sons.

Schore, A. N. (2012) *The Science of the Art of Psychotherapy*. New York, NY: W. W. Norton.

Stern, D. (1985) *The Interpersonal World of the Infant*. New York, NY: Basic Books.

Szalavitz, M. and Perry, B. D. (2010) *Born for Love*. New York, NY: Harper Collins.

van der Kolk, B. A. (2005) 'Developmental trauma disorder: Towards a rational diagnosis for chronically traumatized children.' *Psychiatric Annals 35*, 5, 401–408.

Wilkinson, M. (2010) *Changing Minds in Therapy*. New York, NY: W. W. Norton.

ABOUT THE EDITORS

Anthea Hendry graduated in Sociology and qualified as a teacher (she lectured in Further Education and taught abroad). She then trained as a social worker and worked for Bradford Social Services Fostering and Adoption Unit for 11 years. She did a fine art training and went on to qualify as an art therapist. She was part of a steering group that established After Adoption Yorkshire (now PAC-UK) and was the organization's first manager. She worked for Leeds Child and Adolescent Mental Health Service for 12 years and helped to establish a specialist clinic for adoptive families. She has completed an MA in the Advanced Clinical Practice of Art Psychotherapy at Goldsmiths College, London, and now works in private practice as an art psychotherapist, supervisor and trainer.

Joy Hasler is the founder and a director of Catchpoint Consultancy CIC, a registered Adoption Support Agency. Catchpoint is a team of arts and play therapists offering therapy, support and training for everyone involved with children in adoptive or foster families who have experienced early trauma. She has personal experience of fostering and adoption, which, alongside her training as a teacher and music therapist, gives her insight into her professional field of work – therapy with adopted children and their families. She has been published as an illustrator and as an author on the topic of music therapy with families, and support for adoptive parents.

ABOUT THE CONTRIBUTORS

Marion Allen is a consultant practitioner in education. She is an adoptive parent and a qualified teacher with over 20 years' experience in the early years and primary sector. She attended a credited course at Family Futures on Adoption and Attachment from 2004 to 2006, and then joined the agency to establish an education team supporting children and teachers in schools as an integral part of the therapy programme, promoting the principles of Family Futures' Neuro Physiological Psychotherapy model within education. She is trained in family therapy, Theraplay and Dyadic Developmental Psychotherapy. She delivers training to adoptive parents and education professionals. She has worked closely with Adoption UK, developing their parent training programme and speaking at their annual conference. She is keen to ensure that traumatized children access the same educational and life opportunities as their peers, with provision being made to help them manage the specific challenges related to the impact of their early trauma.

Sarah Ayache is an art psychotherapist and Head of Therapy at the William Henry Smith School, UK, a specialist residential school for boys with severe social, emotional and mental health difficulties. She leads a dynamic, innovative and integrative team of creative psychotherapists, speech and language therapists, occupational therapists and family counsellors. Her theoretical interests lie in the field of neuroscience, attachment and child development. Her recent studies have included training by Jaak Panksepp, Mark Solms, Allan Schore and Margaret Wilkinson. Her ambition is to explore her interests in affective neuroscience at doctorate level. She has presented at numerous national and international conferences in the fields of mental health and education and as a postgraduate lecturer, teaching aspects of art psychotherapy, neuroscience and working with complex clients.

Franca Brenninkmeyer is Head of Child and Family Service –
PAC-UK (formerly Post-Adoption Centre) – London Office. She
has over 25 years of professional adoption experience and has worked
at PAC-UK since 1996. She has a Licenciate in Pedagogical Sciences
(Belgium), equivalent to a BA and MSc in Child and Family Psychology,
as well as an MSc in Counselling Psychology (UK). She is a member
of the British Psychological Society. Franca has attended numerous
additional training courses and conferences, including some in the
USA. She was instrumental in developing PAC-UK's assessments and
intensive therapeutic interventions for adoptive families. She regularly
trains and presents on adoption, trauma and attachment-related topics
and has contributed to a recent publication, *Surviving the Early Years*, by
Acquarone. She also has an interest and experience in therapeutically
supporting adults who experienced childhood trauma.

Alan Burnell has a BSc in Psychology and is a qualified social
worker. He has trained in family therapy and Dyadic Developmental
Psychotherapy and also has a passionate interest in neuroscience. He
is Co-Director of Family Futures CIC and is the Registered Manager.
Alan has over the past 40 years worked directly with adoptive families
and has developed adoption support services. He was adopted as a baby,
which has had a profound impact on his personal and professional life.
Following his degree and social work training he was privileged to
work with some very inspired practitioners who led him to believe
that it is always possible to improve services for each generation of
children. His commitment to adoptive families stems from his own
adoptive parents, who embodied the spirit of adoption at its best, and
from the adoptive families with whom he has worked over the years.

Martin Gibson is Vice Principal, with particular responsibility for
therapy and further education, at the William Henry Smith School.
His background is in psychiatric nursing and he has over 25 years'
experience working within the social, emotional and mental health
sector with specific interests in forensic psychology and the causation
of behaviour. He holds an MA in Education, Learning and Teaching
and a BSc in Psychology. He has been instrumental in developing an
on-site therapy department that caters for the emotional well-being
of students within the school but also delivers therapy to students
referred by local mainstream schools. In an era where childhood
disorders are becoming more and more complex, he is a very keen

advocate for schools to focus on holistic learning and the now well-established (but still largely misunderstood) links between special education needs, social, emotional and behavioural issues, mental health and communication difficulties.

Hannah Guy has a passion for Community Dance, which took her to the University of Birmingham in 2000 to study Dance and Theatre Arts. The choreographic element inspired her to work creatively within her local community, supporting schools and colleges with project work, GCSEs and A-levels. The introduction of dance therapy into her training encouraged Hannah to return to study at Dance Voice, Bristol. She qualified as a dance movement psychotherapist in 2011 and has worked closely with elder populations, trauma and attachment disorders. Her interest in the well-being of the practitioner, as well as that of her clients, encouraged Hannah to train as a creative clinical supervisor and to address her own needs through relaxation, running, drumming and the art of henna.

Molly Holland is a dramatherapist living in Bristol with her husband and daughter. Molly studied drama as an undergraduate and after completing her degree worked for a number of years in special education. During this time, she ran drama and storytelling groups with children with multiple learning difficulties. Molly began working with fostered and adopted children and their families in 2012, during the second year of her dramatherapy training, when she joined the Catchpoint team as part of their therapist apprenticeship programme. Molly is a lover of children's literature and a founding member of the Bristol Playback Theatre group 'Rise and Fall'.

Renée Potgieter Marks works as Consultant Therapist and Clinical Lead at Integrate Families in the North of England. Integrate Families is a National Centre for Child Trauma and Dissociation. She is a national and international trainer on the topic of attachment, emotional regulation, complex trauma and dissociation in children and adolescents. She provides effective therapeutic techniques to therapists and counsellors in working with the more serious and complicated population of traumatized children and adolescents. She is an expert witness and provides clinical supervision and consultation to individual therapists and organizations. She is the co-founder of the British Institute for Child Trauma and Dissociation (BICTD), which provides online training for mental health professionals, social workers, carers and adopters on managing and treating children with complex trauma and dissociation. She also chairs the child and adolescent committee of the European Society on Trauma and Dissociation (ESTD) and is a member of the child and adolescent committee of the International Society on Studies of Trauma and Dissociation (ISSTD).

Janet Smith is a qualified business manager and worked for many years in the commercial banking sector before moving into the charity sector in 2002. In 1991 Janet adopted two children, aged 7 and 5, and this experience led her to change the focus of her working life. Janet enrolled in a university degree course and retrained as an adult teacher/trainer and couple and family therapist. Janet joined Adoption UK in 2003 – initially as Training Manager, and then from 2006 as Director of Adoption Support. There she was responsible for the everyday management and development of adoption support services across the UK. In 2013 she decided she wanted to focus her attentions closer to home and joined Families for Children, a Voluntary Adoption Agency based in the South-West of England, as Practice Manager for Adoption Support. In this role she is responsible for the strategic development and management of the adoption support services.

Elizabeth Taylor Buck has worked as an art psychotherapist in child and adolescent mental health settings for 20 years, initially for the National Society for the Prevention of Cruelty to Children (NSPCC) and then in a National Health Service (NHS) Child and Adolescent Mental Health Service (CAMHS). In addition to core training in art psychotherapy, she has training in Mentalization-Based Therapy with Families (MBT-F), Interpersonal Therapy with Adolescents (IPT-A), 'Watch, Wait and Wonder' and Theraplay. In 2014 she completed a five-year National Institute for Health Research (NIHR) Clinical Doctoral Research Fellowship. Her doctoral research focused on dyadic parent–child art therapy. She is a member of the British Association of Art Therapists (BAAT) SIG Art Therapists Working with Children, Adolescents and Families (ATCAF) and helped develop the ATCAF Principles of Best Practice. She has experience of supervising trainee and qualified art therapists and of offering consultation to other professionals.

Sue Topalian qualified as a social worker in 1980. She has worked as an adoption social worker in a voluntary sector agency, and in local authority teams undertaking case work with children who were fostered, adopted or in residential care. She managed a team for looked after children and a disabled children team before moving into planning and development for children's social care, then multi-agency CAMHS in Bristol. Late in her working life, she unexpectedly but joyously found herself retraining and obtaining an MA in Dance Movement Psychotherapy. She currently works as an attachment therapist with Catchpoint, a therapeutic agency working with adoptive and foster families in Bristol. She has a partner, two adult children and a grandchild, and enjoys dancing, kayaking, playing in her garden and wandering by water, in woods or on the hills.

Jay Vaughan MA, is a state-registered dramatherapist, a certified Dyadic Developmental Psychotherapist, a Theraplay therapist, supervisor and trainer as well as a Somatic Experience practitioner. She is Co-Director of Family Futures CIC and is the Agency's Responsible Person as well as its Clinical Director. Jay continues to work directly with families in the assessment and treatment programme in addition to taking overall clinical responsibility for the service. She has been working with traumatized children since qualifying as a dramatherapist in 1989, and passionately believes in the use of arts, play and body-based approaches in helping traumatized children and their families to heal. She has been instrumental in synergizing Somatic Experience, Theraplay, and Dyadic Developmental Psychotherapy into a neurosequential approach to helping traumatized children. She has helped to shape the Neuro Physiological Psychotherapy model, which has now been shown by research to achieve positive outcomes for traumatized children.

ORGANIZATIONS

Catchpoint Consultancy CIC

www.catchpoint.org

Catchpoint is a registered Adoption Support Agency offering therapy and support for adopted and fostered children and their families. Catchpoint offers a trauma recovery model of therapy with an attachment focus through creative arts and play therapies with parents/carers and children together. The model of therapy is informed by Dyadic Developmental Psychotherapy (DDP), Trauma Focused-Cognitive Behavioural Therapy (TF-CBT), a Neurosequential Model of Therapeutics (NMT) and Theraplay.

Families for Children

www.familiesforchildren.org.uk

Families for Children Trust is a specialist adoption agency and charitable trust based in the South-West of England. Families for Children existed for many years as a joint venture operated by the Exeter Diocesan Board for Christian Care and the Plymouth Diocesan Catholic Children's Society. In 2003 the agency became a separate charity in its own right and is now a specialist adoption agency offering: recruiting, preparing and assessing potential adoptive parents; provision of post-adoption support; adult adoptee counselling for adoptees seeking information about their birth families; and an independent birth relative service for parents of children being placed for adoption by the Bournemouth and Poole Local Authorities.

Family Futures CIC

www.familyfutures.co.uk

Family Futures is a not-for-profit voluntary adoption agency specializing in the assessment and treatment of traumatized children placed in foster families, adoptive families or kinship care. Family Futures offers an assessment and treatment programme entitled Neuro Physiological Psychotherapy. This approach integrates Somatic Experience, Theraplay and Dyadic Developmental Psychotherapy, as well as creative arts therapies as part of the assessment and treatment approach. The approach is systemic and provides 'wrap around' support to families working with the whole system around the child and family.

Integrate Families

www.integratefamilies.co.uk

Integrate Families is an adoption support agency in the North of England with different branches across the country. Integrate Families is a National Centre for Child Trauma and Dissociation. Integrate Families follows an individualized and integrative therapeutic approach with each child and family, based on a comprehensive assessment.

British Institue of Child Trauma and Dissociation

www.bictd.org

BICTD is an online video training website specifically focussing on children with attachment difficulties, trauma and disassociation. This is an international collaborative and training organization that also acts as the training arm of Integrate Families. BICTD harnesses over a century of experience, from some of the world's most seasoned professionals, in the field of child trauma and dissociation.

PAC-UK

www.pac-uk.org

PAC-UK is the largest independent adoption support agency in the country. Its vision is that all people affected by adoption and other forms of permanence are supported and enabled to live their lives to the full. PAC-UK's services include an Advice Line, an Adult Counselling and Intermediary Service, a Child and Family Service (with particular expertise in working therapeutically with families whose children suffered complex trauma), an Education Service, a 'First Family Service' for Birth Parents and Birth Relatives, and a Training Service. PAC-UK's services are staffed by qualified and experienced professionals as well as some volunteers.

SUBJECT INDEX

AUTHOR INDEX